What English Language Teachers Need to Know Volume II: Facilitating Learning

Designed for pre-service teachers and teachers new to the field of ELT, these companion textbooks are organized around the key question: What do teachers need to know and be able to do in order for their students to learn English? All English language teachers need to understand the nature of language and language learning, and with that understanding they need to be able to facilitate student learning.

Volume I, on **understanding learning**, provides the background information that teachers need to know and be able to use in their classroom:

- the characteristics of the context in which they work
- how English works and how it is learned
- their role in the larger professional sphere of English language education

Volume II, on **facilitating learning**, covers the three main facets of teaching:

- planning
- instructing
- assessing

The focus throughout is on outcomes, that is, student learning.

Features of the texts

- Situated in current research in the field of English language teaching and other disciplines that inform it
- Sample data, including classroom vignettes
- Three kinds of activities/tasks designed to create a dialog between text and reader and so help teachers and prospective teachers to understand and apply the material being presented: Explore; Reflect; and Expand

The texts work for teachers across different contexts (countries where English is the dominant language, one of the official languages, or taught as a foreign language); different levels (elementary/primary, secondary, college or university, or adult education); and different learning purposes (general English, workplace English, English for academic purposes, or English for specific purposes).

Denise E. Murray is Professor Emerita, Macquarie University, Australia, and Professor Emerita, San José State University, US.

MaryAnn Christison is Professor, University of Utah, Department of Linguistics and the Urban Institute for Teacher Education, US.

ESL & Applied Linguistics Professional Series
Eli Hinkel, Series Editor

Visit **www.routledge.com/education** for additional information on titles in the ESL & Applied Linguistics Professional Series.

What English Language Teachers Need to Know Volume II

Facilitating Learning

Denise E. Murray and
MaryAnn Christison

Routledge
Taylor & Francis Group

NEW YORK AND LONDON

First published 2011
by Routledge
270 Madison Avenue, New York, NY 10016

Simultaneously published in the UK
by Routledge
2 Park Square, Milton Park, Abingdon, Oxon OX14 4RN

*Routledge is an imprint of the Taylor & Francis Group,
an informa business*

© 2011 Taylor & Francis

The right of Denise E. Murray and MaryAnn Christison to be
identified as authors of this work has been asserted by them in
accordance with sections 77 and 78 of the Copyright, Designs and
Patents Act 1988.

Typeset in Bembo by RefineCatch Limited, Bungay, Suffolk
Printed and bound in the United States of America on acid-free
paper by Walsworth Publishing Company, Marceline, MO

Library of Congress Cataloging-in-Publication Data
Murray, Denise E.
    What English language teachers need to know. Volume II :
    facilitating learning / Denise E. Murray and MaryAnn Christison.
        p. cm.
    Includes index.
    1. English language—Study and teaching—Foreign speakers.
    2. Language and languages—Study and teaching.   3. Language and
    languages—Study and teaching.   I. Christison, MaryAnn.   II. Title.
    PE1128.A2M878 2010
    428.2′4—dc22   2010005349

ISBN13: 978-0-415-80640-4 (hbk)
ISBN13: 978-0-415-80641-1 (pbk)
ISBN13: 978-0-203-84629-2 (ebk)

Brief Contents

PART III
Assessing for Learning 177

Contents

Preface

English language teaching worldwide has become a multibillion dollar enterprise, one that the majority of nations in the world are embarking on to lesser or greater extents. For many countries, English is seen as a commodity through which they will become more competitive in the global marketplace. While English may have national and personal advancement potential, it is also pervasive in the global media. Youth culture in particular is influenced by English-dominant media and marketing. As a result, English is being consumed and transformed transnationally.

The settings where English is taught vary from countries where English is the official and dominant language, such as the United States or Australia, to those where it is an official language, usually as a result of past colonialism, such as India or the Philippines, to those where it is taught in schools as a subject of study, such as Japan or the Czech Republic. In the first set of countries, when English is taught to immigrants or to international students, the language is often called *English as a second language (ESL)*, and its teaching *TESL*. In the second set of countries, where it is taught to citizens and increasingly to international students, it is usually referred to also as ESL. In the third set of countries, the language is often referred to as *English as a foreign language (EFL)*, and its teaching *TEFL*. Because both ESL and EFL carry ideological baggage, there is much discussion in the field about more appropriate terminology and use of alternate terms. Some prefer to use *(T)ESOL* —(teaching) English to speakers of other languages—since it acknowledges that the learners may have more than one previous language and can be used to include both ESL and EFL contexts. Others prefer *(T)EAL*—(teaching) English as an add-itional language—for the same reason, whereas ESL implies there is only English, plus one other. Other terms in use include *English as an international language (EIL)*, and *English language teaching (ELT)*. Whatever the terminology used, distinctions are increasingly becoming blurred as people move around the globe and acquire their English in a variety of different settings, being taught by teachers from a variety of different linguistic backgrounds.

In these volumes, we will use ESL and EFL because they are still the most widely used terms, while recognizing the inherent reification of English in their use. When referring to teaching, we will use ELT to avoid confusion between the field of TESOL and the professional association called TESOL.

Similarly, the terminology used to define the users of English has been contested. The most commonly used terms have been *native speaker (NS)*, in contrast to *nonnative speaker (NNS)*. Both terms assume ideological positions, especially since the NS is valued as the norm and the model for language learning, not only in those countries where English is the dominant language, but also in many EFL settings. Yet, the majority of English language users and teachers do not have English as their mother tongue or dominant language. In some ESL contexts, such as the United States, immigrant learners are referred to as *English language learners (ELLs)*, even though all English speakers, no matter their immigration status, are English language learners—we both are still learning English! Leung, Harris and Rampton (1997) have therefore proposed refining what it means to know and use a language with three terms: *language expertise* (linguistic and cultural knowledge), *language affiliation* (identification and attachment), and *language inheritance* (connectedness and continuity). What is important then about a learner's (or teacher's) language is their linguistic repertoire in relation to each of these criteria, not whether they are a NS. Since there is no general acceptance of such terms, we shall continue to use NS and NNS, while noting that they establish a dichotomy that is neither valid nor descriptive.

Much of the literature also refers to people learning English in formal settings as students and sometimes as learners. We have chosen to use the term learner, except when it leads to infelicitous expressions such as "learners learning." Student implies passivity; learner implies agency. For us, learners are vital collaborators in the educational enterprise.

Who is This Book For?

We are writing this book for pre-service teachers and teachers new to the field of ELT. Whether you are teaching in an English-dominant country, a country where English is one of the official languages, or a country where English is taught as a foreign language, the information in this book is relevant to your context. We have also designed it for whatever level you may be teaching—elementary (primary) school, secondary school, college or university, or adult education. It also includes the information teachers need to teach general English, workplace English, English for academic purposes (EAP), or English for specific purposes (ESP). We realize that this is a big ask, but we have used examples from the diversity of ELT settings. Of course, we cannot include examples from every country or grade level, but we have tried to be inclusive and ensure that whatever your current or future teaching situation, you will find the material relevant to your learners and situation. At the same time, we have been as specific as possible, rather than relying on generic characteristics of the field.

Our own experiences have covered a vast array of different age groups, contexts, and content areas—between us, we have taught in English-dominant countries, EFL contexts in every continent, young people, adults, university students, general English, English for business, English for science and technology, and EAP. We draw on these experiences, so the volumes are representative of a broad range of English language teaching contexts around the world. The volumes therefore are quite different from other ones on theory and methodology for ELT.

What is This Book About?

In order to teach in these different contexts, teachers need understandings about the nature of language and language learning. With those understandings, they need to be able to facilitate student learning. Since student learning is the goal, we have oriented these volumes about the notion of learning, asking the question: *what do teachers need to know and be able to do in order for their students to learn English?*

Therefore, the first book provides the background information teachers need to know and be able to use in their classrooms. Teachers need to know (or know how to find out about) the characteristics of the context in which they work—the nature of their learners, the features of their institution, the policies and expectations of their nation/state, and the broader world with which their learners will engage. They need to know how English works and how it is learned. To become proficient in English, learners need to be able not only to create correct sentences in the classroom, but also to engage in conversations with other English speakers, and to read and write texts for different purposes. To accomplish this, teachers need to know how learning takes place both within the learner and through social inter-action. Finally, teachers need to understand their role in the larger professional sphere of English language education so that they can continue to grow as teachers and expand the profession through their own participation in its various enterprises. They also need to engage in their local communities to be informed of their needs and to inform their communities about the nature of English language learning.

While we have provided separate sections on each of these important themes, the challenge of successful teaching is to know how to blend an understanding of learners, language, and language learning with knowledge of their content goals and how to achieve those goals. This is the subject of Volume II.

Volume II, therefore, is organized around the three main aspects of teaching: planning, instructing, and assessing. However, this is not a linear progression. These three aspects are reiterative. While planning instruction, teachers are assessing what their learners already know and what they need to know to reach their next curriculum goals. While instructing, teachers are constantly assessing whether their learners have acquired the language in focus and planning on the spot by reacting to student learning (or evidence of not learning). While assessing, teachers are con-stantly reviewing instructional goals to determine whether learners have achieved them and if not, why not, and how to plan for revision or next steps.

With the focus always on student learning, Figure 0.1 below illustrates the dynamic, cyclical interaction of these processes.

We include both theoretical perspectives as well as directions for translating these theoretical perspectives into practice. We illustrate with examples from practice to

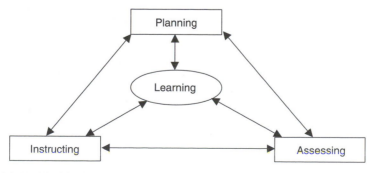

Figure 0.1 Model of the instructional process.

guide the reader in this translation process. It is important to read through and apply these perspectives against the principles elaborated in Volume I. The two books together provide an iterative conversation concerning how to develop language programs that result in optimal student learning. They stem from the view that teaching is a thinking, reasoning, and sociocultural activity in which teachers make decisions based on the context of their classrooms.

The material in these two volumes is based on current research in the field and in other disciplines that can inform English language teaching. These include psychology, neuroscience, pedagogy, sociology, anthropology, cultural studies, and linguistics. The focus throughout the volumes is on outcomes, that is, student learning.

Each chapter begins with a classroom vignette that comes from experiences in English language teaching, many from actual classrooms we have observed or taught. Each chapter also includes activities for the reader—whether to reflect on the information based on your own experiences, to read further on a topic, or to conduct small-scale investigations into teaching and learning. We hope that you will have as much enjoyment engaging with the materials as we have had writing them.

Reference

Leung, C., Harris, R., & Rampton, B. (1997). The idealised native speaker, reified ethnicities, and classroom realities. *TESOL Quarterly, 31,* 543–560.

Acknowledgements

We are grateful to our many students and colleagues over our careers, whose wisdom and experiences have enhanced our own understandings of the field. We are especially grateful to Naomi Silverman for her enthusiastic support of this project and Eli Hinkel for her willingness to read and respond to, yet again, another manuscript from us. And, we are, as always, tremendously thankful for our families, especially Bill Murray, Adrian Palmer, and Cameron Christison, who have supported our work, even when it has meant less time together and sometimes distracted dinner-time conversations! You continue to inspire us to be creative and professional.

Part I

Planning

In Part I, we explore how teachers plan instruction, both prior to class and during class, in order to create the optimum environment for student learning. We begin in Chapter 1 with the larger plan, that is, curriculum, to which the other plans are tied. Curriculum can be conceived of as the entire instructional process, that is, planning, instructing, and assessing, and is often used synonymously with course. Program, on the other hand, is used to refer to all courses of study in a particular institution. Curriculum and syllabus are often used interchangeably in the literature, although some writers make a distinction. Syllabus is often used to refer to the instantiation of a curriculum in a particular class or setting. Further, there are differences in use between the U.K. and U.S., with the latter preferring curriculum. Here we will use curriculum to refer to the entirety of the instructional process, including the delineation of the linguistic and subject matter content of the course, and the sequencing of such content.

In this part, we need to present what is essentially an iterative, dynamic system in a linear format. In Volume 1, Chapter 4, we discussed the various roles teachers play in the language classroom. In this part, we focus on the two major roles teachers have in the classroom (Wright, 1987):

1. to create the conditions under which learning can take place: the social side of teaching
2. to impart, by a variety of means, knowledge to their learners: the task-oriented side of teaching. (pp. 51–2).

We will begin with a discussion on planning the overall framework that guides instruction, that is, curriculum. Then in Chapter 2 we discuss how teachers plan the language and subject content for their specific lessons, using a curriculum framework. Next, we will discuss in Chapter 3 how to plan the structure of classroom activities, and finally, we provide a chapter on how to develop and adapt materials, including textbooks and computer-assisted language learning.

Reference

Wright, T. (1987). *Roles of teachers and learners*. Oxford: Oxford University Press.

Chapter 1

Planning Curriculum

VIGNETTE

I am working with a group of teachers from three different universities in Thailand who are exploring ways to innovate their syllabus. I present my ideas of the process for curriculum design and the group agrees that it wants to embark on that process. They begin with their theoretical framework and come up with a long list of their jointly held beliefs about language and language learning. The discussion around these beliefs is quite intense, but everyone agrees on all but two items on a final list. These are "Language means the ability to analyze the language structure" and "Language is understanding the meaning of vocabulary." Two of the ones they agree on are "Language varies according to contexts, disciplines, and workplaces" and "Language is a functional tool for communication, academic studies, and professional development." They are university-based, teaching both university students and English in the workplace, as can be seen by some of their beliefs. Next they decide to focus on a standard for oral language that is required by their curriculum, "Students will be able to orally present information in their related field." They then develop a list of performance indicators through which learners could demonstrate their ability, such as "can introduce the purpose of the presentation," "can organize the information coherently," and "can use transitional phrases to link ideas." They next develop an assessment task for the standard: "Choose a topic of your interest only from the Internet, research into it, and use the information collected to give an oral presentation to your class." Then they list exactly what learners are to include in their presentation. Because this is an initial workshop, they have some issues that need to be worked through in the next workshop, such as whether searching for information on the Internet should be a separate standard, taught before this one. They also realize they needed to say how long the presentation should be and also be far more explicit about the Internet search, such as how many sites students should consult. [Murray, research notes]

Task: Reflect

1. Why do you think some teachers didn't agree that analyzing language and knowing the meaning of vocabulary were appropriate in their framework?

2.   What are your views about the four belief statements we've included here? Are they part of your beliefs about language and language learning? Why? Why not?

3.   What other performance indicators do you think are needed for this standard?

4.   How would you make the task more explicit? Rewrite it and share with a colleague.

Introduction

Often teachers work to a curriculum determined by others—by the nation, the state, or even the institution where they work. Sometimes, however, teachers need to develop new curricula or adapt a curriculum for their own particular context. It is therefore important for teachers to understand the principles of curriculum design and to practice developing and adapting curricula.

All effective curricula are based on an organizing principle, either agreed upon by its users or determined by its designers. The most common organizing principles in English language teaching are: linguistic, subject matter, learner-centeredness, and learning-centeredness. We shall briefly examine each of these organizing principles because you may find yourself teaching to a curriculum based on any one (or more) of these principles. The curriculum design does not inherently determine the instructional strategies you will use, even though some designs lend themselves more easily to particular strategies.

Task: Reflect

Think about your own language learning. Which organizing principles drove the curriculum design? Respond with "yes" or "no" to each principle. Keep your responses and, after you have completed the chapter, return to this brief set of questions and see whether you agree with your initial reflections now that you know more about each.

____1.   The curriculum was organized around grammatical structures.

____2.   The curriculum was organized around texts.

____3.   The curriculum was organized around themes.

____4.   The curriculum was organized around the content I needed to study.

____5.   The curriculum was organized around competencies I was expected to master.

____6.   The curriculum was organized around tasks I was expected to carry out.

____7.   The curriculum was organized by the class in negotiation with the teachers.

Organizing Principles

Linguistic-based

A number of different approaches are based on linguistic information—grammar-based, functional/notional, and text-/genre-based.

Grammar-based Design

One of the earliest organizing principles was grammatical structures. This approach is often called a structural syllabus. In such a design, each aspect of the curriculum is a grammatical structure, with progression through the curriculum based on what is considered to be most easily learned to most difficult structures. Therefore, these designs often begin with present tense and leave structures such as conditional until later stages. One of the problems with this design is that there is still insufficient research to guide the progression. Further, the structure often takes precedence over meaning and other aspects of language, such as functions, text structures, and appropriacy of language use (see Volume I, Part II, for discussion of these aspects of language). However, even if the main principle is not grammatical structures, any curriculum must ensure that learners are exposed to and have opportunities to practise all the grammatical structures they need in order to use English.

One of the problems with such an approach is that learners may be able to create accurate sentences, but not be able to use them appropriately.

Notional/Functional-based Design

Notional/functional approaches began with the Council of Europe in the 1970s, and were adopted in response to learners and teachers noticing that, while learners might be able to produce grammatically correct utterances, these might not be used appropriately. The focus in this approach, then, is the pragmatic purposes of language use (see Volume I, Chapter 9). Therefore, notional/functional approaches begin with the functions (such as apologizing, asking permission, or refusing/declining an invitation) and include notions (such as time, space, or health) that learners need to perform to be communicatively competent. In functional/notional approaches, the grammatical features taught are dictated by the function.

One of the problems with this approach is that there is no one-to-one correspondence between functions and syntax.

Text- or Genre-based Design

Genre- or text-based approaches begin with the text types that learners will need for the contexts in which they will use the language. In such an approach (see, for example, Feez, 1998), language is seen as a resource for making meaning through whole texts and language learning involves learning how to choose among the different meanings expressed through linguistic systems to communicate effectively in different contexts (see, for example, Feez, 1998; Halliday, 1985; New South Wales Adult Migrant Education Services, 2003). This curriculum model is based on *systemic functional grammar*, where text refers to a stretch of language, whether spoken

, that coheres through meaning and is embedded in the social contexts in is used. While a number of teaching methodologies could be used in a text-based approach, this approach is most commonly used with explicit instruction of the linguistic features of the text and the staging that makes the text coherent. Texts can be oral or written, monologues or dialogs.

One of the difficulties with this approach is that, while the linguistic features of texts/genres can be described, not all genres have been described and users can use a variety of different features and still accomplish a successful text.

Subject-matter-based

A number of approaches begin with subject matter, rather than linguistic features. A content-based curriculum involves the study of language and subject matter where the language structures and the sequence of their presentation are determined by the content, not by any inherent aspect of the language itself. It has been used in a variety of settings and takes different forms in these different settings. In the United States, Canada, and Australia, it is usually referred to as *content-based instruction (CBI)* or is part of bilingual education, whereas in Europe, it is referred to as *content and language integrated learning (CLIL)*. The various instantiations of content-based curriculum design are discussed in Chapter 11, this volume.

One of the difficulties in adopting a content-based approach is that the language taught is not predetermined. Therefore, it is vital in the planning stages that a system is worked out to show what grammar and functions are to be learned.

Learner-centeredness

One would think that all curricula should be learner-centered. However, this term refers to one particular orientation to curriculum design. It is most closely associated with Chris Candlin and David Nunan and their groundbreaking work in the adult migrant English program (AMEP) in Australia in the 1980s. Learner needs were the starting point for syllabus design, the syllabus was negotiated with the learner, and the teacher was seen as curriculum developer (Nunan, 1988).

While such a design empowers learners and teachers, this design has serious shortcomings for most settings. Because much of the course content is negotiated with learners, there is no explicit progression from level to level and so learners (and other stakeholders) may not be able to develop effective pathways for learners. Many learners, especially those coming from backgrounds where teachers take all the responsibility for instructional decisions, feel that their teachers are being "lazy" and not doing their job. Such a bottom–up planning process depends on teacher autonomy and teachers becoming curriculum developers and so makes tremendous demands on their time and may stretch their expertise.

Learning-centeredness

Again, one would expect that all curricula would focus on student learning and certainly all frameworks are interested in what learners learn. However, a learning-centered approach focuses on outcomes, that is, what is learned, and then works back to determine what to include in the curriculum.

A number of different approaches have been adopted that take a focus on learner outcomes as their guiding principle: outcomes, competency, standards, and task-based. While all three have a similar focus, quite different philosophies underlie each of these approaches.

Outcomes-based Design

Outcomes-based education has a long history in general education, where it has had very specific approaches to defining and assessing outcomes (Spady, 1993). Progress towards specific objectives is what governs activity. The curriculum lists desired outcomes in the form of learner behaviors, skills, attitudes, and abilities. Learning experiences are then designed to allow teachers to coach the learners to a mastery level in each outcome. Learners are assessed against the outcomes. Spady advocates transformative outcomes, ones that will help learners become productive citizens, problem-solvers, or autonomous learners. Such outcomes should fundamentally restructure courses and programs.

Like the learner-centered approach of Nunan and others, in Spady's approach students are self-directed.

Competency-based Design

The *competency-based approach*, which emerged in the United States in the 1970s, depends on determining learner needs and then developing a curriculum in which both instructional goals and assessment measures consist of a list of competencies for learners to achieve. These competencies are written in "can do" statements and need to be measurable. Therefore, this approach provides a list of verbs that are acceptable as measurable achievements of learners, such as, *identify, respond, demonstrate, summarize,* and *scan*. In contrast, verbs such as *understand* are not considered measurable. Learners are told the skills they are to achieve and so instruction and assessment are transparent to learners. This approach is not unique to language learning and has been used primarily in adult education, with a focus on learner mastery of skills. Table 1.1 below lists the two most commonly used competency-based approaches, along with a sample competency from each.

CASAS grew out of California's concern in the 1970s at the plethora of instructional models used in adult education and so in 1980 adult ELT adopted CASAS to provide a consistent approach. It was developed by the California Department of Education and a consortium of local adult education agencies. Since then, it has been adopted in all states and elsewhere. Similarly, in Australia at the

Table 1.1 Competency-based Curricula

Curriculum	Sample competency
Comprehensive Adult Student Assessment System (CASAS)	• Complete a personal information form • Clarify or request clarification
Certificates in Spoken and Written Language (CSWE)	• Can conduct a short telephone conversation • Can read a procedural text

same time there was concern about lack of consistency across programs and the Commonwealth Government adopted the CSWE as the national curriculum framework to ensure explicit learner pathways.

Canada also uses a competency-based approach for adult immigrants. However, they use benchmarks that provide a descriptive scale of ESOL proficiency for adult learners; it is not a syllabus. However, curriculum developers can use the benchmarks as a guide in syllabus design.

One of the problems with a competency-based approach is that it can be reduced to checklists that do not ensure that learners can engage in sustained interactions. While a competency-based approach to education works quite well for subject matter that is skills-based, it works less well when dealing with something as fundamental to human expression and identity (see Volume I, Chapter 1) as language.

Standards-based Design

The standards movement began in the United States in the late 1980s in response to government requirements for greater accountability, challenging subject matter, and greater consistency across school districts. Standards usually include not only content objectives regarding what learners should know and be able to do, but also teaching principles and instructional strategies. In the United States, TESOL, the international professional association, engaged in bottom-up development of standards for various contexts of English language education—pre-K–12 learners and teachers in the U.S., adult teachers, and teachers and learners in China. The pre-K–12 learner standards consist of three goals and nine standards. Each standard is elaborated by descriptors, sample progress indicators, and classroom vignettes and discussions. The standards are organized around grade-level clusters—pre-K–3, 4–8 and 9–12. (See TESOL's website for more details of these projects http://www.tesol.org/s_tesol/seccss.asp?CID=86&DID=1556.) Table 1.2 provides an example of the standards.

At the same time, various other initiatives were under way in Australia and Europe and later, in many countries in Asia, such as Thailand. The terminology and organization of the different standards reflect the different views of language and learning by the standards developers. So, for example, the Australian document (McKay & Scarino, 1991) is called the ESL Framework of Stages and consists of the following components: communication goal, objectives, activities, assessment tasks, criteria for assessing student performance, and key indicators for where students lie along a continuum of developmental stages. There is greater specification of language to be learned and also of activities for classroom use. In Europe, *The Common European Framework of Reference for Languages* (CEFR) was designed to set standards across all EU countries for all taught languages and grew out of work in the 1970s on a threshold level for learning modern languages (van Ek, 1976). The CEFR describes "i) the competences necessary for communication, ii) the related knowledge and skills, and iii) the situations and domains of communication. The CEFR defines levels of attainment in different aspects of its descriptive scheme with illustrative descriptors scale" (Council of Europe, n.d.).

In the United Kingdom, there has been recent development of standards for adult learners. The Adult ESOL Core Curriculum offers a framework for English language learning, defines the skills, knowledge and understanding that ESOL learners

Table 1.2 TESOL Pre-K–12 Standards: Samples of Goal 1 for Grades 9–12

Goal	Standard	Sample descriptors	Sample progress indicators
To use English to communicate in social settings	Standard 1: Students will use English to participate in social interactions	• sharing and requesting information • expressing needs, feelings, and ideas	• express feelings through drama, poetry, or song • make an appointment
	Standard 2: Students will interact in, through, and with spoken and written English for personal expression and enjoyment	• expressing personal needs, feelings, and ideas • participating in popular culture	• talk about a favorite food or celebration • express humor through verbal and nonverbal means
	Standard 3: Students will use learning strategies to extend their communicative competence	• self-monitoring and self-evaluating language development • using the primary language to ask for clarification	• test appropriate use of new vocabulary, phrases, and structures • ask someone the meaning of a word

© Teachers of English to Speakers of Other Languages, Inc. (TESOL). Reprinted with permission.

need to demonstrate their achievement of the national standards, and provides a reference tool for ESOL teachers in a variety of different settings (The Adult ESOL Core Curriculum, 2001).

These various standards documents are not of themselves curricula since they do not take into consideration the differences in context in which the standards might be used. They do, however, provide a framework for nations, states, and institutions to develop curricula that are standards-based.

Task-based Design

Tasks have been defined in many different ways and sometimes the term has been used as a synonym for activity. However, most proponents of task-based design agree that the context for the task should have a purpose beyond the display of knowledge or practice of discrete skills; realistic uses of the subject inside and beyond the classroom; a process of talking, thinking, and doing by learners; an integration of knowledge, strategy, and skill; and a product that is more than just language. The various proponents of task-based approaches to curriculum design have aligned themselves with different design types. Breen and Candlin's (1980) proposal, for example, is a negotiated syllabus, which is more usefully conceived of as learner-centered. Prabhu's (1987) procedural syllabus is really a set of different activities. Long and Crookes' (1992) approach is to include focus on form, but the syllabus is not designed around grammatical forms. What all seem to agree on is that task–based curricula should conform to what we know about language learning. It is for this reason that we have included it under learning-centered approaches.

Curriculum Design Process

Many writers have developed schema for delineating the process of curriculum design. We provide a process we have used in our own ELT work. The process we use places learning and therefore student performance as a result of learning at the center of the process. We will describe this process here in a linear fashion. However, the design process is dynamic. The components of the process are provided in Table 1.3.

You might notice that we have not used the terms *method* or *methodology* in the process. These are highly disputed in ELT. The position we take here is that methodology is the activities, tasks, and learning experiences used by the teacher within the teaching and learning process. Methodology has a theoretical basis in the teacher's assumptions about (a) language and second language learning, (b) teacher and learner roles, and (c) learning activities and instructional materials. Therefore, we have chosen here to discuss the specifics of methodology rather than to use a method or methodology as if it were a uniform whole.

Determining Theoretical Framework

Although it may be necessary to analyze stakeholders and learner needs first, many curricula are developed based on particular views of the educational authority, the institution, or the teacher. A brief survey of the literature on curriculum innovation shows that most innovations have begun with a particular view of language and/or

Table 1.3 Process of Curriculum Design

Stage	Sample questions to ask
Determining theoretical framework	What is the broad sociocultural context of learning? What beliefs about language and language learning are to be articulated through the curriculum?
Conducting stakeholder analysis	Who are the stakeholders? What do they expect learners to be able to do?
Conducting needs analysis	What do learners already know and are able to do? What do they need to know and be able to do?
Determining outcomes/goal	What are the intended goals of the course? What will learners have to do to achieve those goals?
Selecting content	What content needs to be taught so learners can achieve these goals?
Sequencing content	How should content be organized?
Selecting learning materials and activities	What materials help learners acquire the content? What activities help learners achieve the course objectives? What roles do teachers and learners take?
Assessing learning	How will I find out what learners have achieved?

learning in mind. For example, Singapore changed its English language teaching curriculum in 2001. This was an example of a top-down, large-scale curriculum change. The Ministry of Education viewed language not as subject matter, but as something to use for information, literary purposes, and social interaction. The goal was to teach learners to communicate effectively in English so that they could use language meaningfully and appropriately for a specific purpose, audience, context, and culture. Further, they understood that language purpose determines the types of texts learners would need. Additional values included a "thinking skill" initiative developed in 1997, information technology (IT), and national education. These beliefs then drove the content of the curriculum (see Goh & Yin, 2008, for a description of the curriculum design process). Thus, for example, the value thinking skill and the focus on texts led to learning outcomes such as students being able to infer and draw conclusions from reading or listening texts by using contextual clues and prior knowledge. The inclusion of IT as a value, along with the focus on texts, rather than discrete linguistic items, led to learning outcomes such as students being able to demonstrate the understanding of language and text types from print/non-print/electronic sources.

Conducting Stakeholder Analysis

Many models for curriculum development do not include this step. We believe it is vital so that the curriculum meets learner needs and is accepted by all stakeholders. Often, in top-down, large-scale curriculum design, such as that for Singapore discussed earlier, teachers' beliefs, expertise, and understandings are not acknowledged and so no attention is paid to the management of the implementation. As a result, the intended curriculum is reinterpreted by teachers. Therefore, teacher expertise and ability to work with the new curriculum is a vital consideration during the stakeholder analysis stage.

In the stakeholder analysis, as well as defining who the stakeholders are, it is necessary to ask global questions about how the language curriculum will meet their needs. What role does English play in the broader community? Is it a subject of study in the school curriculum or is it a language used for wider communication? What variety of English is valued by the community? Is it used in the home? Is it a gatekeeper in the community? What expectations does the community have for its investment in English language education? Does it support economic development?

Task: Explore

Who are the stakeholders in the context in which you teach (or plan to teach)? Design a brief questionnaire to find out what they need and expect from an English language curriculum. Choose two or three people from different stakeholder groups and have them respond to your questionnaire. If these stakeholders are not nearby, send your questionnaire via email. Collate your data and share them with your class or a colleague.

Conducting Needs Analysis

All effective curricula are based on the language learning needs of the specific learners. Interestingly, all of the above curriculum design principles can be based on learner needs (although not all necessarily are).

What Do Learners Need?

Given the wide range of contexts in which English is taught (see Volume I, Chapter 3), learner needs are dependent on the context of learning. To help get some idea of the complexity of learner needs, we provide the following two quite different scenarios.

Scenario 1	Scenario 2
The learners are Grade 3 in primary school in Taiwan. All children are Taiwanese. They are in a classroom with a local Taiwanese teacher, who has limited English speaking skills. A native speaker teacher is provided for the school to assist the classroom teachers. The goal of the government is to develop bilingualism and make English the official second language. Once these learners are in high school, they will take many of the secondary subjects in English, and so they need to develop sufficient proficiency in primary school to be successful with secondary level academic language. Parents want their children to become bilingual so that they can get prestigious and financially remunerative work in global companies.	The learners are recent immigrants and refugees to Australia. They come from more than 140 language backgrounds, and countries as varied as China, Iraq, Lebanon, Sudan, and Russia. Some learners are not literate in their home language, some have graduate degrees, and some have irregularly attended school for several years. Ages range from 18 to seniors 60 and older. Some have been in refugee camps for much of their life; others held professional positions in their country of origin. The government's goal is to help all learners settle in their new country, acquiring sufficient English proficiency to be able to manage their day-to-day encounters with Australian-born and other immigrants and to be work-ready.

To determine learner needs, curriculum designers need to conduct a needs analysis. Earlier models of needs analysis focused on interviewing learners about their needs. However, as can be seen from the scenarios above, learners are not the only stakeholders involved and with investment in learner outcomes. Hence the step we described earlier. To determine learner needs, teachers need to ask questions about learner identity, experiences, and goals. For more proficient learners, these questions can be asked in an interview. For beginner learners, you can use simple agree/disagree statements. Table 1.4 provides a sample questionnaire. This is not a complete questionnaire for a specific group of learners, but includes items for different types of learners. For example, 5b and 5c would be appropriate for an

Table 1.4 Needs Analysis Questionnaire

---

1. What is your age?
2. How long have you been learning English?
3. Where did you learn English?
4. What will you do when you finish this course?
5. How difficult are these tasks for you in English? Very difficult   ok   easy
   a. Asking questions in class
   b. Doing a formal presentation
   c. Writing essays
   d. Reading labels on food
   e. Talking to the doctor
6. How do you like to learn? Rank your choices.
   a. In groups
   b. By reading
   c. By thinking by myself
   d. Being told by the teacher
   e. By rote

---

academic curriculum, while 5d and 5e might be appropriate for immigrants. The table is provided to give you some idea of the types of questions to ask for your particular contexts.

Learner Identity

What is their age? Educational level? Occupation? Gender? Motivation? Family or other circumstances that might affect learning? Race? Ethnicity? See Volume 1, Chapter 1, for a discussion of learner identity.

Learner Experiences

What are their previous language learning experiences? What do learners already know and what are they able to do in English? What attitudes do they have towards English?

The question of what learners already know and can do requires a language assessment, so they can be placed in appropriate classes and also to determine where to start teaching. See Chapters 12 and 13, this volume, for discussions on placement assessment.

Learner Goals

To pass a school subject? To pass a gatekeeping examination? To settle in an English–dominant country? To work for a multinational company? To study in an English–medium university?

Determining Outcomes/Goals

For goals and objectives to be useful, they need to be measurable since assessment of learning will involve assessment of the extent to which the learners have achieved the curriculum goals. One often overlooked set of goals is the learning process.

Learners who can reflect on their own learning can develop learning strategies that are appropriate for their own preferred learning styles and become more effective language learners. These are often referred to as learning-how-to-learn strategies and goals. When the curriculum is for a very specific purpose and context, for example, to prepare students for a nursing course, to prepare students for entry to an accounting degree at a university, or to help managers in the electronics industry to give presentations, one method for determining needs is to observe communications in the actual setting. Most curricula have a small, limited set of goals (usually around five or six) for which specific sets of objectives are developed. Table 1.5 provides sample goals (both language and learning-how-to-learn) and some possible specific objectives. These are taken from the Australian Language Levels Guidelines for K–12 (McKay & Scarino, 1991).

Selecting Content

Content includes both the language to be taught and the subject matter in which the language is embedded. In some literature on curriculum this is referred to as *scope*. In terms of language, we need to select items from the following list of language characteristics:

- language structures
- skills
- genres
- registers
- speech acts/functions
- sociocultural appropriacy
- process/product
- generic skills, and
- nonlanguage outcomes.

Educators also need to decide what subject matter content needs to be included in order to help meet learners' needs and help them achieve the goals of the course. Both of these aspects of content are discussed in detail in Chapter 10.

Table 1.5 Sample Goals and Objectives

Goals	Related objectives
Language	Learners will be able to:
To enable learners to obtain information by searching for specific details in spoken or written text and then process and use the information obtained	• extract information from a range of spoken texts • understand a process and be able to explain the process to another learner • follow instructions • write a summary • extract information from charts and tables
Learning how to learn	
To develop cognitive processing strategies	• ask for repetition • ask for further explanation

Sequencing Content

Having selected the content, you then need to decide how to sequence it. You need to ask questions such as: what subject matter knowledge builds on other knowledge? What language functions build on other functions, texts, and grammar? What grammar needs to be included so learners have the language to create texts or engage in tasks? This is a critical phase of curriculum design and, in many ways, the most tricky. It's difficult because, unlike some other areas such as arithmetic, there is no predefined linear progression and much depends on what learners achieve along the way. However, as each section of the curriculum is decided, you must decide the next steps towards learners achieving the goals and objectives of the course.

Selecting Learning Materials and Activities

This stage involves selecting materials and activities that will translate the goals and objectives into learning experiences for students. In other words, materials and activities are not selected because they seem like a good idea or because students might find them fun, but because they will help learners meet the goals and objectives of the course. We have therefore devoted separate chapters to each of these topics (Chapters 3 and 4).

Assessing Learning

As Broadfoot (1991) claims, assessment is a celebration of learning. Therefore, any curriculum needs to include assessment that is tied to the goals and objectives of the course. We include this here because it is an essential part of the process. However, because assessment is the ultimate planning and evaluation tool, we provide details of assessment in Part III of this book.

Adapting Curriculum

As mentioned earlier, most teachers work from an existing curriculum. However, most curricula do not provide a day-by-day, hour-by-hour description of what is to be taught and how. The exception often is when a textbook is prescribed and teachers are asked to work through it. Teachers therefore need to work from the existing curriculum to develop their lessons, and choose their activities and materials. In working from a textbook, teachers still need to supplement so they meet the needs of the learners in their particular context. We will come back to these issues in Chapters 2, 3, and 4.

Curriculum in Practice

While the curriculum teachers develop or work with may have been developed following the most effective principles of curriculum design, it is really a "statement of intent" (Nunan, 1992). How the curriculum is resourced, implemented, and its effect on learning can be quite different from the intent. These differences result from decisions made by institutions, teachers, and learners. Adamson, Kwan, and

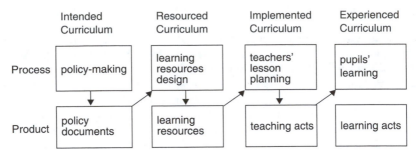

Figure 1.1 Steps in Curriculum Decision-making.

Reprinted with permission from Adamson et al. (2000). *Changing the curriculum: The impact of reform on primary schooling in Hong Kong.* Hong Kong: Hong Kong University Press.

Chan (2000), in discussing the implementation of a new curriculum in Hong Kong primary schools, capture these different perspectives in Figure 1.1 (p. 146).

Conclusion

Curricula are embedded in the sociocultural setting in which they are used. Therefore curricula need to reflect the beliefs and values of language and language learning in the local community. For this reason, curricula do not travel well. If teachers have the opportunity to design their own curriculum, either by themselves or with colleagues, they will need to follow the dynamic process described earlier. The only proof that the curriculum is working is through assessing students' learning. Having assessed whether learners are achieving the goals and objectives, teachers then need to go back to the curriculum and adjust where needed.

Task: Expand

Feez, S. (1998). *Text-based syllabus design.* Sydney: NCELTR.

This is the most thorough description of a curriculum based on text. Feez also provides a useful overview of other types of curriculum design.

Nunan, D. (1988). *The learner-centred curriculum: A study in second-language teaching.* Cambridge: Cambridge University Press.

In this volume, Nunan describes the implementation of a learner-centered curriculum in Australia's Adult Migrant English Program in the 1980s.

Questions for Discussion

1. Explain the overarching organizing principles used in designing language curricula.
2. What are the advantages and disadvantages of a learner-centered approach to curriculum design?

3. In this chapter you read about standards–based curricula. Explain how the curriculum designer moves from broad goals to actual learner outcomes.
4. What is a needs analysis? How can it be conducted? Why is it important in planning instruction?
5. Explain the different steps in curriculum decision–making. Who do you think should be involved in the various stages?
6. Why (and how) do curricula change as they go from intent to resources, to implementation, to experience?

References

Adamson, B., Kwan, T., & Chan, K. K. (Eds.). (2000). *Changing the curriculum: The impact of reform on primary schooling in Hong Kong*. Hong Kong: Hong Kong University Press.

Breen, M. P., & Candlin, C. N. (1980). The essentials of a communicative curriculum in language teaching. *Applied Linguistics*, *1*(2), 89–112.

Broadfoot, P. (1991). *Assessment: A celebration of learning*. Belconnon, ACT: Australian Curriculum Studies Association.

Council of Europe. (n.d.). The Common European Reference for Languages: Learning, Teaching, Assessment. Retrieved from http://www.coe.int/T/DG4/Linguistic/CADRE_EN.asp

Feez, S. (1998). *Text-based syllabus design*. Sydney: NCELTR.

Goh, C. C. M., & Yin, T. M. (2008). Implementing the English Language Syllabus 2001 in Singapore Schools: Interpretations and Re-interpretations. In D. E. Murray (Ed.), *Planning change, changing plans: Innovations in second language teaching* (pp. 85–107). Ann Arbor, MI: University of Michigan Press.

Halliday, M. A. K. (1985). *An introduction to functional grammar*. London: Edward Arnold.

Long, M., & Crookes, G. (1992). Three approaches to task-based syllabus design. *TESOL Quarterly*, *26*, 27–56.

McKay, P., & Scarino, A. (1991). *ESL framework of stages: An approach to ESL learning in schools*. Melbourne: Curriculum Corporation.

New South Wales Adult Migrant Education Services. (2003). *Certificate I in spoken and written English*. Sydney: NSW AMES.

Nunan, D. (1988). *The learner-centred curriculum: A study in second-language teaching*. Cambridge: Cambridge University Press.

Nunan, D. (1992). Toward a collaborative approach to curriculum development: A case study. In D. Nunan (Ed.), *Collaborative language learning and teaching* (pp. 230–253). Cambridge: Cambridge University Press.

Prabhu, N. S. (1987). *Second language pedagogy*. Oxford: Oxford University Press.

Spady, W. (1993). *Outcome-based education*. Belconnen, ACT: Australian Curriculum Studies Association.

The Adult ESOL Core Curriculum. (2001). Retrieved from http://www.dcsf.gov.uk/readwriteplus/ESOL

van Ek, J. A. (1976). *The threshold level for modern language learning in schools*. London: Longman.

Planning Lesson Content

VIGNETTE

Peter was teaching an adult class of 19 recently arrived immigrants and refugees to Australia. They had intermediate proficiency in English and a variety of language and educational backgrounds. The curriculum goal for the course that term was for students to be able to produce a written report of 100–200 words. The curriculum does not mandate topic content and so Peter had to decide what content he would use to teach students how to write a report and also what topic they should use for their own reports. He was dismayed "at students' frequent lack of knowledge and interest in world events, news, and current affairs" outside of their own area of interest (usually events in their home country). He thought that using the Internet to access content might motivate his students to learn about world events. He therefore "maintained a constant news focus during the term in general listening/speaking/reading exercises and encouraged discussion/ awareness of current affairs in the classroom." However, while initially almost half the class chose a topic stimulated by a recent news item they had read or listened to (e.g,. World Trade Center Twin Towers, aircraft "black boxes," land mines, "Big Brother TV series"), only five actually wrote on a topic that was both related in some way to a news item they had read and outside of their existing knowledge. Others wrote on a city in their home country or on an Australian animal or other miscellaneous topics. On reflection after the course, Peter decided that one of the problems was the serendipitous nature of news items. Students' ability to choose a suitable topic was constrained by what news there was on the day they had to search the Internet websites for news that could stimulate a report. (Norton, 2002)

Task: Reflect

1. Although Peter's students produced appropriate written reports, they were not all on the topic of news that he had asked for. How would you handle this if these were your students?
2. To what extent do you think using the Internet might have helped or hindered students in choosing a topic for their reports?

3.   Why do you think so many students chose to write on a city in their home country or Australian animals?
4.   How could Peter have anticipated and planned to avoid the serendipitous nature of current events?

Introduction

In Chapter 1, we explained how to develop a curriculum. Many teachers have no or limited autonomy regarding what to teach, whether at the level of curriculum or individual lesson. In some contexts, teachers work from a prescribed textbook; in others, they can adapt, add to, and select from a prescribed textbook; in yet other contexts, they have the freedom to develop their own lessons, as long as their learners achieve the curriculum outcomes developed by the institution or state. Most teachers have to work from a general curriculum framework to develop specific teaching units to meet the curriculum goals. To do this requires knowing not only what to teach, but also how to teach. In Chapters 2–4 we explain how to develop a teaching program, develop and select the activities (Chapter 3) and materials (Chapter 4) to support learning goals. In this chapter, we begin by presenting some general principles concerning planning instruction. We then discuss the types of content teachers need to include in their teaching and present the principles for creating a unit of work and an individual lesson plan. By **unit of work**, we mean a coherent, integrated, and sequenced series of lessons that meet specific curriculum goals. The unit may cover one or more weeks of instruction. Different countries and traditions use different terms for this concept. By **individual lesson**, we refer to one meeting of teacher and learners, which may be for 50 minutes or three hours.

Principles for Planning Instruction

We begin with some general principles because instruction should facilitate learning. There are two types of planning: preparation prior to teaching and planning in situ. The former refers to a teacher deciding what to teach and how to teach it and this will be the major focus of this chapter. It includes teachers' changing their plans based on student learning. In the vignette above, for example, Peter could have changed his plan in the middle of the course and chosen old news items for students to choose from, once he realized his students were having a difficult time finding an appropriate topic. This would, of course, have drastically changed his goals of trying to interest learners in world events and in giving them autonomy over their report topic.

In addition to this change of plans based on student learning or other aspects of the context, in situ planning also occurs. During a lesson, teachers notice that learners are "not getting it," that the materials they have chosen are too difficult or too easy. Teachers make decisions on the spot to change their activities to ensure learning takes place, rather than sticking to their plan regardless of what happens in the classroom. Effective teachers constantly monitor their own and their learners' behaviors and language use, evaluating what is working and what needs to be changed. As well as planning in situ because the original lesson plan is not working, teachers also seize opportunities for learning that arise from student questions or other behaviors in the classroom. This is referred to as "a teachable moment," or **interactive decisions** (Richards & Lockhart, 1994). An example illustrates. One of us was teaching the practicum class in an M.A. program and students were reporting on their observations in different settings. One student, Kaye, was observing in a K–12 school and on this particular occasion was observing a pull-out special reading tutoring session. This particular reading program was designed for learners having difficulty learning to read and was highly prescriptive, with each tutoring session scripted for the tutor. Teachers were trained not to deviate from the script. Kaye was observing the tutoring session when the young boy suddenly interjected, "My dog died last night." The teacher responded, "Oh, I'm sorry" and proceeded with the lesson script. Kaye was disturbed and asked our class if this was appropriate and suggested that the teacher could have used this as an opportunity to engage the young boy about his dog, perhaps having him draw the dog. Other students jumped in with lots of other suggestions such as having the young boy write the dog's name or even dictate a story about him and his dog to the teacher, who could write it down and then use it as a reading text (see Volume I, Chapter 5, on the language experience approach). The teacher of this young boy missed the opportunities presented by this teachable moment by adhering so strictly to her lesson plan.

The research literature refers to these teacher behaviors as decision-making (Shavelson, 1973) or reasoning (Johnson, 1999). Shavelson notes that *the* most important skills that differentiate average teachers from exceptional ones are the decisions they make, whether conscious or unconscious. For the novice teacher, in situ decision-making is quite difficult and often teachers fall back on teaching the way they were taught. However, with constant reflection on one's practice, teachers can acquire the ability to reason among the dynamic, complex, moment-to-moment events that occur in the classroom. We explore techniques for examining one's own practice in Chapter 11, this volume.

When planning instruction, based on what is known about learning and teaching (explained in detail in Volume I), instruction should:

- build on what learners already know
- present new information in chunks that learners can digest
- include teacher input that is comprehensible to learners
- challenge learners to move beyond their current level of language
- include opportunities for learners to practise new skills and knowledge
- provide feedback (from teachers and/or peers)
- provide a supportive environment
- be responsive to learning opportunities that occur in the classroom.

As well as adhering to these specific principles, teachers must also be aware of the social nature of instruction, which we discussed in detail in Volume 1, Part I. In planning, therefore, it is important to consider the social as well as the pedagogical components. There may be a mismatch between the teacher's plans and the learners' view of instruction. As Prabhu (1992) notes:

> [A] recommended teaching procedure may incorporate the principle that learners' efforts should precede the teacher's input, such that much of the learning takes place as a form of discovery by the learner, and the teacher's

input is responsive to the learner's effort, rather than pre-emptive of it. But the classroom lesson as a social genre often includes the notion that it is a part of the teacher's role to provide the necessary inputs and that it is therefore unfair or incompetent of the teacher to demand effort by learners in the absence of such inputs. (pp. 230–1)

While Prabhu refers here only to a procedure, this can be equally true for choice of content or materials. In the vignette above, Peter deliberately wanted to choose topic content that learners were not familiar with and may even not have been interested in. While teachers may, like Peter, choose topic content that learners may be uncomfortable with, they may also choose to have learners choose their own topic content. Peter did this as well, by making the actual choice of topic for the report of the learners' own choosing. Similarly, many learners want to learn grammar rules, while the teacher may want to teach by modeling and practice.

Similarly, teachers need to determine the extent of L1 use in a particular lesson. As we noted in Volume 1, the use of L1 can support the acquisition of English. However, if the L1 is used for all instructional language in the classroom and English only for models and practice, learners are exposed to a very limited range of English use. Often, the most authentic uses of English are those in which teachers ask questions or give instructions to learners.

Task: Reflect

If you wanted to use an approach or content that you thought students might be uncomfortable with, what would you do? How would you introduce the approach or content? To what extent do you think teachers should allow learners to choose their own content or way of learning? Or do you think the choice of content should be solely that of the teacher? Discuss this with a colleague.

Types of Content

In language teaching, the goal is to help learners become proficient users of the target language. This is rather different from teaching a body of knowledge such as mathematics or science. Rather, it requires teaching a skill. In teaching other skills such as automotive repair, language is the vehicle for teaching the skills. The paradox in language teaching is that the language is both the vehicle for teaching and the goal. In many programs, therefore, the language is taught not as a skill, but as subject matter with rules that need to be learned. In other words, learners are being taught *about* language, not how to use the language. In many contexts, this view has been rejected and many countries around the world have mandated more communicative approaches, that is, teaching situations in which learners get to use the language, preferably in life-like situations. The result of such curriculum innovation means that teachers need to choose some topics for learners to talk about. Therefore, in our view the content of language instruction as having two intersecting parts—*language* and *topics*, both of which we discuss below.

Language

Many programs divide language into its four components—listening, speaking, reading, and writing—with separate classes for each mode. Others use an integrated approach in which all four modes are taught in the one class. In one sense, it is not possible to teach each mode separately, as all lessons involve speaking and listening, while writing (also called composition) classes require learners to read texts so that they have something to write about other than their own personal experiences. Here we take an integrated approach to language content, while recognizing that in some contexts, teachers will focus on individual language modes for specific lessons (or even programs).

As we presented in Volume 1, Part II, language consists of sounds, words, sentences, and texts, as well as the conditions for using the particular linguistic item. So, when planning content, it is not sufficient to choose which linguistic items to teach, such as **questions** or **requests**. Teachers must also decide what contexts the language will occur in. For example, while it might be appropriate to say to a friend, "*Hey, why don't you open the window?*" or "*It's too hot in here*" as requests to open a window, in a formal setting or in a train with strangers, it would be more appropriate to say, "*I'm really hot. Do you think you could open the window?*" or "*Would you mind opening the window? It's really hot in here.*" Therefore, the teacher needs to decide whether to teach requests in informal situations or in formal situations, or both. Again, if teaching present continuous, what context would be appropriate? Often materials present *present continuous* to describe an action going on while someone is watching. This happens to be a rather infrequent use, except for sports announcers. A common use of present continuous is to complain, such as in *She's always talking on her cell phone*. Additionally, teachers need to decide what sequence they want to present language. Some of these choices depend on the curriculum approach the teacher wants to take. If the curriculum is content-based (see Chapter 10, this volume), the subject matter content will determine the language to be taught. Similarly, if the approach is task-based or project-based, the language results from the task, although many researchers on task-based language teaching have found it is difficult to predict what language learners will use to perform the task.

Topics

In some contexts, the topics are mandated. For example, some learners are in compulsory school settings where the regular school curriculum is being taught using English (see Volume 1, Chapter 3, for a discussion on such programs). Then, the topics teachers can use are constrained by the school curriculum. In many other settings, teachers have autonomy in choosing what topics will best facilitate the language they need to teach. Topics can be ones learners need for their lives, such as *going to the doctor* for new immigrants, or *accounting principles* for students preparing to study accounting at university. Topics can also be chosen because they appeal to the particular learners, such as *rap musicians* for teenagers or *the environment* for adults interested in world affairs.

Creating a Unit of Work

As we discussed in detail in Volume 1, language teaching is more than the transfer of information from teacher to learner. The language classroom is also a social event where the culture and roles of teachers and learners, and the context in which teaching takes place, interact to facilitate or resist learning. Therefore, as teachers plan the teaching program, they need to consider their specific context, including learners' perspectives, and arrange for classroom interactions that help learners achieve their language learning goals, as well as the language and topic content discussed above.

In developing a unit of work, teachers need to plan both the **scope** and **sequence** of instruction. By scope, we mean what content will be taught. By sequence, we mean in what order linguistic items and topics will be presented. We illustrate by presenting a unit of work of a teacher in one of our research projects. Peter Norton was teaching a mixed language adult class of 19 students for 8 weeks. The class met three times a week, including a 90-minute session in the computer lab. The specific linguistic curriculum goal for the class was report writing. Although the major goal was a written text, the curriculum integrated speaking, listening, reading, and writing. Peter decided to use world news as the topic content for this unit. The unit assignment was:

Written report

To prepare a written report (100–200 words) on a topic you have chosen from current events reported in the news.

    You can choose any story that is interesting to you. Then choose something from that story that you would like to research and write a report on.

    To choose a news story, you can use either the English language *Easy News* website or an Internet newspaper in your language from the *Paperboy* website.

Peter followed the teaching/learning cycle that is common in his program:

1. building the context
2. modeling and deconstructing the text
3. joint construction of the text
4. independent construction of the text
5. linking the current text type to related texts.

We present his planned unit of work in Table 2.1. Note that this class took place just after the September 11, 2001, attacks in the U.S.

Because the instructional goal was a written report on a topic of the students' own choosing (but related to recent news), the major language teaching was the structure and language of reports (see Volume I, Chapter 9, for these features). This was conducted in English because it was a multilingual class, but the use of L1 by learners to each other for clarification was encouraged. However, students were

Table 2.1 Unit of Work for Learning Outcome: Written Report

	Week 1	Week 2	Week 3	Week 4	Week 5	Week 6	Week 7	Week 8
Language	Recent news vocabulary, structures	News vocabulary and texts	Features of a written report	Describing a town or city	Web search terms			
Topic content	Recent news events	News	Australian cities	Cabramatta (their current town)	Student's home town	Student's own guided choice		
Materials	Survey on student access to news BBC news website	EasyNews¹ website	Website on Australian cities—Sydney	Local council brochures	Websites— LonelyPlanet, Encarta	News websites		
Activities	Complete survey Explore the website	Exercises on the website at different levels of proficiency	Read report online Complete cloze on Sydney	Pairs write a report on Cabramatta	Revise web search skills Write report on home town or country	Exercises on how to choose topics Choose topic for report Consult with teacher Begin Internet search	Internet searching Drafting report	Internet searching Writing report
Outcomes	Complete survey Reading news on website	Listening to items on EasyNews website	Understand features of written report	Collaborative report	Individual report	Topic chosen Net search started	Draft outline of report submitted	Submitted report online

1 *EasyNews* is a website designed for ESL/EFL learners. It contains extracts from radio news programs from SBS (Australia's multilingual, multicultural media broadcaster), arranged by level (beginner, intermediate, advanced) and includes listening comprehension questions.

permitted to use L1 news websites to find a news item that could be the catalyst for the topic of their report. So, for example, one student read a Vietnamese newspaper from the website *Paperboy*, choosing a news item about a typhoon in Vietnam in the previous weeks that had damaged many houses. She then chose to write her report on typhoons in general.

Task: Explore

Re-read the vignette of Peter's experience. Using that information and the overall scope and sequence in the unit of work in Table 2.1, decide how Peter based his planning on the principles of instruction we discussed earlier:

1. building on what learners already know
2. presenting new information in chunks that learners can digest
3. including teacher input that is comprehensible to learners
4. challenging learners to move beyond their current level of language
5. including opportunities for learners to practise new skills and knowledge
6. providing feedback (from teachers and/or peers)
7. providing a supportive environment
8. being responsive to learning opportunities that occur in the classroom.

Planning Lessons

Once teachers have planned the overall unit of work, they then need to plan each lesson in more detail. However, because, as we explained above, learning does not necessarily take place exactly as planned, it is best not to plan individual lessons too far ahead at one time. This allows the teacher to adjust individual components of the unit of work to accommodate what actually happens in the classroom.

The most important first decision is what learning outcomes should be achieved. The lesson objectives should be tied to the overall unit of work and curriculum. Further, they should be in behavioral terms, that is, what learners will know and be able to do as a result of instruction. Work on how teachers frame objectives (Brindley, 1984) has shown that teachers tend to write objectives that are:

- instructional goals (what teachers will do)
- descriptions of course content (language and topic), or
- learning materials to be used.

Other teachers discover a new activity or text and base the lesson on the activity or text. While all these aspects of the lesson need to be considered, they are in fact in the service of the behavioral objectives. Behavioral objectives therefore should be in terms of *doing* verbs within the concepts *understand, apply, analyze, evaluate, create*. Within these concepts, teachers need to think how learners can demonstrate them. For the concept understand, for example, teachers could write the objective in terms of *comparing, classifying,* or perhaps *explaining*. Not only do such specific objectives help teachers assess learning, they also help learners understand what is expected of them. Verbs such as *know* or *appreciate* do not tell teacher or learner what actual performance is expected. Once teachers decide what learners will know and be able to do at the end of the lesson, they can then make decisions about what content needs to be taught and used, what activities will help learners practise the content, and what materials can best present the content.

The following format is helpful when planning a lesson. By using this format teachers become aware of all the issues they need to attend to. Although experienced teachers might omit some of these items, beginning teachers need to be constantly aware of their context and adapt instruction to the specifics of that context.

Lesson plan guidelines

Teacher:	(first and last name)
Date/Time:	(day, date, and time)
School/Room:	(school, building, and room)
Level/Subject:	(level/subject area)
Student body:	(number, age, gender, ethnicity of the students, differences in level or interests or attitudes)
Book:	(what book or computer program the students are using, if any)
Seating:	(what the seating arrangement is)
Materials:	(e.g., handouts, blackboard, audiotape, video, CALL)
Prior lesson(s):	(What content—both language and topic content—was learned in the previous lesson(s) that will be built on in this lesson?)

Objective(s) of the lesson:

(Objectives should be specific—what students will know and be able to do as a result of the lesson)

Rationale or relevance of the objective(s):

(Why is this objective important for the students?)

(What evidence is there that students need work in this area?)

Approach or philosophy:

(Is the lesson driven by any particular approach? Why have you chosen that approach? How will students respond to it? What, if any, L1 will be used and/or encouraged?)

Procedure:

(Housekeeping tasks: announcements, attendance, homework collection, etc.)

Introduction or staging: (approx. number of minutes)

(How will you frame the lesson? How will you give students the learning objective(s), e.g., outline the lesson on the blackboard? Elicit background information to activate what students already know.)

Presentation: (approx. number of minutes)

(What materials or activities will you use to present the new content? How do you expect students to respond, e.g., listening, reading, questioning?)

Practice: (approx. number of minutes)

(What activities/tasks will you give students to practice in attaining the objective(s)? Will activities be controlled, partly free, or completely free? What modes will you use for the activities, e.g., group work, pair work, role play, reading, writing? Will you need to pre-teach vocabulary? Will there be pronunciation difficulties for students? What learning do you expect to take place during these activities?)

Evaluation:

(How will both teacher and students know that progress is being made toward the objective(s)? Will you provide feedback throughout the lesson? How do you expect students to respond to your feedback?)

Summary or wrap-up: (approx. number of minutes)

(How will you review or pull together the main points at the end of the lesson?)

Homework and information about the next class:

(Is there a follow-up assignment? How do you let students know what will happen in the next class?)

Difficulties:

(What might go wrong? Do you have alternate plans? If using groups, what if there aren't enough students? What if some students arrive late?)

We now provide a sample lesson plan from a teacher in one of our research projects. Katherine was teaching a class of nine adults from six different countries. All students had completed high school or college in their home countries and were planning on gaining professional qualifications in an English-speaking country. Her overall unit of work was to teach the students how to write reports, with subgoals including reading information texts, extracting and using information from websites, reading a procedural text, note-taking, and responding to spoken instructions. In the first lesson, her goal was to teach students how to skim and scan printed text. The lesson plan below is adapted from Katherine's action research report (Hail, 2005).

Level/Subject:	Post-beginner
Student body:	5 males, 4 females
	1 Dutch, 1 Indian, 2 Russian, 2 Serbian, 1 Korean, 2 Sudanese
Book:	No textbook
Seating:	Movable chairs and desks
Materials:	Worksheet on *How to read information texts*
	A model information text about Australia, with comprehension questions
Prior lesson(s):	The previous lesson had explained the objectives of the course and the general outline of what the course would cover.

Objective(s) of the lesson:

Learners will be able to skim and scan printed text and extract information from it. They will develop confidence in reading so they will not feel they had to read every word. They will rely less on dictionaries to translate every word they don't know. L1 will be encouraged between learners for clarification.

Rationale or relevance of the objective(s):

Learners do not have the time or proficiency to be able to understand every word of a written text, but they think they should. Vocabulary load is always an issue, but they can obtain the information they need without understanding every word.

Approach or philosophy:

Important to scaffold lessons, build on learners' prior knowledge, and provide feedback and support as needed.

Procedure:

Introduction or staging:

- In groups, learners discuss how they found information in a text quickly.
- Whole class pooling of ideas.
- Elicit more ideas.

Presentation:

- Display worksheet *How to read information texts* on overhead projector.
- Read with class.

- Discuss with class.
- Clarify misunderstandings.

Practice: (approx. number of minutes)

- Give students handout of comprehension questions for *Australia – a model text*.
- Discuss key words in question 3 as whole class.
- Have students underline key words in remaining questions.
- In pairs, students compare their decisions.
- Discuss decisions as whole class; reteach what a key word is if necessary.
- Display on overhead projector the headings of the text *Australia – a model text*.
- Elicit from students the type of information they would expect in each section, based on the heading.
- Elicit from students which questions are related to each section; ask them how they know.
- Learners read the text and, without dictionaries, answer the questions as quickly as possible.
- Discuss answers with whole class, clarifying where needed.
- In pairs, students write brief reports about Australia.

Evaluation:

Constantly check for understanding and provide feedback to learners; answers to questions and reports used to confirm what students learn.

Summary or wrap-up:

Summarize how to read information texts; remind students of what they achieved without knowing every word.

Homework and information about the next class:

Advise students they will do the same thing in the next lesson, but using a text I will choose from the Internet.

Notice that both Peter and Katherine used topic content related to students' lives and with which they might already be somewhat familiar. Students (and teachers) were living in Australia and so both chose information texts on Sydney. Peter also had students investigate content even closer to their homes, by having them use materials about Cabramatta, the area of Sydney where they lived. Katherine, on the other hand, did not choose her own city (Adelaide) for the skim and scan lesson. However, she used a text on Adelaide in the next lesson where learners skimmed and scanned an information text on the Internet. Both teachers began by finding out what learners could already do—Peter through a survey, Katherine through group and then whole class discussion. In this way, they could build on learners' skills and knowledge. The contexts for both Peter and Katherine were similar, therefore we will now present a less detailed lesson plan in a very different context and focus only on choice of content.

Level/Subject:	High intermediate
School:	Private language school in U.K.
Course:	4-week intensive course with focus on spoken language
Student body:	7 males, 8 females (all European, 5 from same country)
Seating:	Movable chairs and desks
Materials:	Handout with workplace conversation
	Handout with telephone conversation
	Handouts with different situations for making excuses
Prior lesson(s):	The previous lesson learned and practised how to make excuses and accept excuses in informal situations among friends.

Objective(s) of the lesson:

Learners will be able to refuse an offer in formal situations. Learners will be able to recognize when someone accepts their formal excuse.

Rationale or relevance of the objective(s):

Learners use limited forms for refusing offers and do not follow English conventions.

Approach or philosophy:

Learners need to use English, even in pairs with speakers of their own language.

Procedure:

Introduction or staging:

- Have students in pairs practise an informal offer/refusal from the previous day.
- Ask them for formal situations they've been in when they've needed to refuse an offer.

Presentation:

- Display dialog on overhead projector.
- Read with class.
- Explain new vocabulary (write words on board).
- Check and practise pronunciation.
- Elicit schematic structure: write stages on board:
Situation
Offer
Refusal of offer—apology
Reason for refusal

Attempt at persuasion

Very polite refusal

Reason for refusal (not just repetition of former excuse)

Practice:

- Divide class in half and have one half take Stefan's part and the other half take Joe's.

Excuse dialog

Stefan works for Joe, who is his supervisor at the coffee shop. Stefan has pulled Joe aside, out of hearing of customers.

Stefan: *Well, Joe. Marco has called in sick and I need someone to cover his shift this evening. Can you work until 8pm and do the clean-up?*

Joe: *I'm really sorry, Stefan. I have a previous commitment. I promised my wife that I'd stay home and look after the children while she goes to her evening class.*

Stefan: *That's a pity because we could pay you extra for the evening shift.*

Joe: *That would be nice, but it's too late to arrange a babysitter.*

Stefan: *OK. Another time perhaps.*

The teacher has tried to choose a realistic situation and one that the learners might themselves be in. They might work in a coffee shop or elsewhere in the English-speaking world. Because functions do not have one-to-one correspondence with language, the teacher also chooses a very different situation for the second presentation dialog—a telephone conversation, in which a doctor's receptionist calls to cancel an appointment and try to arrange a new date, which the recipient can't make. The teacher particularly wants to focus on the need to provide an excuse, not just refuse an offer, and that in the workplace the excuse needs to be substantial. The teacher compares this to one of the situations they practised the previous day where a friend was handing around candy and Stefan could just say "*no thanks.*"

Conclusion

In this chapter we have provided some overall guidance on how to design instruction at the unit level and the individual class level. The focus has primarily been on content, but because instruction is integrated, we have touched on activities and materials, which will be discussed in greater detail in Chapters 3 and 4 respectively. We have tried to capture the dynamic nature of language teaching and show how planning is therefore iterative and in situ. While this complexity is often overwhelming for novice teachers, careful planning and continuous reflection on one's own practice lead to student learning and a sense of achievement for the teacher.

> **Task: Expand**
>
> http://www.bbc.co.uk/worldservice/learningenglish/teach/lessonplans/
>
> This BBC website provides a range of lesson plans for intermediate to advanced learners. The topics are based on BBC world news stories. The plans include materials and exercises.
>
> http://www.tesol.org/s_tesol/trc_genform.asp?CID=1253&DID=7561
>
> The professional association, TESOL, has a resource center that includes lesson plans, but is available to members only.
>
> http://iteslj.org/Lessons/
>
> The Internet TESL Journal includes a lesson plan section on its website.

Questions for Discussion

1. Why do teachers need to carefully plan ahead, but also plan in situ?
2. Why do teachers begin lessons by activating learners' background knowledge?
3. How can teachers check that their language is comprehensible, but also challenging for learners?
4. How can teachers select language for their lessons? What aspects of language need to be planned? You may want to reread Chapters 6–9 in Volume I to help answer this question.
5. How can teachers ensure learners acquire the grammar they need when using a task-based or content-based approach?

References

Brindley, G. P. (1984). *Needs analysis and objective setting in the Adult Migrant Education Program.* Sydney: AMES.

Hail, K. (2005). Strategies for extracting information from websites. In D. E. Murray & P. McPherson (Eds.), *Navigating to reading; Reading to navigate* (pp. 46–57). Sydney: NCELTR.

Johnson, K. E. (1999). *Understanding language teaching: Reasoning in action.* Boston: Heinle & Heinle Publishers.

Norton, P. (2002). *Using internet resources in the AMEP.* Unpublished action research report. Sydney: ACL.

Prabhu, N. S. (1992). The dynamics of the language lesson. *TESOL Quarterly, 26*(2), 225–310.

Richards, J. C., & Lockhart, C. (1994). *Reflective teaching in second language classrooms.* Cambridge: Cambridge University Press.

Shavelson, R. (1973). What is the basic teaching skill? *Journal of Teacher Education, 24*(2), 144–151.

Chapter 3

Planning Activities and Managing Classroom Interaction

VIGNETTE

As Alice headed to her classroom, she could see a smiling woman with glasses standing in the doorway and greeting students. "Hello, I'm Mrs. Michaelson," she said. "And you are . . . ?"

"Alice Walker."

"I'm so glad you'll be in my class. Your seat is in the second row. Please go to your desk now, and you'll find a paper that you will need to fill out. It's a special interview form—everyone in the class has one—and it will give us a chance to get to know each other better. Be sure to look at the classroom rules that are posted on the board as you go in. These are very important, and I will explain them to all of you this morning."

As Alice entered the room, she stopped a minute to read the classroom rules.

1. *Always raise your hand to talk. Also, raise your hand if you need help.*
2. *Respect other people's rights and feelings. Do not make fun of others.*
3. *Always walk in the class. Do not run.*
4. *Respect other people's property.*

Walking to her desk, Alice noticed that many students, some unknown and some familiar, were already filling out their forms, and many were quietly chuckling as they did so.

"I wonder what's on that form," thought Alice as she slipped into her seat.

[from Sadker & Sadker, 1994, p. 38]

Task: Reflect

Research shows that effective classroom managers are nearly always good planners. They establish rules and follow principles that guide both their own and students' behaviors in the classroom, and they arrange their classrooms to make certain that instruction can proceed efficiently. What rules and principles did the teacher in the vignette above establish to manage her classroom? In what context do you think she worked? Do you have any of the same rules and principles in your own classroom? Do you have rules and principles to manage your classroom that are different from the teacher in the above scenario? What rules and principles from the above classroom would work in yours? Which ones would not? What adjustments would you have to make?

Introduction

In Chapter 1 we presented some basic principles that govern the development of curriculum and provided a curriculum design process. Chapter 2 focused on two steps in the curriculum design process—selecting and sequencing content through lesson planning. In Chapter 3, we take the process of curriculum design a step further by turning our attention to the task of planning activities for learning and managing classroom interaction. In doing this we will focus on two stages in the lesson planning process—the presentation and practice stages. The purpose of these stages in lesson planning is to give learners practice in attaining the objectives (i.e., what learners know and are able to do). In the presentation stage of lesson planning, teachers are principally concerned with identifying the materials or activities they will use to present the new content and determining how students will respond to the selected activities, e.g., listening, reading, questioning. The focus in the practice stage is on the implementation of these activities requiring that teachers think about answers to questions, such as what modes will be used, how transitions between activities will be accomplished, and how much freedom in responding will be given to students.

Modern language classrooms are complex environments that require teachers to carefully plan activities and manage interaction. We have been classroom observers for a combined total of more than 50 years and are well aware of the fact that well-managed classrooms do not come about as a result of magic. Instead, they are products of hard work and the application of carefully established principles. In the vignette above, the teacher established some very clear principles that guided how she envisioned managing her classroom. For example, she arrived at the class before her students in order to create a positive learning environment and, in the case of younger learners, before any sort of disruption or noise had a chance to build. In this chapter, we will cover some basic principles related to planning for classroom activity and managing content that we believe to be most important for teachers working in different contexts with learners who vary in both age and language proficiency.

Planning Activities

Working with Objectives

In order to carry out these tasks, teachers must first think about planning activities for their learners that focus on helping them achieve the intended objectives, thereby creating an optimal environment for learning. The most important factor governing the selection of activities for the classroom is to determine how they might support the lesson objectives. Objectives serve as road maps for both teachers and learners, clearly marking important stops along the way, as well as indicating how to reach the final destination. The purpose of writing objectives is twofold. First, objectives help teachers create lesson plans that focus on learners and learning, and they provide learners with a clear understanding of what they are expected to learn and how they will learn it. Because objectives focus on student performance, they are called **performance objectives**. For the purposes of planning for activities, we review the four key components for writing objectives.

There are four key components in writing performance objectives. The first component focuses on what students will be able to do (e.g., identify, list, categorize, tell). The second component identifies what they are expected to learn, and this will vary greatly depending on the type of class you are teaching. For example, in a skills-based reading class, you may be focused on specific content related to the reading. In a skills-based writing course, you may be focused on the organizational structure of an essay or a story. In a grammar course, the focus may be language itself, such as working with the different ways to express past time in English. In a content-based instruction (CBI) course, you may be teaching language through content, such as history, biology, or social studies. The third component in writing objectives is particularly important for this chapter because it focuses on how students will demonstrate what they have learned (i.e., what activities will they do to help with this task). The purpose of classroom activities is to provide practice opportunities for learners so that they can achieve the lesson objectives. The selection of activities can only take place once objectives have been established. The final component in writing objectives is to establish the conditions for the practice (e.g., What grouping strategy will be used? How much time will they get? What type of input will be used? What type of response will be expected?).

In the example objective below, each of the four components is evident.

> *Students will be able to (SWBAT) [identify] [four characteristics specific to each of the seven American Indian tribes covered in the chapter] [by completing a graphic organizer] [in pairs].*

The first component is *identify*—what the learners will be able to do. This is followed by what they are expected to learn—*four characteristics specific to each of the seven American Indian tribes covered in the chapter*. The third component is how students will demonstrate what they know—*by completing a graphic organizer*. The final component specifies the conditions—*in pairs*. In order to achieve this objective students will need practice in identifying the characteristics specific to each of the seven American Indian tribes covered in the chapter, so that they will be successful in completing the graphic organizer. During the practice session, they might participate in a categorizing and sorting activity. In a categorizing and sorting activity each of the pairs or groups of students receives a list of tribal characteristics and a list of the tribes. Students work together to match each characteristic with its correct tribe. Learners could also participate in a search and find activity wherein they are given the graphic organizer and told to work in pairs to search the chapter, find information about each tribe, and record their answers on a graphic organizer. Both of these activities prepare learners for the final task of completing the graphic organizer without support from the text or other sources.

Demonstrating Student Learning

Because demonstrating student learning is such an essential aspect of planning activities, we focus on one particular type of activity that teachers can use, namely, **graphic organizers**. Graphic organizers are visual representations of knowledge, concepts, or ideas. They support learners in understanding text and provide a framework or structure for capturing the main points of what is being read. Figure 3.1 presents six common graphic organizers—Venn diagram, T-chart, semantic map, KWL, timelines, and process. Venn diagrams are used to help compare or contrast ideas, such as comparing two different countries. In a Venn diagram the information that is different (i.e., in contrast) about each country is written in one of the nonoverlapping pieces of the circle. The information that is the same about the two countries is written where the circles overlap with each other. A T-chart is used when teachers want students to analyze two facets of a topic, such as the pros and cons associated with it. A semantic map (also called semantic webs) is used to help students visually organize information and graphically show relationships. Semantic maps are used to help students organize their own ideas for writing and to organize the ideas found in a text. KWL charts have been used successfully in activating background knowledge and in working with text. In the K column, students write what they already know about a topic before reading a text. In the W column, they write what they would like to know. At the end of the unit or the activity, they write what they have learned in the L column. Students can then compare what they have learned with what they wanted to learn and with what information was covered in the text. Timelines work well with texts that are chronologically organized, such as history texts or grammar time sequences. The key events are identified, listed in the boxes, and given a date. The date is entered on the timeline. Process graphic organizers work well in science and in business. The sequential steps are identified from the prose and organized sequentially on the graphic organizer.

Task: Explore

Look at the sample performance objectives below. See if you can identify the four components in each one. In what type of class would you use each of these objectives? What type of activities would help students in achieving these objectives?

1.   Students will be able to generate two examples of the different ways to refer to the past in English by writing two sample sentences for each way with correct verb forms in pairs.
2.   Students will be able to evaluate the effectives of five sample paragraphs by completing a short rubric individually for each paragraph.

In addition to planning activities that support performance objectives, there are numerous other factors that teachers must take into consideration. For the purposes of this chapter, we have focused on six additional factors that govern planning and selecting activities—managing transitions, questioning strategies, establishing variety, pacing, responding to learners, and sequencing activities.

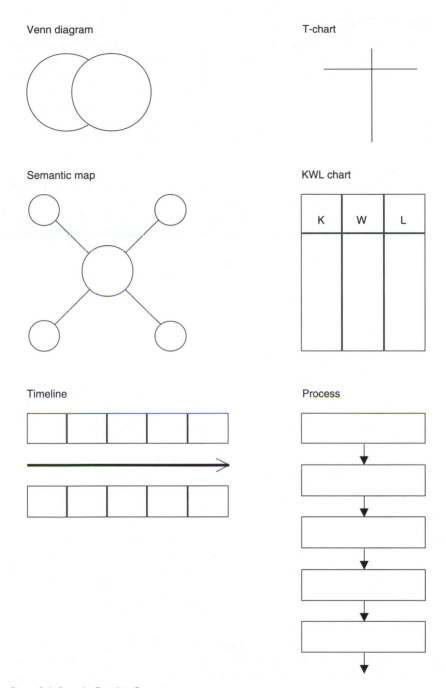

Figure 3.1 Sample Graphic Organizers.

Managing Transitions

In order to support learners in meeting performance objectives, teachers must develop expertise in making connections between previously learned information and new information (i.e., making connections between lessons). In addition, teachers must make connections with lessons. **Transitions** are the strategies that are used to make these two types of connections in order to develop lesson plans that flow from one stage of the lesson to the next, from activity to activity, and from one lesson to the following lesson. In addition, you want to be mindful of connections within the activity itself. Our classroom observations indicate that full-time teachers (i.e., those who teach multiple classes) manage about 30 major transitions each day. These transitions encompass moving from one lesson or content area on to another, through different instructional activities within a lesson, and through many different "housekeeping" routines, such as handing out papers, getting students into groups, and taking roll, etc. About four decades ago, Kounin (1970) identified five common patterns that can derail the process of effective transitioning for learning. Although these appear as a list of "do nots" below, embedded in each type of pitfall are the strategies themselves. We share them with you in order to get you thinking about your own practice as it relates to transitioning.

Flip-Flopping

This pattern occurs in transitioning when teachers terminate one activity, begin a new one, and then return to the original activity because of something they may have forgotten. For example, when the class finishes an activity, the teacher says, "Good job. Now let's move on to our next activity. Oh, yes, before I forget, how many of you got all of the problems correct on this part of your homework?" This comment is followed by a five-minute discussion over homework results before returning to the next task. It would have been better to say, "Before we move on to the next activity, let's talk about the problems you missed on the homework assignment. Do you have questions?" In transitioning, it is best to keep the momentum moving forward.

Fragmentation

Have you ever been to a class when the students took no action to begin an activity or the teacher was bombarded with questions from learners because they didn't know what to do? "Excuse me, teacher, but what should I do?" "Can you explain again?" "I don't understand." "Do we stay in our groups now or should we switch groups?" Transitional fragmentation occurs most frequently when teachers are introducing and setting up new activities or giving directions. For example, "OK, what I'd like you to do now is put away your books. You shouldn't have any other papers on your desk either. That includes all notebooks as well. You should not have papers that belong to anyone else either, and these should be off of your desk. You can have a pencil, but not papers," instead of the simpler instructions, "Clear your desk of all paper and books. Keep a pencil." Language learners need focused, step-by-step instructions so they know on what content and language to focus (see Chapter 11, this volume, on L2 teacher talk). If the instructions are multistep, L2 teachers must reinforce oral instructions with written ones.

Overdwelling

This pattern occurs when teachers spend more time than is necessary giving instructions or perhaps correcting an infraction of a classroom rule (such as disruptive behavior in small groups or arriving late to class). In giving multistep instructions, teachers need to plan out what to say step by step in order to avoid spending too much time on this process and, as a result, robbing students of interactive practice time. When correcting an infraction of a classroom rule, teachers should try to state the problem in one simple sentence. When teachers spend too much time on these processes, learners stop paying attention and are not certain on what they are supposed to focus.

Dangles

This problem in transitioning occurs when teachers start something only to leave it hanging. For example, "Would you please read the first paragraph on page 94? Oh, yes, did I tell you that we will have a guest speaker during the last 30 minutes of class? I don't know how I could have forgotten about that. This is going to be a very exciting day . . ." Student are left wondering about the paragraph on p. 94. That topic has been left dangling indefinitely.

Thrusts

Although thrusts are not directly concerned with making connections between lessons or within lessons, we include mention of them under transitions because, like the previous four concepts, they affect the optimal flow of classroom activity. Thrusts occur when classroom momentum is interrupted. This interruption most frequently occurs when teachers voice random thoughts that just seem to "pop" into their heads or tell personal stories that are only tangentially related to the topic of instruction. For example, the class is engaged in silent reading when their quiet concentration is broken by the teacher who says, "Where's Dori? I thought I saw her earlier today." or "How are you enjoying this book? It reminds me of a time when . . ." After this type of interruption, it takes quite some time for learners to get back into reading or to refocus their attention on the sequence of concepts. If this type of interruption happens often, it seriously disrupts learning and makes it hard for learners to concentrate or enjoy working on a learning task without interruption or reading during time devoted to silent reading.

Planning and managing activities must include planning for how to transition between activities within lessons and between lessons and how to maintain momentum within activities in order to avoid the common pitfalls outlined above.

Task: Expand

From Kounin's list of transitioning pitfalls above, develop a list of strategies (i.e., to dos) for L2 teachers to follow.

Questioning Strategies

Managing Questions

Good questioning is at the very heart of good teaching. It is also a key element in guiding learning and is an essential part of almost any activity you choose; therefore, teachers should develop sound principles for using questioning in the classroom. All learners should have equal access to classroom questions, so the first step in managing questions is for teachers to be aware of patterns that can interfere with this goal. Research shows that male students are asked more questions than female students. In addition, teachers ask more questions to students who sit in the front of the classroom and are also seated directly in front of them (see Chapter 11 in this volume on the action zone). Boys are more likely to call out the answers to questions without raising their hands or using another agreed upon protocol for turn-taking. When girls call out answers, teachers often tell them to raise their hands. While raising hands is certainly a way to mediate turn-taking, it is also true that in the rapid pace of classroom interaction, teachers can often forget their own rules. We believe that questioning is an important part of professional decision-making in the classroom and teachers should be aware of the possible pitfalls in questioning, have principles that guide this interaction, and communicate these principles to their learners. We believe that learners should be a part of this process. When teachers violate their own principles, learners can be called on to remind them to get back on track.

Asking Questions

One of the most widely used systems for managing demands on cognitions during questioning was developed by Bloom (1956). In Bloom's taxonomy, there are six different levels representing different demands on cognition (see Table 3.1).

The first three levels (i.e., Levels 1–3) are known as lower-order levels of questioning and the top three levels (i.e., Levels 4–6) are known as higher-order

Table 3.1 Levels of Questioning

Level on the taxonomy	Description
Level 1: Knowledge	Requires learners to recall or reorganize information.
Level 2: Comprehension	Requires learners to arrange or reorganize information mentally or in writing.
Level 3: Application	Requires learners to apply previously learned information to solve a problem.
Level 4: Analysis	Requires learners to break concepts into component parts or to identify causes or motives.
Level 5: Synthesis	Requires learners to make predictions, solve problems for which there are no specific answers, or use original and creative thinking.
Level 6: Evaluation	Requires students to judge the merits of a piece of work and back the judgment with appropriate and logical facts.

levels of questioning. Differentiating between factual or **lower-order questions** and thought-provoking or **higher-order questions** is important for teachers of L2 learners. In the questioning process, L2 teachers are managing demands on cognition (i.e., lower- or higher-order questions) and the difficulty of the language (i.e., concrete, here-and-now language vs. abstract concepts). Lower-order questions can be answered through the use of memory and recall and without consulting outside references. If a text is available, the information can be found almost verbatim in the text. Example lower-order questions might be, *What are the countries that share a border with Thailand? What is the capital of France?* Higher-order questions require more demanding thought before responding. These questions may require evaluations, making comparisons, establishing cause and effect, or solving problems. Example higher-order questions might be, *How can you raise money to travel to Australia from the United States this summer? In Shakespeare's play King Lear, why do you think that the king misjudged his daughter?*

Use lower-order questions when students are being introduced to new information, are practising new information, are reviewing previously learned information, or when they are working with familiar content with new language concepts. Use higher-order questions when a knowledge base has been established and you want learners to manipulate information in a more sophisticated way, when learners are solving problems, and when learners are asked to make judgments.

Task: Expand

Write a sample question for each of the levels of Bloom's Taxonomy. If you are teaching, write questions based on one of your own lessons. Share your sample questions with a colleague by presenting your questions in random order and asking your colleague to identify the level of the question from Bloom's Taxonomy. Discuss any differences you have.

Establishing Variety

If you have ever listened to a lecture for an hour and found your initial interest in the topic lapse into thinking of other things or if you have ever watched your own students fall apart during a seat assignment that required concentration into behavior such as passing notes, talking, and even flying paper airplanes, you have experienced what happens as both a learner and a teacher when there is not sufficient variety in a learning episode.

In planning activities, L2 teachers must provide variety in both content and process. Content varies from context to context. For example, in a large binational center[1] in South America, one of us (Christison) observed teachers providing variety by moving from a vocabulary building exercise to an activity that focused on finding the main and supporting ideas, both within the same reading. Another teacher varied the process by conducting two very different activities (matching and information gap activities[2]) within the same English grammar point.

The following is a list of sample activities that L2 teachers can use to maintain student interest by varying activity types:

- art activities
- board work
- brainstorming sessions
- contests
- cooperative learning activities
- creative writing
- debates
- field trips
- games
- guest speakers
- guided practice
- independent seatwork
- information gap activities
- jigsaw activities[3]
- learning centers
- lectures
- movies, tapes, and other audio–visual presentations
- musical activities
- panel discussions
- plays
- role plays
- silent reading
- simulations
- small group discussions
- spot quizzes
- student presentations
- students tutoring one another
- tests
- tutoring.

Research has shown that learners who spend more time pursuing academic content learn more and that teachers vary greatly (as do schools and programs) on the amount of time devoted to instruction (Goodlad, 1984). This general research on learning has implications for language teachers. Learning time can be thought of in different ways. **Allocated time** is the amount of time a teacher is scheduled to teach a subject or, in the case of elementary school, the amount of time a teacher schedules for each subject. It is not the allocated time that makes a difference in how much students learn. Allocated time is quite different from **engaged time**, and it is engaged time on which we want to focus. Engaged time is the time that students spend actively participating in learning. When students are daydreaming, doodling, writing off-topic notes to each other, whispering, talking off topic with their peers in groups, or waiting for instructions, they are not involved in engaged time. Learner engagement is affected by how challenged learners are by the concepts or activities, how much control they have over their learning, and what choices they get to make in the process of learning (Guthrie, 2008). Teachers must carefully plan the time devoted to instruction in order to get as much engaged time as possible.

Pacing

The speed with which one delivers a lesson is known as **pacing**. When dealing with many different types of learners from a variety of cultural and language backgrounds, it is important to pay attention to the speed at which a lesson is conducted. There are many things a teacher can think about or do to ensure that the pace of each lesson is appropriate for the content and for the students.

A student's attention span is about one-half of his or her age up to adulthood. Keep this in mind when planning the number of activities to include in a learning episode. If you are working with very young learners, you will need to have many short activities for them. As learners get older they can attend for longer periods of time, especially if they have a history as classroom learners. Learners get frustrated when too little time is given to a task, and too much time on a task allows learners to become bored. It is not easy to strike the perfect balance. Each classroom activity should be assigned a time appropriate for the learners' collective attention span. A nine-year-old language learner with beginning level language proficiency will take longer to complete a written assignment than a 16-year-old who has high intermediate level language proficiency. Experience helps teachers develop the flexibility needed to anticipate how much time an activity will take to complete. Changing activities before learners have had time to finish or process them completely is frustrating and works to diminish motivation. If you frequently find yourself in this situation, you should plan for fewer activities during class time.

In order to guide teachers in developing skills in lesson pacing, we offer these few guidelines:

1. Teachers need to understand their own natural pace before making changes in their classroom behaviors. Ask a colleague to view your class or tape your class and review your teaching later. Answer the following questions about your pacing: Is it too fast? Is it too slow? Do I tend to repeat things more often than is necessary for the learners in my classroom? Do I vary content? Do I vary processes? Is the presentation over- or underactive relative to movement?
2. Teachers should make decisions about pacing by responding to their learners' needs; consequently, teachers must pay attention to learner behavior throughout the lesson. What behaviors signal that learners do not understand? When teachers see these behaviors, they should slow down. What behaviors signal that learners are bored? When teachers see these behaviors, they should speed up.
3. Movement is important. Think of how you can give your learners opportunities to move about. Too much seatwork can be boring. Take short energy breaks! Have students stand up and follow a few TPR (Total Physical Response) commands. Energy breaks provide learning interludes so that learners can stay on task when they return to their work.

Responding to Learners

Teachers must decide how to respond to learners during classroom activities. Learning is increased when learners receive feedback and guidance on improving their performance. Many educators emphasize the importance of providing feedback to learners based on specific principles.

Feedback should be:

- based on behavior that teachers want to encourage
- specific, indicating what aspect of a learner's behavior is noteworthy
- sincere
- varied and dependent on the situation
- related to success or effort
- based on past performance as a context for describing present performance.

Feedback should not be routine or automatic and teachers should avoid using the same phrases over and over. When all learners receive the same praise or feedback, the feedback becomes meaningless.

Sequencing Activities

There are a number of different factors that can influence how teachers decide to sequence activities, such as difficulty of content, amount of self-disclosure required, or difficulty of the language involved in the activity. The Gradual Release Learning Model (Pearson & Gallagher, 1983) provides a useful framework for thinking about sequencing classroom activities based on the level of learner control in activities (see Figure 3.2).

In this model activities are sequenced according to the amount of control given to the learners (see also Guthrie, 2008). At one end of the continuum are activities in which the learner has little or no control, such as when a teacher is giving a demonstration or instructions on how to do an activity. As learners develop skills, teachers select activities that move along the continuum and gradually release control to the learner. Learner control increases and teacher control decreases until the activities selected fall on the end of the continuum in which learners take most of the control and require very little from the teachers, such as when they work on problem-solving or jigsaw activities in small groups. The research on the impact of teaching students strategies geared toward personal responsibility in learning is strong (Marzano, Marzano, & Pickering, 2003), so most experienced language

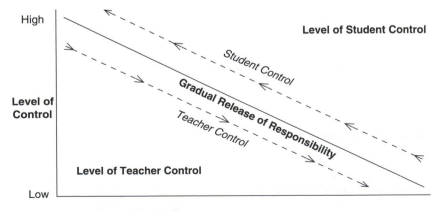

Figure 3.2 Gradual Release Model of Learning.

teachers pay careful attention to the principles of gradual release in their personal philosophy of classroom management.

Managing Classroom Interaction

One of the most useful taxonomies for managing classroom interaction was proposed by Christison and Bassano (1995). In this taxonomy for classroom interaction, activities are divided into six strategy types—restructuring, one-centered, unified, dyad, small group, and large group. The six different strategies function together to help learners and teachers manage interaction and release responsibility to learners. Most L2 learners enter classrooms with certain expectations about how the classroom will be managed and what types of activities they will encounter. Many of the interactive activities (e.g., information gap and jigsaw) that have become standard within the field of English language teaching constitute unfamiliar instructional practice for many students. In order to move students from where they are in terms of their expectations and tolerance for unfamiliar instructional practice to where you may want them to be (i.e., open to new types of interactive activities), you must carefully sequence and manage classroom interaction. The sequencing of strategies systematically helps break down student stereotypes about classroom procedures. Students learn step-by-step interaction techniques that help them develop language skills at the same time as group trust is being developed. In this system, all interpersonal interaction moves from low-risk, nonpersonal content, such as games, information-gathering, reporting, problem-solving, etc., to activities which provide learners with an opportunity to share personal values and beliefs in their interactions if they so desire.

Restructuring Activities

English learners come from many different linguistic and cultural backgrounds and bring with them different expectations about learning English in a classroom setting. Some learners have very traditional expectations, expecting to sit in straight rows facing the teacher who is in the front of the room directing learning. They expect the teacher to accept most of the responsibility for learning. Other learners are already familiar with small group work and are ready to work independently. In order to make certain that all learners are prepared to accept more responsibility for their own learning and for instructional practice where interaction with other students is expected, Christison and Bassano (1995) suggest using *restructuring activities*. Restructuring activities often get students out of their seats and interacting with others on a specific task for a short period of time. In restructuring activities, most of the control still rests with the teacher, but learners are given certain responsibilities. An example of a restructuring activity would be *line-ups*. Learners are asked to line up in various ways, such as by the day and month in which they were born, in alphabetical order by last name or by the name of the town in which they were born. The content chosen for the line-up is based on the content of the lesson. Students must briefly interact with each other in order to line up correctly. Students control with whom they interact and what they will say in order to find their place in the line. Once students have lined up, teachers check the line for accuracy. Students can then return to their seats or try to line up again using other content. KWL charts are also common restructuring activities. Students make three columns on a piece of paper with K, W, and L as column headers. In the K column they write what they already know, in the W column they write what they want to know, and then they share the information with three different people. At the end of the unit, students complete the L column—what they learned. Restructuring activities provide opportunities for learners to participate in limited group interaction that is quite controlled and of a short duration. The activities are designed to restructure their thinking about expected instructional practice.

One-centered Activities

Some learners are by nature very quiet and shy and have difficulty interacting with others in either the L1 or L2. Other learners are very verbal, wanting to be the center of attention and often overwhelm a small group of learners. One-centered activities are designed to focus attention on one learner in a group for a short duration of time. For shy and quiet learners, one-centered activities provide positive interaction with their peers and an opportunity for them to succeed in an activity wherein both the processes and language needed are predictable. These two factors work to build learner self-confidence. One-centered activities also serve students who are more verbal and require more attention. Once these learners receive attention from the rest of the class or group, they seem to require less attention and become better listeners and group members. An example of a one-centered activity is called *Five on Focus*. The teacher gives students five questions to answer about themselves, such as *What schools have you attended? What countries have you visited? Who are the members of your family? What do you like to study? What is one goal you have for the future?* Learners work independently to answer questions. Teachers create specific questions for each group of learners, so the questions change from class to class. One learner is selected to be "on focus" for one minute while the other students ask questions. Five learners are selected each day until all have had a chance to be on focus.

Unified Group Activities

Unified group activities are designed to balance the effects of one-centered activities and promote successful group learning. In these activities there is no success for individuals, only success for the group. If individuals in the group choose not to participate, there can be no success for the group since the role of each individual group member is important in achieving success. Jigsaw (see endnote, this chapter) is an example of one type of unified group activity.

Dyad Work

Working one on one with each member of the class or group in a partnership provides an opportunity for learners to get to know each other. Dyad work prepares learners for small and large group participation later on. An example of a low-risk activity that can be done in partners is an information gap activity such as, *Where do I put it?* In this activity students are seated back to back or next to each other with a barrier in between them, such as a folder or a notebook. Each student has a paper with a small grid on which nine squares have been marked and a small envelope with cards. Students take turns dictating where to put the cards.

Small Groups

Once students have had opportunities to work in pairs with other students, they are ready to start working in groups. Group work not only provides opportunities for students to develop trust and cooperation with other group members, it also is an essential feature of communicative language teaching. In addition, it increases language practice opportunities, improves the quality of student talk, promotes a positive affective climate, helps to individualize instruction, and motivates students to learn (Long & Porter, 1984). Group interaction can promote the kind of input and opportunities for output that promote L2 acquisition. Students working in small groups produce more language of a greater quality than students in teacher-fronted classroom settings (Long, Adams, McLean, & Castanos, 1976).

Large Groups

The objectives for large groups are basically the same as for small groups. The major difference is the inclusion of a wider range of individuals whom the students have learned to trust. Examples of activities that can be done in both large and small groups are problem-solving and decision-making activities of various types, such as those that have one correct answer and those that require students to justify the answer at which they arrive.

Although there are no hard-and-fast rules about the proper time to introduce the strategy types to your students, our experience has been that restructuring activities are appropriate when groups and classes are just forming. Restructuring is followed by one-centered and unified group activities, since these activities begin to change student attitudes about what learning together entails. Pair work usually precedes small group work, and large group work most often follows small group work. All strategies can be recycled if teachers believe that students can benefit from the reinforcement of strategies introduced earlier in the sequence.

Conclusion

In this chapter, we first focused on planning activities by introducing performance objectives, the four key components necessary in writing objectives, and the importance of planning for and selecting activities that provide opportunities for students to achieve the objectives. We also introduced six additional factors that influence selecting and managing classroom activities—managing transitions, questioning strategies, establishing variety, pacing, responding to learners, and sequencing activities. Finally, we presented a taxonomy for use in developing effective group interaction with language learners.

Task: Explore

Find two different websites that give you additional information about planning activities and managing classroom interaction. Make a list of three additional pieces of information that you find useful in your own classroom. Share your list with at least one other person. Add their suggestions to your own list.

Questions for Discussion

1. Work with a partner or in a small group. Write three sample performance objectives of your own. Evaluate the objectives you have written using the checklist below.

   Checklist ✔
   Does the objective state . . .
   _____ what students are able to do?
   _____ what students are expected to learn?
   _____ what activities they will do?
   _____ under what conditions they will demonstrate learning?

2. Work with a partner or in a small group to identify or create one activity for each of the six different interactive strategy types—restructuring, one-centered, unified group, dyad, small group, and large group—and share your ideas with another group or partnership.

Notes

1. Binational center is a term used to refer to a number of private English language teaching centers in Mexico and South America although they occur to a lesser extent elsewhere in the world. Because many of these centers originated as U.S.-funded or a combination of locally funded and U.S.-funded institutions, they were in origin binational. Although the U.S. government no longer provides operational funding for these centers, the name "binational" has persisted. The U.S. government still provides some ongoing professional development support by funding American ELT professionals known as academic specialists for short two- to six-week visits to work on teacher and curriculum development.
2. Information gap is a type of interactive activity in which each member of a partnership has information, often in the form of charts or graphs, that the other person does not have. Without looking at each other's materials, they figure out how to communicate the missing information to each other.
3. Jigsaw is a type of interactive learning activity in which each learner has a piece of information necessary to solving a problem. Learners must work together, decide how to share the information with each other, and determine the usefulness of the information in solving the problem.

References

Brumfit, C. (1984). *Communicative methodology in language teaching*. Cambridge: Cambridge University Press.

Christison, M. A., & Bassano, S. K. (1995). *Look who's talking*. Burlingame, CA: Alta Book Center Publishers.

Goodlad, J. (1984). *A place called school.* New York: McGraw-Hill.

Guthrie, J. T. (2008). *Engaging adolescents in reading.* Thousand Oaks, CA: Corwin Press.

Kounin, J. (1970). *Discipline and group management in classrooms.* New York: Holt, Rinehard, & Winston.

Long, M., Adams, L., McLean, M., & Castanos, F. (1976). Doing things with words: verbal interaction in lockstep and small group classroom situations (pp. 137–153). In J. Fanselow & R. Crymes (Eds.), *On TESOL '76.* Washington, D.C.: TESOL.

Long, M., & Porter, P. (1985). Group work, interlanguage talk, and second language acquisition. *TESOL Quarterly, 19,* 207–28.

Marzano, R. J., Marzano, J. S., & Pickering, D. J. (2003). *Classroom management that works.* Alexandria, VA: ASCD.

Pearson, D. P., & Gallagher, M. C. (1983). The instruction of reading comprehension. *Contemporary Educational Psychology, 8,* 317–344.

Sadker, M. P., & Sadker, D. M. (1994). *Teachers, schools, and society* (3rd ed.). New York: McGraw-Hill.

Chapter 4

Selecting and Adapting Materials

VIGNETTE

Yuko teaches in an elementary school in Japan, where the school administration has chosen one of the textbook packages approved by the Ministry of Education. The textbook package includes the textbook, CDs, story cards, word cards, and teachers' books (slightly altered copies of the student textbook, and fuller, trans-lated versions with teaching presentation ideas and detailed explanation of the language points to be taught). The ministry had introduced a communicative curriculum, although not mandating what methodology teachers use to teach. The particular textbook in Yuko's school includes structured reading, cloze, vocabulary translation, and repetition of key points, with major grammar points in boxed text and translated. All exercises have one right answer, allowing for no initiation on the part of learners. The focus is on teacher control of input and student learning, with no opportunities for speaking. But even the teacher's role is conditioned by the materials so that their own creativity, innovation, and judgement are diminished. The materials also do not lend themselves to pair or group work. Most teachers at her school can in fact use Japanese as the medium of instruction and learners and teacher only use English to complete the exercises in the textbook. Both learners and teacher often prefer this so they don't have to display their lack of speaking ability in the classroom. They have little motivation to practice English speaking because speaking is not tested in examinations. Yuko, however, believes she should be more responsive to the communicative curriculum and wants to supplement the required materials with more communicative and creative activities. [Murray, research notes]

Task: Reflect

1. Reflect on your own language learning experiences. What types of required textbooks were used? How similar were they to the one used in Yuko's school? Did teachers supplement the textbook materials? If so, what did they use?
2. Why do you think the ministry has required a communicative curriculum, but does not test speaking?

3. Think about activities Yuko could use with her learners. Share your ideas with a colleague.
4. How do you think Yuko's colleagues and the school administrators will feel if she supplements the textbook package and uses a more communicative approach?

Introduction

In Volume I, Chapter 4, we referred to the roles teachers and learners play in the language classroom and indicated that materials also play a role and all three roles interact. As can be seen in the vignette, the textbook package chosen by Yuko's school "reduce[s] the teacher's role to one of managing or overseeing preplanned events" (Littlejohn, Hutchinson, & Torres 1994, p. 316). The textbook package itself takes many of the roles of instruction. In Volume I, Chapter 4, we provided a list of roles teachers take in the language classroom, namely:

- transmitter of information (about language)
- manager of learning—both content and activities
- manager of classrooms—including discipline
- a subject matter expert
- model of language use
- a monitor of progress.

The textbook package Yuko is using takes all of these roles, except manager of the classroom, severely diminishing the teacher's autonomy. The range of materials in this package is common in well-resourced language teaching contexts. However, many teachers are working in under-resourced contexts. While this is especially the case in some of the Expanding Circle countries, it may also be the case in the Inner and Outer Circles.

In this chapter we provide tools for how to plan materials—whether a textbook, a handout, or a blackboard. We begin with principles for selecting textbooks and then discuss how to adapt and supplement textbooks. We then explore the range of computer-assisted materials available to teachers and end with a section on teaching in under-resourced contexts.

Selecting Textbooks

As we demonstrated in the vignette, in some contexts teachers have no control over the textbooks they use; rather they are mandated—by the state, by the institution, or by a course coordinator. Here we will use **textbook** as shorthand to cover all types of published materials, such as those in the textbook package used by Yuko. Despite these restrictions, most teachers at some stage in their careers have the autonomy to make their own decisions about the textbook they want to use or, like Yuko, want to supplement the textbook to provide more opportunities for student learning. Allwright (1981) has suggested two views regarding published materials—**deficiency view** and **difference view**. The deficiency view is that the role of published materials compensates for lack of knowledge on the part of teachers.

Many educators and others agree that textbooks should be "teacher-proof," that is, their design and explanations should be sufficiently detailed that almost anyone could teach from them. Such people usually assume that experienced teachers will select and supplement, based on the particular needs of their learners. In the difference view, in contrast, published materials and teachers are complementary. The textbook provides expertise that the teacher may not have and teachers use their own areas of expertise. Published teaching materials, however, reflect the writer's beliefs about language and how it is learned, beliefs that may conflict with those of the teacher using the textbook. Most textbooks, to be profitable, have to be designed for the broadest market possible. Consequently, they avoid controversial topics and try to be culturally neutral such that they are often bland, homogeneous, and reflect the middle-class values of their writers. Even textbooks that are designed for very specific learners may be constrained by local conditions. In Chapter 1, this volume, we provided a curriculum implementation model developed by Adamson, Kwan, and Chan (2000) in which they identified one change that occurs during implementation as the resourced curriculum, such as textbooks. An example of how trying to implement a curriculum comes up against local issues that affect textbook development is described by Katz, Beyrkun, and Sullivan (2008) concerning assisting foreign language textbook writers to develop an up-to-date framework for writing new language textbooks geared to young learners. As the consultants worked with the experienced textbook developers, all agreed on a framework for textbook development, which was discussed and written in English so the American consultant could understand what they had achieved. The difficulties came when they tried to translate their framework back into Ukrainian to present to the Ministry of Education and Science. It was not just a question of translation, but of differences in discourse. *Skills*, which in English they meant to refer to listening, speaking, reading, and writing, had traditionally referred to automatic habits of using phonemes and grammar. More importantly, the documents in Ukrainian were deliberately written vaguely, whereas in English the criteria had been written as explicitly as possible to provide as much guidance to textbook writers as possible. By the end of the project, no solution to this dilemma was arrived at.

If teachers have the autonomy to choose their own textbooks, they need criteria for evaluating and choosing textbooks. Often the textbook publisher claims the textbook has a particular orientation, such as communicative or task-based, but on closer examination, it can be seen that the textbook provides limited, if any, opportunities for interaction and so teachers cannot rely on what the publisher (and even the author) claims about the textbooks. To help teachers select, we provide a list of questions for teachers to ask before choosing a textbook. First, teachers need to examine their needs and their learners' needs and then evaluate the textbook against those needs:

1. Who are the learners and what are their needs?

    a. What language level—for each skill of speaking, listening, reading, and writing?

    b. What literacy in L1 (see Volume 1, Chapter 9)?

    c. What previous language learning?

    d.   What learner goals—enter workplace, study, pass language examinations?

    e.   What preferred ways of learning (see Volume I, Chapter 13)?

2.   What are the course objectives (see Chapters 2 and 3, this volume)?

    a.   What is the subject matter content?

    b.   What is the language content?

3.   What are the teacher's preferred ways of teaching (see Chapter 11, this volume)?

4.   How does the textbook position teachers and learners in terms of their roles (see Volume I, Chapter 4)?

5.   Is the subject matter relevant to learners? Is the language level appropriate (including instructional language)? Is the type of L1 support (if any) appropriate?

6.   Are the activities of interest to learners? Will they help them learn and become autonomous learners?

7.   Is the layout appropriate (e.g., picture, diagrams) to the teaching context?

8.   Is the approach compatible with the teacher's views of language and language learning?

Task: Explore

Choose a textbook you have used or plan to use. Evaluate it for the following aspects:

- approaches to language and learning
- view of culture
- roles of teachers and learners
- context assumed by the textbook
- approaches to assessment
- use of L1.

Adapting and Supplementing Textbooks

> [T]eachers are very autonomous in their textbook use and . . . it is likely that only a minority of teachers really follow the text in the page-by-page manner suggested in the literature. (Stodolsky, 1989, p. 176)

In other words, textbooks do not always drive the teaching-learning process, but rather provide a scaffold on which teachers and learners can build. Because textbooks are mostly written for a wide range of learners, teachers find they need to adapt a textbook that they or their institutions have chosen. This may include making changes to activities and texts in the textbook or supplementing the textbook with additional materials, either from other sources or written by the teacher. For example, in many situations the textbook does not include sufficient local situations or language to be useful for learners. When one of us (Denise) was teaching in Australia in the 1970s, only one Australian textbook series was available and it didn't have some of the most recent approaches to language teaching. The only other textbooks available were from the U.K. or U.S., using either British or American English. These varieties differ from Australian English primarily in pronunciation and vocabulary, but also in grammar. Such models were not helpful for learners who were either going on to study in Australia or had immigrated and needed to understand Australian speech patterns. Learners in fact said they found Australian English too fast and difficult to understand. As teachers, we had an obligation to help learners understand and use this variety. The only Australian models learners had were their teachers, but even some of them were in fact immigrants from Britain and used British English. We therefore analyzed local interactions, wrote scripts, and recorded conversations, listening passages, and lectures to supplement the texts. Such supplementing is the most common form of adaptation that teachers use.

Adapting the Textbook

However, teachers also take activities from textbooks and rewrite them for local conditions. For example, many textbooks include a street map with the names of different stores or offices for students to learn and practise directions. However, these are usually of a generic town. Teachers adapt such maps by substituting local street names and buildings with which learners are familiar. They use the local map for presenting the material and for initial, scaffolded practice. They then use the textbook map of an unknown town for students to practise without support.

Adapting for Cultural Learning

As well as having to adapt textbooks for local language and situations, teachers also often need to adapt because the cultural values inherent in the textbook are alien to their context, or treat culture as unproblematic. The content of textbooks rarely addresses social issues; instead it portrays stereotypical families and cultures that are apparently homogeneous, whereas the societies in which English is used as a *lingua franca* are complex, multilingual, multicultural, and where culture is contested (Kramsch, 1988). See Volume I, Chapter 4, for a discussion of the role of culture in language teaching. Teachers therefore often want to both explore and explode the cultural myths perpetuated in the textbook.

If teachers are using a textbook that has all the men going out to work and all the women staying at home, looking after children, cleaning, washing, and cooking, they may want to discuss with learners whether this is typical of their home, of the homes of their friends, or of the homes they see on television. Teachers may also want to supplement, using some of the visuals and dialogs in the textbook, but substituting male names for female and vice versa. If all the men working in factories are minorities, while all the ones working in offices or as supervisors or managers are white, teachers might again want to discuss with learners and/or adapt by changing the names and faces on the different visuals or in the dialogs.

Many textbooks have an exercise on learners' families, often introducing the vocabulary for names of family members such as *mother, father, sister, brother*. They then ask learners to complete a family chart with names and position in the family. This task can be quite difficult for beginning learners who come from cultures where extended family members (or even close friends) are often called *father* or *uncle* or *cousin*. There may be no one-to-one correspondence of concept between an English word and an L1 translation. Yet, being able to identify these words and the appropriate person is often essential when filling out official forms if the learner is an immigrant or refugee. Additionally, learners who may have lost family members because of war or other trauma may not want to engage in such an activity at all. Teachers therefore need to be careful when working with learners from cultures with which they are not familiar and seek out bilingual aides or others to help with these explanations. Or, they can substitute a neutral family to identify the names for relationships on a genealogy chart.

As we discussed in Volume I, Chapter 4, textbooks also simplify interactions, presenting what Carter (1996) has called a can-do society with smooth interaction, no interruptions, cooperation between interactants, speakers using complete sentences, and with the interaction being predictable. This, as we described in Volume I, Chapter 10, is not the messy, overlapping turns, competing for the floor, misunderstandings, and jerky speech in actual conversations. Teachers therefore need to draw this to the learners' attention. This can be done by using a transcript of actual conversation and comparing it with the idealized version in the textbook.

Task: Explore

The following telephone conversation is typical of that found in many textbooks. After the teacher presents the dialog, students are asked to practice, taking turns as speakers Peter, Mr. Jones, and John. Learners have already been introduced to the Jones family. Peter is one of John's friends from school.

Peter:	*Can I speak to John, please?*
Mr. Jones:	*Sure. Who's calling?*
Peter:	*Peter.*
Mr. Jones:	*OK. Hold on a minute. I'll go get him.*
Peter:	*Thank you.*
John:	*It's John here.*
Peter:	*Hi John. This is Peter.*
John:	*Hi, Peter.*
Peter:	*Can I come over? We can do our homework together.*
John:	*Sure. See you soon.*

1. Think about telephone conversations you have had like this. How do you think this is different? What else would have been said? What would have been said differently? Why?
2. Next time you answer the telephone, write down the conversation as soon as possible afterwards. How did that conversation differ from the one in the textbook?
3. How could you adapt the conversation above, without making the text too difficult for your learners?

Supplementing Textbooks

At the beginning of this section on adapting and supplementing textbooks, we demonstrated how programs in Australia developed supplemental materials to bring the outside into the classroom. We now provide some principles for selecting and writing supplemental materials.

Selecting Reading and Writing Materials

At almost all levels, teachers find they need to choose additional texts for learners to read, either because they want to focus on particular content or they need more examples of particular text types (genres). Wallace (1992, p. 71) identifies six criteria for choosing reading texts in the foreign or second language classroom. She says the text:

- should be a vehicle for teaching specific language structure and vocabulary
- should offer opportunity to promote key reading strategies
- should present content which is familiar and of interest to the learners
- should be at the appropriate language level
- should be authentic, that is, naturally occurring text, not specially written for pedagogic purposes
- should be exploitable in the classroom, that is, lead to a range of classroom activities.

While we would agree with Wallace's criteria, the use of naturally occurring text can be problematic. Often the vocabulary, grammar, and text structure are beyond the level of the learners and it is inappropriate, for example, to choose a children's text for use with young people or adults, even if the language level is appropriate. Therefore teachers make adjustments to the naturally occurring text, changing vocabulary and simplifying the grammar. There is no evidence, however, that simple sentences are easier to understand than compound or complex ones (see Volume I, Chapter 8). In fact, a string of simple sentences without discourse markers can be more difficult for the learner because there are no cues regarding the relationships between ideas. Similarly, simplifying vocabulary is fraught with problems. Colloquial, idiomatic vocabulary may be easier for native speakers who are learning literacy because they already are proficient in the spoken language. For English language learners, however, more formal vocabulary may be what they have had more exposure to.

Some of the literature refers to naturally occurring language (whether written or spoken) as *authentic*. We prefer *naturally occurring* because, while the text may be authentic, the tasks required of learners may not be authentic communication. For example, comprehension questions are authentic only in educational settings. Most people read for information, perhaps sharing some particular piece with a friend, not to answer questions about the text. However, when teachers develop their own reading comprehension questions, they need to trial them to ensure that they are actually checking comprehension and are not just giving learners a pattern matching activity (see Volume I, Chapter 9). They also need to decide what cognitive activity they want learners to use: skimming, scanning, finding facts, note-taking, guessing meaning from context, reacting by giving opinions, synthesizing, inferencing, or critical reading (see Volume I, Chapter 9 for characteristics of critical reading).

Writing materials can vary from gap-filling exercises to essay prompts, depending on the objectives and language level of the learners. When developing writing tasks, teachers need to decide what text type (genre) they want learners to produce. The prompt should be sufficiently transparent that learners don't have to guess what the teacher wants. The stimulus for writing can be nonlanguage, such as pictures (see, for example, the vignette for Chapter 7, this volume), graphs, diagrams, flow charts, or even sounds. These suggestions for developing learner tasks for writing apply equally to listening materials, which we discuss below.

Selecting and Writing Listening and Speaking Materials

Often listening materials are inappropriate for the particular learners, perhaps because the rate of speed is beyond their current comprehension or the English variety is unfamiliar or not the target. Some of our research (Murray, 2005) has found that literate learners find it helpful if teachers scaffold the listening activity with written support. For example, learners may have the written text and can at first follow along or the teacher provides some of the written material and the learners fill in the gaps, as in the activity in Figure 4.1 where students are learning different language for apologies.

Another scaffolding activity for listening can be a matching exercise where learners are provided with some of the target language items in the chart and have to match with either a simplified definition or other response in the listening text (as in Table 4.1), or true/false response (as in Figure 4.2). Picture to word matching is especially useful for beginning literacy. The activity in Table 4.1 follows learners listening to an interviewer at a fast food restaurant asking for personal contact details of someone applying for a job.

Teachers can easily construct matching exercises such as this to test for listening comprehension. This type of matching can also be used to teach an extension of a grammar point made in a listening exercise. For example, if the passage or conversation introduces an adverb of frequency, the teacher can create a chart with the range of adverbs of frequency in sentences and with their different meanings and have learners match the sentences with the meanings, e.g., *I never eat breakfast* to be matched to *not at all*.

True/false responses to statements can also help learners match the alphabet and the words they see written to what they are hearing; this type of activity puts

Table 4.1 Sample Matching Activity

Name	234-567-890
Age	mhamed@computer.net
Address	098-765-432
Phone number	Jamiyl Rashid
Cell phone number	28
Email	Apt. 4, 235 Willow Street Oxington
Emergency contact person	Mohammed Hamed

42

Activity 66

🎧 Listen and write a word from the box in the correct sentence.

all right	~~sorry~~	apologise	sorry
okay	Excuse	mean	all right

Example

1. Sissy: Oh, _____ sorry _____ , Ari. I didn't _____ to hurt you.

   Ari: That's _____ .

2. Win: _____ me, Toomas. But I was here first.

   Toomas: Oh really? _____ about that.

   Win: It's _____ .

3. Ari: I wanted to _____ for making trouble.

   Theresa: That's _____ , Ari. I was happy to help you.

Figure 4.1 Gap-filling Listening Activity.

minimal cognitive load on learners because the response is only true or false. The example below is an activity responding to a video clip so that the video provides additional scaffolding for learners because they can see nonverbal interaction, as well as the verbal interaction. Note also that in Figure 4.2, the text provides a learning tip, helping learners to understand that not all lack of comprehension is linguistic. This provides the teacher with a jumping-off point for discussion.

Matching can also be used for practice of vocabulary or speech acts and their appropriate responses. For young learners or beginners, matching pictures or symbols to words can be used in instruction when realia cannot be brought into the classroom.

While naturally occurring DVDs and videos provide models for learners, like naturally occurring written texts, they are often beyond the level of competence of the learners. Therefore teachers may have to adapt and supplement them. For example, teachers often select very small segments, and use activities such as KWL (see Chapter 3, this volume) to help learners understand. Teachers also use naturally occurring DVDs and videos without the sound, to have learners focus on nonverbal cues and have learners guess what is happening and what language is being used. Learners can then write their own dialogs. More advanced learners can compare their own creative dialogs with those in the original.

Games can be useful materials for helping learners enjoy their lessons. There are many websites that have games, including ones that help teachers design their own crossword puzzles, making them an almost effortless exercise. However, teachers do need to keep in mind that the games need to be tied to lesson objectives, such as consolidating vocabulary in the case of crosswords.

We will not discuss any further activities for speaking because they have been covered in detail in Chapter 3, this volume.

Computer-Assisted Language Learning (CALL)

We use the term **CALL**, although a number of terms have been used. Outside education (and even in education in Europe), information and communications technology (ICT) has been preferred. Cyberspace was trendy for a while, but rejected by language educators such as Warschauer (2001) because "[t]he notion of 'cyberspace' suggests that there exists a virtual, online world that is distinct from our real world . . . I would contend, in contrast, that the significance of online communication lies not in its separation from the real world, but rather in how it is impacting nearly every single aspect of the real world" (p. 1). Technology-enhanced language learning (TELL), computer-assisted instruction (CAI), computer-based instruction (CBI), computer-based training (CBT), have also been used. Elsewhere (Murray, 2007), we have rejected these usages because "enhanced" is evaluative, CAI places a focus on instruction, and CBI and CBT both place the computer at the center of instruction. CALL, on the other hand, by its choice of "assisted" and "learning" implies, we contend, that the teacher chooses this particular technology from among others to facilitate student learning.

We provide a separate section on CALL, even though CALL is one among many types of materials available to teachers. The choice of CALL should be based on the learning objectives of the lesson. For example, in Chapter 2, Peter chose to have learners use the web for news sites in the hope that this would be more motivating

Unit 2 What did I do wrong?

Ari's story

Activity 50

 Watch Unit 2 of the DVD.

Activity 51
Circle True or False.

Example

Ari thought Sissy liked him.	(True)	False
1. Ari wanted to embarrass Sissy.	True	False
2. Ari scared Sissy.	True	False
3. Theresa wanted to know why Ari harassed Sissy.	True	False
4. Ari thought Sissy was silly to be upset with him.	True	False
5. Theresa asked Sissy to listen to Ari's story.	True	False
6. Ari apologised to Sissy.	True	False
7. Sissy will change to another class.	True	False

Learning tip

Sometimes cultural differences can stop us from understanding
each other, but it is important to keep talking.

Figure 4.2 True/False Response Activity for Listening.

than other materials, such as newspapers or weekly magazines. Additionally, computer technology is not ubiquitous in all countries. In some technology-rich countries, it is widely used in education; however, more than half the world's population still does not have access to the Internet and in some countries and sectors of even affluent countries, there is limited, if any, access.

We provide a separate section because CALL has particular features, some of which teachers may not be familiar with for classroom use.

CALL includes a variety of uses of the computer:

- CALL language learning programs, either on CDs, DVDs, or the web—these are either complete courses or sets of materials focusing on particular skills such as pronunciation
- the Internet for person-to-person communication, such as email, chat, instant messaging, blogs, Facebook, Twitter
- the web as a source of information.

Selecting CALL Language Programs

CALL programs use the computer as a tutor, that is, a temporary instructor (Taylor, 1980). The programs have changed from early implementations where the computer acted primarily as a competent and untiring drill master. Now, however, programs have been developed that seek to teach all four skills as communicatively as possible. The questions we provided for selecting textbooks also need to be asked about CALL programs. In addition, "our research has shown the characteristics of best practice, that is, that closely mirror effective instruction by human teachers. In particular, we have found best practice involves:

- models
- explicit instruction
- feedback" (Murray, 2009, p. 14).

As we have recommended before, text structure needs to be explicitly taught. Therefore, it is important to ensure that CALL programs provide such instruction and provide the models for learners. Feedback has always been one of the limitations of technological approaches to language teaching. While CALL programs cannot replicate the interaction between people, they can achieve interactivity. By interactivity, we mean timely, multimodal, and explicit feedback. So, for example, teachers need to use programs that, in addition to telling the learner they have chosen the correct or incorrect answer, explain why their answer is correct or incorrect. The feedback should not be at the end of several activities, but as soon as the learner has made a choice. And, the feedback should be visual, linguistic, and aural. Some language teachers have been experimenting with programs built on natural language processing (Heift & Schulze, 2007), calling it ICALL (intelligent CALL). These have been successful so far only in restricted domains. As Salaberry noted in 1996, and is still the case today, "AI [artificial intelligence] architecture is still a long way from being able to create anything close to mirror the complex system of communication instantiated in any human language and is, hence, unable to introduce any qualitative leap in the design of CALL programs" (p. 11).

Therefore, teachers need to choose CALL language programs that are interactive and provide learners with models and explicit instruction.

The Internet for Communication

This form of communication is usually referred to as **computer-mediated communication (CMC)**. Using CMC requires teachers to develop their own materials and activities because this mode is using the computer as tool (Taylor, 1980). In other words, the application has a purpose other than language instruction. CMC gives learners the opportunity for purposeful communication, either synchronously or asynchronously. The application teachers have used most has been the asynchronous CMC tool of email, although some have used the synchronous tool of chat. Although chat provides immediate feedback, it is constrained by typing speed and the speed with which the messages cross the Internet. Email, on the other hand, gives learners an opportunity to plan their text and read responses carefully. Research has shown that chat can facilitate fluency, but not accuracy (Beauvois, 1992; Lee, 2002). Blogs, Facebook, and Twitter have only recently begun to be used for educational purposes. Teachers need to determine whether the use of email or other Internet communication tools provides learners with opportunities for learning the particular content or discourse goals of the curriculum. One use of CMC that has been widely used and researched is **telecollaboration** (Warschauer & Kern, 2000), where learners across countries or schools collaborate via the Internet to interact or work together on a project. Such interaction via CMC meets the need for authentic communication (Debski, 2006), and it leads to pragmatic competence (Belz & Kinginger, 2002). Teachers need to be aware that the language modeled in these interactions, while authentic, is different from that in face-to-face or telephone conversations. It uses a simplified register (see Volume I, Chapter 9 for an explanation of simplified registers) with abbreviations, reduced forms, and deleted function words.

Salaberry (1996) provides a useful list of characteristics of CMC, many of which are compatible with language learning theory and have been shown to facilitate that learning:

- the learner addresses a specific audience for purposes other than demonstrating a skill
- expansion of the network of peers (sharing the work with fellow students)
- increased access to crosscultural information (sharing information with other communities)
- increased access to experts' advice/guidance (expert-novice interaction, native speaker-nonnative speaker contacts, etc.)
- freedom from time and location constraints (e.g., nonaccessible regions or conflicting schedules)
- emergence of new discursive environments: absence of nonverbal cues (e.g., more spontaneous participation in group work, increased participation of minorities)
- emotional involvement (increased motivation)
- unparalleled access to information databases and help online
- emergence and expansion of a new asynchronous mode of communication (e.g., email)

- safer environment in which learners may try to communicate with more advanced speakers without "losing face" (p. 18).

Thus, CMC can be a useful tool for the language classroom, especially in settings where learners have little or no access to authentic communication with speakers of English.

The Web as a Source of Information

Many teachers have learners go to the web to retrieve information on content they are working on in class, such as Peter did in Chapter 2. Others have learners go to websites that have language exercises for learners. We have found that using the web for such activities needs to be carefully planned and taught (Murray & McPherson, 2005). Many learners are not proficient at web searching and then at deciding which websites will provide them with the information they need. Some teachers therefore scaffold by at first giving learners explicit URLs, then explicitly teaching search skills. In other words, learners need to acquire web literacy in English, the ability to navigate to find specific information. A further aspect of web literacy teachers need to teach explicitly is how to read web pages once the learners have made a selection. Texts on the web can be identical to those in print—there are narratives, reports, argumentative essays, and so on. However, the web page itself is a genre specific to the Internet. For example, visual literacy plays a much larger part in conveying ideas than it does in traditional print, even though newspapers and magazines do include visual elements. Research has shown that reading online is not the same as reading print (Thurstun, 2004; Tindale, 2005). For example, online reading involves understanding the nature of hypermedia, which is the linking of different texts and other media across the web through clicking on specific items. If these two volumes had been online, we could, for example, have provided links to exactly the place in another chapter that is related to something the reader is currently reading. The web structure is very different from that in print text, such as a novel, which is structured linearly, or even a newspaper, which is not linear, but not as complex as the web. Some teachers therefore teach reading of web pages first by printing them out so that learners are not distracted by the colors and pop-ups and other physical features of the screen. Others choose simple web page screens that follow the traditional three-part structure and have few pop-ups or menus, in order to introduce learners to some of these complexities.

Materials in Under-resourced Contexts

Although many teachers have limited, if any, access to CALL in their settings, many are in settings where there are no textbooks or ones that have poor print quality and no visuals. Still other teachers have to work with large classes with only a blackboard and with learners who have no paper and pencil or pen. Materials therefore need to be taken from the world in which they live, that is, realia. Activities may have to depend more on memorization and choral work before embarking on pair or group work. Teacher blackboard work then becomes critical for learners. As well as writing clearly, teachers need to model the language on the board; they may need to make stick person drawings (although this can be difficult for young learners or preliterate learners to comprehend, as we discuss in Chapter 7, this volume). They can have learners help produce materials from discarded newspapers or other waste. These contexts are very challenging for teachers, who need to exercise all their creativity.

Conclusion

In this chapter, we have focused on how teachers can adapt published materials and also develop their own. This chapter needs to be read in conjunction with Chapter 3, where we provide ideas for how to structure classroom activities. To some extent, the division between materials and activities is arbitrary and we have discussed them separately for the convenience of the reader. The selecting and writing of materials needs to be based on the course objectives, not on having found something interesting in a workshop or the media or because the technology is available, whether that technology be computers or DVDs or even the textbook. While materials play a role in the language classroom, teachers and learners need to drive instruction.

Task: Expand

See the websites we provided in Chapter 2 on planning lesson content on p. 32. These websites provide materials as well as lesson plans.

Murray, D. E., & McPherson, P. (Eds.). (2005). *Navigating to read; reading to navigate*. Sydney: NCELTR.

This is a collection of action research reports written by teachers in Australia. They provide real-life examples of the difficulties of teaching using the web, and the solutions the teachers used. In addition, the first part of the book includes three chapters summarizing the research findings concerning the difference between reading print and reading online.

Questions for Discussion

1. Why don't most teachers teach from the textbook?
2. What principles do teachers need to use when selecting textbooks?
3. How can teachers ensure that the materials they produce themselves are effective?
4. What are the disadvantages and advantages of using naturally occurring written and spoken texts?
5. How can computers be used to teach language?
6. Will technological advances such as computers, the Internet, and wireless communication change English language teaching irrevocably? Why? Why not?

References

Adamson, B., Kwan, T., & Chan, K. K. (Eds.). (2000). *Changing the curriculum: The impact of reform on primary schooling in Hong Kong*. Hong Kong: Hong Kong University Press.

Allwright, R. (1981). What do we want teaching materials for? *ELT Journal, 36*(1), 5–18.

Beauvois, M. H. (1992). Computer-assisted classroom discussion in the foreign language classroom: Conversation in slow motion. *Foreign Language Annals, 25*(5), 455–464.

Belz, A. J., & Kinginger, C. (2002). The cross-linguistic development of address form use in telecollaborative language learning: Two case studies. *The Canadian Modern Language Review, 59*(2), 189–214.

Carter, R. (1996). *Speaking Englishes, speaking cultures.* Paper presented at the IATEFL Conference.

Debski, R. (2006). *Project-based language teaching with technology.* Sydney: NCELTR.

Heift, T., & Schulze, M. (2007). *Errors and intelligence in computer-assisted language learning.* New York: Routledge.

Katz, A., Beyrkun, L., & Sullivan, P. (2008). Challenges in translating change into practice: Textbook development in Ukraine. In D. E. Murray (Ed.), *Planning change; changing plans: Innovations in second language teaching* (pp. 43–61). Ann Arbor, MI: University of Michigan Press.

Kramsch, C. (1988). The cultural discourse of foreign language textbooks. In A. J. Singerman (Ed.), *Towards a new integration of language and culture* (pp. 63–68). Middlebury, VT: NCTFL.

Lee, L. (2002). Synchronous online exchanges: A study of modification devices on non-native discourse. *System, 30*(3), 275–288.

Littlejohn, A. L., Hutchison, T., & Torres, E. (1994). The textbook as agent of change. *ELT Journal, 48*(4), 315–328.

Murray, D. E. (2009, May). *Transforming the role of ICT in pedagogy.* Paper presented at the 26th International Conference on English Teaching and Learning in the R.O.C., National Tsing Hua University, Taiwan.

Murray, D. E. (2007). Creating a technology-rich English language learning environment. In J. Cummins & C. Davison (Eds.), *International handbook of English language teaching* (Vol. II, pp. 747–762). New York: Springer.

Murray, D. E. (2005). Teaching for learning using new technology. In Y.-J. Chen & Y.-N. Leung (Eds.), *Selected papers from the fourteenth international symposium on English teaching* (pp. 103–111). Taipei: English Teachers' Association-Republic of China.

Murray, D. E., & McPherson, P. (Eds.). (2005). *Navigating to read; reading to navigate.* Sydney: NCELTR.

Salaberry, M. R. (1996). A theoretical foundation for the development of pedagogical tasks in computer mediated communication. *CALICO, 14*(1), 5–34.

Stodolsky, S. (1989). Is teaching really in the book? In P. W. Jackson & S. Haroutunian-Gordon (Eds.), *From Socrates to software: The teacher as text and the text as teacher* (pp. 159–184). Chicago: The National Society for the Study of Education.

Taylor, R. P. (1980). *The computer in the school: Tutor, tool, tutee.* New York: Teacher's College Press.

Thurstun, J. (2004). Teaching and learning the reading of homepages. *Prospect, 19*(2), 56–71.

Tindale, J. (2005). Reading print and electronic texts. In D. E. Murray & P. McPherson (Eds.), *Navigating to read; reading to navigate* (pp. 2–15). Sydney: NCELTR.

Wallace, C. (1992). *Reading.* Oxford: Oxford University Press.

Warschauer, M. (2001). The death of cyberspace and the rebirth of CALL. In P. Brett (Ed.), *CALL in the 21st century* (CD-Rom). Whitstable, Kent: IATEFL.

Warschauer, M., & Kern, R. (2000). *Network-based language teaching: Concepts and practice.* Cambridge: Cambridge University Press.

Part II

Instructing for Learning

Part II is entitled *Instructing for Learning* and contains seven chapters. This section needs to be read in the light of Part I on planning, and the theoretical underpinnings of instructing for learning presented in Volume I. Four chapters focus on particular types of learners—young learners (Chapter 5), adolescents (Chapter 6), adult immigrants and refugees (Chapter 7), and postsecondary adults (Chapter 8). We address learners in different contexts around the world—those learning in Inner Circle countries, in Outer Circle countries, and in the Expanding Circle (Kachru, 1986). In an introductory volume such as this, we cannot cover all countries and all issues, so we focus on issues in common and major differences in the different contexts. In Chapter 9, we focus not on specific learners, but on instructional content, the workplace. We include programs to prepare learners for the workplace, as well as those that are conducted in workplace settings to help workers become successful and have the skills that help them achieve promotion to other positions. In Part I, we provided a chapter on planning language and subject matter content (Chapter 2). In Chapter 10, we build on this to provide a more in-depth model of how to develop effective content-based instruction. Research has shown that effective teachers develop their instructional practice throughout their careers (Bailey & Nunan, 1996; Borg, 2006). A key component of such development is exploring one's own practice. Therefore, we end this part with a chapter (11) that provides teachers with tools for examining their own practice.

References

Bailey, K. M., & Nunan, D. (Eds.). (1996). *Voices from the classroom: Qualitative research in second language education.* Cambridge: Cambridge University Press.

Borg, S. (2006). *Teacher cognition and language education: Research and practice.* London: Continuum.

Kachru, B. B. (1986). *The alchemy of English: The spread, functions and models of non-native Englishes.* Oxford: Pergamon Press.

Chapter 5

Teaching Young Learners

VIGNETTE

I am working as a consultant for a large English language-teaching center in Jakarta, Indonesia. The center has about 4,000 adolescent and adult students aged 12–50 studying English as a foreign language. The center has enjoyed a reputation for offering high-quality English language instruction for over 30 years. In the past year they have added a new program for young learners aged 3–11 and have hired me to spend a week with them, offering workshops for the teachers in the new program and reviewing and offering feedback on the curriculum they are developing. Even though the program is very new, they have over 500 young learners enrolled so far and are offering programs three afternoons and two mornings a week and all day on the weekends. Some adult-level teachers have moved to the young learners program, some adult teachers are teaching additional courses in the young learners program, and the center has hired new teachers and many of them have never taught young learners. Since the program was added so quickly and the program grew much faster than anticipated, there was not enough time to create an effective curriculum. Consequently, some important concepts are not being taught. In the absence of appropriate materials, some adult-level teachers are using materials from their adult courses. The program is experiencing a number of growing pains and the administrators are eager to discuss them with me and to generate solutions to the difficulties they are facing. In my initial meeting with the center's administrators and the Directors for the Young Learners Programs I asked some questions in order to better understand their motivation for adding the Young Learner Program and allowing it to expand so quickly. [Personal notes – Christison]

Task: Reflect

What questions do you think the consultant in the vignette above intended to ask the program administrators? Why do you think the center added a program for young learners? Is the teaching of young learners different from teaching adolescents and adults? Do you think the adult teachers in the center above will have difficulties teaching young learners? What might some of those difficulties be? Why are English language teaching programs for young learners becoming so popular around the world?

Introduction

In the past two decades, there has been a steady increase in the number of young learners in English classes around the world. The increase is due to the growing demand worldwide that English be taught at younger and younger ages. Many parents are of the belief that younger is better when it comes to learning English; in addition, they see that English language skills are tied to high-level jobs in business and industry and want to give their children competitive educational and economic advantages (Phillips, 1993). In addition to the private English language teaching centers that offer programs for young learners, ministries of education have become interested in this large-scale expansion so that English courses are now being included in primary curricula. The introduction of English into the primary curricula in public schools for the first time presents numerous challenges. In Outer and Expanding Circle contexts, primary language teachers are most often nonnative speakers of English with varying levels of English proficiency. This corps of teachers may be trained teachers of young learners, but they may not be trained language teachers or proficient. In Inner Circle contexts, primary teachers are most often native speakers of English who are trained in content area instruction but not in teaching second and foreign languages, and very often they are monolingual English speakers. Private language schools face somewhat different challenges, such as is depicted in the vignette above. The center has a cadre of excellent English language teachers, but they are not trained as teachers of young learners. The education that young learners receive in English is extremely important for their intellectual, physical, emotional, and social development (Linse, 2005). In this chapter we will focus on the concerns related to the different ways in which young learners develop and how the instruction they receive should be consistent with this development. In addition, we will focus on characteristics of young English language learners in worldwide contexts and then offer suggestions for providing instruction for learning and for organizing learning environments.

Characteristics of Young Learners

As a group, young learners are very diverse. They come from many different backgrounds, have many different profiles, and learn English in many varied contexts. Young language learners vary greatly in terms of their language competence even within the same age group. In addition, learners may vary in terms of the skills they have acquired in their home language(s), depending on their age and how many languages they use in daily communication. Learners may also vary in terms of their proficiency level in the different language skills—reading, writing speaking, and listening. Some learners may understand almost everything said in English but may not be able to speak confidently. Other learners may be able to read and write quite well, but become completely lost in casual conversations. In terms of experience with literacy, the differences are huge; some learners demonstrate literacy skills in their native language while others, even in the same age group, do not. In addition, young learners differ in how they learn best. They also differ in terms of their socioeconomic status, as well as the countries in which they are learning English (see Volume I, Chapter 2). All teachers working with young learners can benefit from understanding more about the diversity represented in this population.

In Volume I, Chapter 2, we explained the distinction between Inner, Outer, and Expanding Circle countries (Kachru, 1986) and discussed the pros and cons of using this paradigm to describe the contexts in which English language teachers work; therefore, we will not review this discussion here. Nevertheless, for the reasons explained in Volume I, Chapter 2, we will use the paradigm here to describe the characteristics of young learners.

Young English Learners in Inner Circle Countries

The demographics in public schools in Inner Circle countries have changed dramatically in the past two decades. For example, in Australia one in four children speak English as a second language (Gibbons, 1993) and the numbers continue to increase. In public schools in the United States, there are 5.1 million English language learners (ELLs), approximately 10% of the total school population (National Clearinghouse for English Language Acquisition, 2006).

Young learners in these countries fall into one of three categories—children who are newly arrived, were born in an Inner Circle country, or have had some schooling in English. Learners in the newly arrived group have had a variety of experiences. They may have:

- spent time in refugee camps
- had no previous schooling in any language
- had periods of interrupted schooling
- developed written skills but no oral skills
- developed good oral and literacy skills in their first language.

Some children may have been born in Inner Circle countries but enter school speaking little or no English because they don't speak English at home. In addition, they interact mostly with their home language community. Still other young learners may or may not have been born in an Inner Circle country but come from homes where English is not used, English is not the only language used, or English is a second language for the parents. Many of these children develop some skills in English, but not adequate skills to cope with the demands of an academic curriculum that requires them to learn English and acquire the skills and knowledge necessary for success in content-area subjects (Becker, 2001).

Young Learners in Outer and Expanding Circle Countries

As mentioned in both the vignette and the chapter introduction above, the demand for English instruction for young learners is increasing in both the context of public school primary education and private education in both K–12 schools and English language centers. In public school primary education, learners have many different profiles and often their socioeconomic status varies greatly. The emphasis on English in primary schools also varies from country to country, so it is difficult to draw conclusions about the learners, the teachers, or the curriculum. In private K–12 schools and English language centers, learner profiles may vary, but most children come from families with a higher than average socioeconomic status. Most parents take an interest in their children's English education because they see English as a pathway towards upward mobility for their children. Learners in private language schools are usually well educated and English is encouraged at home and in social situations.

Instructing for Learning

Standards for Young Learners

TESOL, the international professional association of teachers to speakers of other languages, has developed ESL standards for pre-K–12 students (TESOL, 2010). The Standards are organized around goals (the overarching areas in which learners need to develop competence), standards (what students should know and be able to do with English), and descriptors (broad categories of discrete, representative behaviors that students exhibit when they meet the standard). The activities and issues we discuss in this section fall within this framework; namely, that they support the three major goals of the standards—to use English to communicate in social settings, to use English to achieve academically in all content areas in school settings, and to use English in socially and culturally appropriate ways. The ESL pre-K–12 standards also explain how the proficiency levels—beginning, intermediate, and advanced—should be interpreted with each of the nine standards. In addition, the vignettes offer examples for the different levels of proficiency for different grade or age levels. For the purposes of the sample progress indicators for the nine standards, they are presented in terms of the following age groups: grades pre-K–3 (aged 4–8), grades 4–8 (aged 9–13), and grades 9–12 (aged 14–18). Young learners are aged 4–9 and fall into preschool, kindergarten, and grades 1–4 in the standards.

Although we believe that these standards can play a role in designing effective instruction for young learners in all contexts, it must be noted that they were developed for pre-K–12 learners in U.S. public schools; therefore, the standards, descriptors, and vignettes are written for the U.S. context. For example, Goal 2—to use English to achieve academically in all content areas in school settings—is very Inner Circle directed. However, Goal 2 could also pertain to Outer or Expanding countries where content may be taught in English, such as in some programs in The Netherlands, Germany, and Malaysia. TESOL's standards provide an excellent starting point for thinking about instructional design for young learners and help teachers and administrators develop a clear understanding of what must go into creating a useful set of standards for young learners that are specifically directed to other contexts.

The ESL pre-K–12 standards outline a number of general principles for language acquisition that teachers of young language learners should keep in mind. These principles are derived from current research and theory and are briefly described below:

- Language is a means of communication; consequently, successful language learning and teaching should emphasize functional literacy.

- Language comes in different varieties and varies according to person, topic, purpose, and situation. Young language learners should learn both the oral and written language varieties that are used in school and in the communities where English is spoken.
- Programs for young learners must acknowledge that patterns of language use vary across cultures and help learners develop an understanding and respect for cultural diversity.
- Second language acquisition happens over time with young learners moving through a series of developmental stages. Programs for young learners must recognize that the rate of acquisition is influenced by multiple factors, such as age, first language background, learning styles, cognitive styles, and motivation.
- Second language acquisition takes place when learners interact with others using language that they comprehend to accomplish specific tasks.
- The use of language in the real world requires the use of different language modalities simultaneously (i.e., speaking, listening, reading, and writing); therefore, young language learners need to develop language abilities using an integrated approach by participating in activities that require multiple modalities.
- Native language proficiency contributes to second language proficiency, and native language correlates positively with the acquisition of literacy in a second language.

Task: Explore

Work with a partner. Discuss the relationship between the three goals for TESOL's pre-K–12 ESL standards and the principles for language acquisition described above.

Stages of Cognitive Development

It is important for teachers of young learners to understand the general developmental characteristics essential for learning at different ages. Given that the trend is for English instruction to begin at younger and younger ages, teachers must think about these stages as they plan lessons or make recommendations to program administrators about when to begin instruction within their programs. Piaget (1963) identified four stages of cognitive and affective development that are important for English language teachers to consider as they plan instruction for young learners.

Sensory-motor Stage

This stage occurs from 0–2 years. Behavior at this stage is primarily motor or physical. The child does not yet internally represent events and think conceptually.

Preoperational Stage

This stage occurs between 2 and 7 years. Language develops during the preoperational stage as does rapid conceptual development. Because children are very egocentric during this period of time, this stage is called prelogical or semilogical. Children can focus on a specific feature in a situation, but they cannot focus on multifeatures.

Concrete Operations

This stage occurs between 7 and 11 years of age when the child develops the ability to apply logical thought to concrete problems. Children also begin using language to exchange information and become more social and less egocentric.

Characteristics of Learners at Each Stage of Development

In addition to understanding the cognitive stages, it is important to understand how to translate these stages into learner behaviors at each stage.

Preschool (ages 2–4)

This is a sensitive period for language development. Children at this stage are usually quite good imitators of speech sounds. They do not work well in groups and prefer to work alone on something that interests them although they enjoy parallel play (i.e., playing alongside other children but not directly with them). They have very short attention spans and love to repeat the same activity over and over again. They need concrete experiences.

Grades K–2 (ages 5–7)

Like preschoolers, they need concrete experiences and love to name objects, define things, and learn about objects in their own world. They learn new concepts best when they are taught in binary opposites. They learn the meaning of *large* by referencing it with something in their world that is *small*. Children at this age also have vivid imaginations and respond well to stories of fantasy. At this age, they learn best through oral language, so they love being told stories with a solid beginning, middle, and end. It is important for teachers to remember that young learners at this age are unskilled in using the small muscles (e.g., the intrinsic muscles) and coordinating fine-tuned motor skills. Reinforcing regular routines helps learners at this age.

Grades 3–5 (ages 8–10)

At this stage, children begin to develop characteristics of concrete operations, such as the ability to understand cause and effect. They are also most open at this age to people, situations, and ideas that are different from their own experiences. Introducing children to information about other cultures and countries at this stage is very important. In addition, children at this age can learn how to work with other students, particularly in groups, and they like writing notes to each other and to pen pals, and creating skits and participating in role plays. Like children in younger grades, they continue to benefit from imaginative and creative play, and they also like a story that has a definite beginning, middle, and end. Using rubrics and peer assessments can be used with children at this age.

> **Task: Explore**
>
> Review the general learning guidelines offered for each age group above. Then, based on the information provided above, generate two specific language-learning activities that you might use with each group.

Characteristics of Learner Language

Two Types of Language

Skuttnabb–Kangas and Toukamaa (1976) were the first researchers to make a distinction between two types of language—playground and classroom. Cummins (1996) took this idea further in making his distinction between **basic interpersonal communicative skills (BICS)** and **cognitive academic language proficiency (CALP)**.[1] BICS develops quickly in about two years; however, CALP takes about seven years to develop and must be explicitly taught. The distinction is particularly useful in determining how to plan instruction for young language learners because the types of activities that learners need to help them develop these two types of language are very different.

Language Skills

It is important to recognize behaviors associated with each of the four skills that young language learners are likely to exhibit. Recognizing these behaviors is important for teachers in all contexts (Gibbons, 1993).

LISTENING

Young language learners:

- have difficulty in consistently following a series of instructions
- have difficulty attending
- have a shorter attention span than other students
- have difficulty in predicting what is about to be said
- cannot differentiate among different genres
- do not understand key words in phrases which can alter meaning, such as *although, however, except*, and *unless.*

SPEAKING

Young language learners:

- have difficulty adjusting register and may sound impolite in formal situations with adults
- use language that is known and often say the same thing many times

- make mistakes with basic sentence structures that are not typical of native English speakers
- appear to have difficulty sequencing thoughts.

READING

Young language learners:

- read slowly
- have poor comprehension if the topic is unfamiliar
- have trouble paraphrasing and isolating the main idea
- have trouble predicting what will come next in a narrative
- cannot differentiate among different genres
- have difficulty reading for meaning
- rarely self-correct when reading aloud.

WRITING

Young language learners:

- have generally poor written language skills
- can write sentences but have difficulty writing a paragraph
- write only in an informal style characteristic of spoken language
- use a limited vocabulary
- use mostly simple sentence structures
- make grammatical errors not typical of native speakers
- have poor spelling
- lack confidence to write at length
- do not have mastery of different genres
- tend to write the same thing over and over again.

Language Functions

Adult learners often treat second or foreign language learning as an intellectual game or an abstract system. This is quite different from young learners who respond to language based on what it does or what they can do with it, in other words, its functions. A useful starting point in planning instruction for young learners is to identify the language functions that learners will need in the classroom because these functions are closely tied to academic language and Cummins' notion of CALP mentioned above. In addition, these functions are useful outside of the classroom as children interact with other children or adults who may speak English. The list in Table 5.1 is not meant to be exhaustive, but identifies some of the most common language functions.

Armed with this list of language functions, teachers can then think of the ways in which these different functions can be used with learners in their specific contexts. For example, telling someone how to place something on a grid, how to do a homework assignment, or how to play a game are all examples of the language function associated with *giving instructions*.

Table 5.1 Language Functions

agreeing and disagreeing
apologizing
asking for directions
asking for permission
classifying
comparing
denying
describing
evaluating
expressing likes and dislikes
explaining
giving instructions
hypothesizing
identifying
inferring
planning and predicting
questioning
refusing
reporting
sequencing
suggesting
warning
wishing and hoping

Adjusting Language for Young Learners

Within any of these language functions in Table 5.1, there are many ways of expressing similar ideas. For example, the function of *asking for permission* can be expressed as simply as saying, "May I open the door?" to a more complicated "Do you mind if I open the door for a few minutes until it cools off in here?" Native speakers and proficient nonnative speakers of English should make a point of offering a range of alternate wordings for learners. When teaching new functions, we believe it is a good idea to model the simplest version first and make adjustments as learners demonstrate understanding of the concepts. The examples that follow suggest how the same basic concept of *cause and effect* can be conveyed to learners in different ways:

- It snowed. The weather was very cold this morning.
- It snowed, so the weather became very cold.
- Because it snowed, the weather turned very cold.
- The weather turning cold was a result of the snowstorm we had yesterday.
- The cold weather was caused by the snowstorm we had yesterday.

Of course, it is impossible to accurately predict language use for all learners, but if you start low and work your way up the scale of difficulty you lessen the risk of leaving some learners behind. Additional characteristics of L2 teacher talk are outlined in Chapter 11 of this volume.

Determining which Language to Use

In Outer and Expanding Circle contexts, teachers are often working with young learners who not only speak the same native language, but also share the teacher's native language; consequently, the question of whether or not to use the mother tongue in the English classroom is one that is frequently discussed. Our belief is that in Outer and Expanding Circle contexts, it is important to use as much English in the classroom as possible since the classroom provides the main opportunity for input in English. Keeping the class in English takes careful planning. Basic routine instructions that are related to running the class should be given in English. If teachers use gestures as well, children will eventually become used to receiving the instructions in English and begin to understand what is being expected of them. When activities are designed specifically to help them develop their spoken language, learners should be encouraged to use English. However, it is also important to realize that comprehension precedes production and that many young learners will understand teacher language before they are ready to talk.

Many teachers who work in Inner Circle contexts have classes of young English language learners (ELLs) who come from many different linguistic and cultural backgrounds in one class. Teachers may not know the home languages of any of the children. In addition, teachers may have mother tongue speakers of English in the same classroom. In these contexts, teachers cannot use any language other than English in the classroom. There are numerous English language teachers who are able to adjust their teacher talk (see Chapter 11, this volume) in order to make their classroom language comprehensible to the English learners.

Language for Communication

Classrooms should be structured around communication to develop both oral and literacy skills. Creating a classroom that is focused on communication is particularly difficult to do when teachers are working with young learners who have beginning levels of English proficiency. Nevertheless, it is important to remember some basic concepts about communication. When language in the classroom is limited to lists, labeling, one-word responses, memorized patterns and dialogs, songs not integrated into the curriculum, recitation, and choral reading, the class is likely not to be a communicative one (Curtain & Dahlberg, 2010). If the goal of learning English is for communicative purposes, then classroom activity should be about communicating (see below for suggested activities).

Organizing for Learning

Organizing the Physical Classroom

The physical arrangement of the classroom is very important. Classrooms for young language learners work best when chairs, tables, and desks can be moved around to accommodate different learning activities. Young learners also need visual stimuli, so permanent display boards are important so that learners' work can be posted. Many of the activities for young learners that we suggest below are product-oriented, meaning that learners create such items as pictures, graphs, or stories as part of the activity. In addition, teachers can use these boards to reinforce concepts they are learning, such as creating a word wall. Teachers can create word walls simply and easily by placing key words from the lesson on poster board cards and taping them to the wall. It is likely that teachers in content area classes that include ELLs may have several word walls around the room. In these cases, each word wall is also labeled to identify the specific content area. Display boards are constantly changing, so notebooks and folders are excellent ways to store and collect student work when old work is taken down and new work is posted (see Chapter 12, this volume).

Selecting Activities for Communication

General Guidelines

There are many factors that influence how children will respond to activities in the classroom—their cultural background, the environment (do they live in a rural community or a city?), their gender, their family background, and the expectations they have for classroom learning. The type of activity a teacher selects is influenced not only by the age of the learners (see "Stages in cognitive development" above), but also by the circumstances surrounding learning, the attitudes of the learners, and the interests they have. The following list offers teachers of young learners a set of general guidelines to follow in selecting activities:

- Activities for young learners should be simple enough so that they can under-stand what is expected of them. The younger the child, the simpler the activity should be, both in terms of the processes and the demand on cognition.
- Because human development progresses through a series of stages, teachers must consider what young learners are capable of doing. The goal of the activity needs to be achievable, and the activity itself needs to be stimulating. This is not an easy balance to achieve.
- For very young learners and for beginning English learners, activities should be orally based—directed toward listening and speaking.
- The ordering of skills for young learners should be listening, speaking, reading, and writing. Children should only be asked to write words they can read. They should only read words they can talk about, and they should only be asked to talk about words and concepts they have listened to and can recognize in spoken language (Peregoy & Boyle, 2010).
- Written activities should be used sparingly until children have had the chance to master the mechanics of writing. Some young learners are slow to develop fine motor skills. Even though they may understand literacy concepts, they are not able to demonstrate that understanding until their fine motor skills develop.
- Activities that help young children develop balance and spatial awareness at the same time they are learning language are ideal activities, such as variations of TPR (see below).
- Building literacy skills works best in young learners when they learn to read and write about ideas and concepts they already use in their oral communication.
- Activities that help children develop social skills in conjunction with language are also desirable. Children need to become aware of themselves in relation to others, to share and cooperate, and to be assertive without being aggressive.

These skills can all be learned in the classroom with carefully designed and implemented activities.

• Children also need to learn how to learn. In order to help them achieve this goal, their learning must not be confined exclusively to the classroom, the textbooks, and the teacher. As teachers, we want to help young learners acquire strategies for learning (see Volume I, Chapter 13) and independence (see Chapter 3, this volume).

• Activities for young learners should give them an opportunity to experiment with different ways of learning and organizing their work, so that they become aware of themselves as learners and can determine their preferred ways of learning (see Volume I, Chapter 13).

• Activities should promote a positive affective climate in the classroom so that learners feel comfortable responding and look forward to classroom tasks and interacting with others.

Grouping Strategies

In Chapter 3 of this volume, we discussed the importance of grouping strategies and presented a taxonomy for thinking about how to organize group work (Christison & Bassano, 1995). Although we believe that it is important for teachers of young learners to use different grouping strategies, we also believe that it is important to recognize that the concept of working in groups may be new to children, and they may find it difficult at first. Therefore, it is important to begin with restructuring activities (see Chapter 3) and to gradually transition them toward more independence (see Figure 3.2 in Chapter 3, this volume) in learning tasks.

Activities for Language Development

There are numerous activity types for teachers to choose from. The list of activity types below is not meant to be exhaustive, but rather provides teachers with some of the most common activity types for the development of all four skills.

TOTAL PHYSICAL RESPONSE

Total physical response (TPR) (Asher, 1969) is an extremely useful activity for young learners because it requires learners to respond to a teacher's commands with physical actions, thereby making it easy for the teacher to determine whether the learners have understood or not. The activity known as *Simon says* is a common extension of TPR. In this version of TPR, some commands are preceded by the phrase *Simon says*, for example, "Simon says, sit down," so learners should respond and sit down. Other commands are not preceded by the phrase *Simon says*, so learners should not respond. TPR activities vary from simple listen and do to sequenced activities that complete a process or tell a story.

TPR can also be combined with simple oral drills using pictures. First, vocabulary is introduced verbally and via pictures and each picture is cued with an appropriate gesture. Each word is introduced slowly and used over and over again. Then the teacher gives commands to the learners, getting them to manipulate the realia or pictures, such as *pick up, put down, point to, touch, show me*, and *give*. Then the teacher elicits one-word responses, e.g., *Is it a coat? Is it a hat?* After students have exchanged pictures, teachers ask, *Who has the coat? Who has the hat?* Pictures can even be put into a simple story sequence that beginners can learn and then retell.

SEQUENCING

Many different things can be sequenced—letters can be sequenced to form words, words can be sequenced to form sentences, and sentences can be sequenced to form short stories or paragraphs, as in Table 5.2. All sequencing activities can be done orally or at desks with papers or manipulatives.

CLASSIFYING AND SORTING

There are many different ways in which teachers can use this activity type. With beginners, learners can sort written vocabulary words into their appropriate categories, such as *animals, food, furniture, clothes.* In a content area class, learners can sort vocabulary based on the key concepts covered in class. Teachers can also give students a set of cards depicting animals or objects and ask learners to categorize them in as many different ways as possible.

GRID ACTIVITIES

A grid is a way of organizing information. Grids can be used in many different communicative activities involving all four skills—reading, writing, speaking, and listening—and they work equally well in activities involving individuals working alone, in pairs, or small and large groups. Information gap is one common way to use grids. Students receive complementary grids (i.e., Grid A has all of the missing information from Grid B, and vice versa) and must ask and answer questions with a partner in order to find the missing information.

MATCHING

There are many items that children can match depending on their age level and language ability—pictures to sounds, pictures to words, words to definitions, questions to words, and missing words to their sentences. Matching activities can be done individually at desks or interactively. The interactive version of this activity is known as *Find Your Partner* and requires students to mill around with their picture, definition, word, question, or answer and ask questions of each other until they find their partner or match.

Table 5.2 Examples of Sequencing

Letters to words									
S	E	Q	U	E	N	C	I	N	G
Words to sentences									
This	chapter	is		about		teaching	young	learners.	

JIGSAW

In a jigsaw activity, each student gets a part of the information to share with the group. The group cannot complete the main problem-solving activity until all group members have successfully shared their information (see, for example, Curtain & Dahlberg, 2010, pp. 109–112).

SURVEYS AND QUESTIONNAIRES

Surveys and questionnaires are excellent for developing social skills and both oral and written language. Each student gets a simple survey or questionnaire and must find a specific number of individuals (within or outside of the class) to complete the survey by asking questions and recording answers on a tally sheet. Once all surveys have been completed, the class analyzes and discusses the results. The topics for surveys and questionnaires can vary depending on the interests of the class.

PLAYS AND ROLE-PLAYS

Role-plays are for intermediate-level learners. They move learners a step beyond the traditional dialogs and place students in a new situation. In role-plays learners are asked to use material that they have memorized and become familiar with through dialog drills, and other types of classroom activities, as a basis for expanding and personalizing the information. For example, the role-play may spring from a dialog about shopping or going to a party. Learners are called on to use the dialog they learned, substitute and change words and phrases to create a role-play about shopping or going to a party that is consistent with their own personal experiences.

SONGS AND RHYMES

Another important way in which teachers can link language with action is through song and rhymes. Many songs and rhymes for young children are designed to incorporate actions. Once children learn the songs, they will want to do them over and over again. Songs work best when they can be integrated into the thematic context of instruction.

Task: Explore

Work with a partner. Using the suggested activity types above, create a specific activity for young learners. Describe the context in which you see the activity being used.

Activities for Developing Literacy Skills

In order to read efficiently in English, young learners must learn to recognize words. Automatic word recognition depends on the ability to rapidly and efficiently decode, and, in turn, decoding is dependent on the foundational skills of reading—

print concepts, alphabet principle, and phonemic awareness. **Print concepts** is an umbrella term that refers to the features of written language and the way the text is organized that underpin literacy development. The **alphabet principle** is the ability to visually recognize and name the letters of the alphabet. **Phonemic awareness** is the conscious understanding that spoken language is composed of phonemes or speech sounds. Some individuals use the term **phonological awareness**, but we make a distinction here. Phonological awareness is an umbrella term that includes phonemic awareness, but it also includes skills such as breaking sentences into words, breaking words into syllables, and recognizing and producing rhyming words.

It is beyond the scope of this chapter to provide an in-depth discussion of teaching reading to young learners; instead, we focus on learner indicators for print concepts, alphabet recognition, and phonemic awareness and the questions that teachers can ask learners that help determine learner skills in relation to each of the three concepts. We focus attention here because many teachers of young learners are working with these foundational concepts. Table 5.3 presents a summary of the benchmarks and teacher questions.

Table 5.3 Summary of Foundational Concepts for Reading in English

Foundational Reading Concepts	Indicators	Teacher questions
Print concepts	Ability to discriminate between a letter and a word. Ability to recognize word boundaries and sentences. Ability to name and understand the role of common punctuation marks. Ability to recognize print in varying forms. Ability to track from left to right. Ability to make a return sweep to the next line.	Can you point to a letter? Can you point to a word? Count the words in the last sentence. Can you show me a "stop mark" or a "full stop?" Can you show me a question mark? Can you show me the first letter in this word? When you come to the end of this line, where do you read next?
Alphabet recognition	Ability to recognize letters in printed form. Ability to identify names of letters. Ability to recognize similarities and differences in letter shapes. Ability to correctly write letters of the alphabet. Ability to recognize letters in words. Ability to match letters. Ability to recognize specific letters in context.	What is this letter? (*Pointing to a circled letter*) Is this letter the same as this letter? (*Pointing to the same letter circled in two places*) Show me how you write the letter A. Where do you put the pencil when you start to write it? How is this letter different from the one you wrote? How is it the same? (*Point to an example printed letter*)
Phonemic awareness	Ability to recognize sounds as the same or different.	Which two words begin with the same sound: *cat, cup, dog?*

(*Continued overleaf*)

Table 5.3 Continued

Foundational Reading Concepts	Indicators	Teacher questions
	Ability to recognize words that begin or end with the same sound.	What is the last sound you hear in this word: *cup?*
	Ability to recognize words with the same middle sound.	What is the first sound you hear in this word: *cat?*
	Ability to combine sounds to create a word.	What is the middle sound you hear in this word: *dog?*
	Ability to separate sounds in a word.	Can you guess which word I am trying to say: /k/ /u/ /p/?
		How many sounds do you hear in this word: *cat?*
		Say *seat* without /s/: (eat)
		Say *mat.* Now instead of /t/ say /p/. What's the new word? (*map*)

Although we have focused above on the **bottom–up processing model**, we also acknowledge that fluent reading is achieved as a result of both bottom–up and **top–down processing** (see also Volume I, Chapter 9). A top–down processing model proposes that readers access stored experiences that help them make sense of the information encountered while reading (Herrera, Perez, & Escamilla, 2010). Teachers who use the top–down model are most often described as **whole language** teachers because they see that their responsibility is to guide understanding of the reading process by tapping into learners' prior knowledge. In working with young language learners, we subscribe to an **interactive processing model** (Reutzel & Cooter, 2000) that makes use of both bottom–up and top–down processing.

Conclusion

In this chapter we have provided an overview of the characteristics of young learners who are learning English worldwide, recognizing that learners in private English language centers in Expanding Circle contexts may have needs that are different from learners in public school contexts in Inner Circle countries. Nevertheless, there are important principles that are overlapping among contexts, and it is on those principles we have tried to focus. In the section of the chapter devoted to instructing for learning, we have tried to make the point that children are not simply small adults and in terms of human development they have very special needs and requirements for learning. In addition, we focused on learner language, such as how to use language functions, adjust language, and create classrooms for communication. In the section of the chapter devoted to organizing for learning, we offered suggestions for the physical classroom and for selecting activities. Finally, we offered sample activities for developing both oral language and literacy.

Task: Expand

www. ncela.gwu.edu
The National Clearinghouse for English Language Acquisition collects, coordinates and conveys a broad range of research and resources in support of an inclusive approach to high quality education for ELLs. To fulfill its mission NCELA supports high quality networking among state-level administrators of Title III programs in the U.S. www.cambridgeesol.org/exams/young-learners/yle/html
This website outlines the Cambridge ESOL qualifications for young learners.

Questions for Discussion

1. What advice would you give a teacher of young learners about using a language other than English in the classroom?
2. What are the two different types of language that young learners have to master? Provide an example of each one. What evidence exists to support these two types of language?
3. Explain how teachers can tell whether young learners have the skills for learning to read in a second language.

Note

1. The distinction between basic interpersonal communicative skills (BICS) and cognitive academic language proficiency (CALP) is an important one for young learners in all contexts. The distinction suggests that young language learners should first have an opportunity to engage in meaningful language use and interaction in the target language to build BICS and that CALP skills are better built in a second language once children have acquired these skills in their first language.

References

Asher, J. (1969). The total physical response approach to second language learning. *Modern Language Journal, 53*, 3–17.

Becker, H. (2001). *Teaching ESL K-12: Views from the classroom.* Boston, MA: Heinle and Heinle.

Christison, M. A., & Bassano, S. K. (1995). *Look who's talking.* Burlingame, CA: Alta Book Center Publishers.

Cummins, J. (1996). *Negotiating identities: Education for empowerment in a diverse society.* Ontario, CA: California Association for Bilingual Education.

Curtain, H., & Dahlberg, C. A., (2010). *Languages and children. Making the match: New languages for young learners, Grades K-8.* Boston, MA: Pearson.

Gibbons, P. (1993). *Learning to learn in a second language.* Portsmouth, NH: Heinemann.

Herrera, S. G., Perez, D. R., & Escamilla, K. (2010). *Teaching reading to English language learners: Differentiated literacies.* Boston: Allyn & Bacon.

Kachru, B. B. (1986). *The alchemy of English: The spread, functions and models of non-native Englishes.* Oxford: Pergamon Press.

Linse, C. (2005). *Practical English language teaching: Young learners.* New York: McGraw Hill International.

National Clearinghouse for English Language Acquisition (2006). Retrieved from http://www.ncela.gwu.edu/faqs

Peregoy, S. F., & Boyle, O. F. (2008). *Reading, writing, and learning in ESL: A resource book for K-12 teachers*. Boston: Pearson.

Phillips, S. (1993). *Young learners*. Oxford: Oxford University Press.

Piaget, J. (1963). *The language and thought of the child*. New York: W.W. Norton.

Reutzel, D. R., & Cooter, R. B., Jr. (2000). *Teaching children to read: Putting the pieces together*. Upper Saddle River, NJ: Prentice-Hall.

Skuttnabb-Kangas, T., & Toukamaa, T. (1976). *Teaching migrant children's mother tongue and learning the language of the host community*. Helsinki: Finnish National Commission for UNESCO.

TESOL ESL Standards for Pre-K-12 Students. (2010). Online version. Retrieved from http://www.tesol.org/s_tesol/seccss.asp?CID=113&DID=1583

Chapter 6

Teaching Adolescent Learners

VIGNETTE

For the past three years we have been working on a U.S. federal grant with a group of content area teachers in a local school district. Five middle schools[1] are involved in the project and 26 content area teachers. We meet with the teachers for inservice workshops (six hours) about every eight weeks to help them implement an instructional model designed to improve reading skills for at-risk learners, including English language learners. We are in the second semester of the project, and today I am visiting classes for the first time at one of the middle schools. I must admit to being a bit shell-shocked! I worked in a middle school years ago, so I know that today's experience was quite normal for middle schools; in fact, this is an exceptional middle school. No students are really misbehaving; nevertheless, the sheer level of noise is overwhelming in hallways between classes and in classrooms before instruction begins. It feels like everyone in the entire school is speaking at the same time. And, there is constant interpersonal drama in the hallways between classes—girls slamming lockers, boys rough-housing with each other, boys bopping girls and other boys on the head with books and pencils to get attention, boys bumping into girls and knocking everyone in nearest proximity to the event slightly off balance, including me on one occasion. The energy level is both exhilarating and exhausting.

I am now watching an 8th grade science class, and it is certainly an education. The teacher has to spend so much time just trying to control the undercurrent of adolescent energy. It seems like it's one extreme or the other—either they are bouncing off of the walls with energy, or they are bored. It's hard for even the most proficient teacher to engage them as learners. One young man is tapping his pencil, another is softly kicking the side of a table, and a third is drawing illustrations on the front of his notebook. Two girls are staring blankly out the window, watching nothing and everything; one is practising threading her pencil through her fingers. At the back of the room, a couple of other students are whispering to each other. I am impressed by the patience of the teacher that I am observing and have great admiration for the job she does. She is a wonderfully competent science teacher who obviously knows her subject matter. In addition, she has developed superb classroom management skills. She somehow manages to get the students' attention and gets them working on their group projects about rocks. I can tell she enjoys her students, and they genuinely like her. [Christison personal notes, February 2006]

Task: Reflect

1.　Based on the description provided in the vignette above, what would you say are the defining characteristics of adolescent learners?
2.　Have you worked with or taught adolescent learners? Were they L1 or L2 speakers of English? In what context?
3.　If you have worked with adolescent learners, are your experiences similar to or different from the middle school described in the vignette?
4.　Have you talked to teachers of adolescent learners? If yes, what information have they shared with you about teaching adolescent learners?
5.　What are your own memories of school during your adolescent years? Are your experiences similar to or different from the middle school described in the vignette?

Introduction

Adolescents are often the neglected group of language learners in terms of focus and specific teacher preparation in most English language teaching contexts. As a profession, language teachers and researchers have spent much of their efforts on understanding and educating adult academic learners, and, in the past decade, have added young learners to the mix; however, adolescent learners do not fit into either group. The context for the vignette above is young adolescent learners in U.S. public schools; however, the behaviors of the adolescent learners in this context are typical of adolescents in other contexts. Although adolescence technically spans the ages of 10 to 18, we are focusing this chapter on young adolescents between the ages of 10 and 14 because it is this group that has received the least attention in the research and in teacher education programs. In addition, older adolescents are more similar to young adult language learners in postsecondary contexts in terms of their academic needs, and many features of this group will be covered in Chapter 8 on adult learners in academic contexts.

As the author of the vignette suggests, young adolescent learners can be challenging. They are different from young learners because they have had a more diverse set of experiences, including social and academic experiences; yet, they are not adults because they do not have the breadth and depth of experience nor the cognitive maturity of adults. From about the ages of 10 to 14, learners grow and develop more rapidly than at any other stage in life, except for infancy. In addition, adolescents are often very much aware of their growth and development, and this awareness can make the changes they are experiencing uncomfortable and difficult.

In this chapter we will focus first on the contexts for learning and then discuss characteristics of adolescent development in five key areas—intellectual, social, physical, emotional, and moral—because the instruction adolescents receive should be consistent with their development. In order to help teachers meet the needs of adolescent language learners, we then turn our attention to issues concerning second language literacy by looking at some of the research and some research-based principles for second language reading instruction.

Characteristics of Adolescent Learners

As a group, young adolescent learners vary greatly. They vary in terms of their L2 language competence even within the same age group, as well as the proficiency level they have acquired with their home language(s). Learners may also vary in terms of their academic backgrounds (Waggoner, 1999) and in the range of proficiency levels with different skills—reading, writing, speaking, and listening —within the same language. We believe that all teachers working with adolescent learners can benefit from understanding more about the diversity represented in this population.

In Volume I, Chapter 2, we explained the distinction between Inner, Outer, and Expanding Circle countries (Kachru, 1986) and discussed the pros and cons of using this paradigm to describe the contexts for English language teaching. In Volume II, Chapter 5, we used this paradigm to discuss the context and characteristics of young learners. We will also use Kachru's paradigm in Chapter 6 to provide a summary of the contexts for adolescent L2 learners of English.

Adolescent English Learners in Inner Circle Countries

The changing demographics in Inner Circle countries have not only affected the number of young learners in public school, they have also affected the number of adolescent learners. In terms of demographics, adolescent L2 learners also fall into two categories—those who are newly arrived and those who were born in an Inner Circle country. In terms of English, they also fall into two categories—those who have had some schooling in English and those who have not.

Adolescent learners in the newly arrived group have had a variety of experiences; and consequently have different learner profiles. They may have:

- spent time in refugee camps
- experienced trauma escaping or moving from their home country
- had no previous schooling in any language
- had periods of interrupted schooling
- developed written skills but few oral skills or vice versa
- developed good oracy and literacy skills in their first language
- ambivalent attitudes to learning English and consider it as purely an academic requirement, with no relevance to their future lives.

Some adolescent learners speak little or no English at home. If they are newly arrived to an Inner Circle country, they may enter school speaking little or no English. In addition, they may interact outside of class almost exclusively with their home language community. Other adolescent learners may have been born in an Inner Circle country but come from homes where English is not the only language used, or is a second language for the caregivers. Many of these adolescent learners develop some basic interpersonal communicative skills (BICS) (Cummins, 1996) in English (see Volume II, Chapter 5) but not adequate skills to cope with the demands of an academic curriculum that requires them to learn English and acquire the cognitive academic language proficiency (CALP) (Cummins, 1996) and knowledge necessary for success in content area subjects (Becker, 2001).

Adolescent Learners in Outer and Expanding Circle Countries

In Outer and Expanding Circle contexts, the demand for English instruction for adolescent learners is increasing in both the context of public school and private education. The emphasis on English in public schools varies greatly from country to country, so we do not wish to draw definitive conclusions about learners, the teachers, or the curriculum in these contexts. For example, different countries provide learners with quite different exposure to English outside the classroom, depending on the role of English in that country. In private English language centers, most adolescent learners come from families with a higher than average socioeconomic status, and most parents take an interest in their children's English education because they see English as a pathway towards upward mobility for their children. Learners in private language schools are usually well educated, and English is often encouraged at home and in social situations. In many Outer and Expanding Circle countries there are also private coaching and tutoring schools that focus on English as well as content area subjects.

Instructing for Learning

TESOL, the international professional association of teachers to speakers of other languages, has developed ESL standards for pre-K–12 students (TESOL, 1997). The standards are organized around goals (the overarching areas in which learners need to develop competence), standards (what students should know and be able to do with English), and descriptors (broad categories of discrete, representative behaviors that students exhibit when they meet the standard). The activities and issues we discuss in this section fall within this framework; namely, that they support the three major goals of the standards—to use English to communicate in social settings, to use English to achieve academically in all content areas in school settings, and to use English in socially and culturally appropriate ways. The ESL pre-K–12 standards also explain how the proficiency levels—beginning, intermediate, and advanced—should be interpreted with each of the standards. In addition, the vignettes offer examples for the different levels of proficiency for different grade levels. For the purposes of the sample progress indicators for the nine standards, they are presented in terms of the following age groups: grades pre-K–3, grades 4–8, and grades 9–12. Adolescent learners are aged 10 to 14 and fall into grades 5–9 in the standards.

Although we believe that these standards can play a role in designing effective instruction for adolescent learners in all contexts, it must be noted that they were developed for pre-K–12 learners in U.S. public schools; therefore, the standards, descriptors, and vignettes are written for the U.S. context. For example, as we mentioned in Chapter 5, Goal 2 in TESOL's Pre-K–12 ESL Standards—to use English to achieve academically in all content areas in school settings—seems very Inner Circle directed. However, Goal 2 could also pertain to Outer or Expanding Circle countries where content may be taught in English, such as in some programs in The Netherlands, Germany, and Malaysia. TESOL's standards provide an excellent starting point for thinking about instructional design for adolescent learners and help teachers and program administrators develop a clear understanding of what must go into creating a useful set of standards for adolescent learners in other contexts.

The ESL pre-K–12 standards also outline a number of general principles for language acquisition that teachers of adolescent language learners should keep in mind regardless of the context in which they work. These principles were outlined in Chapter 5 on young learners in this volume; we encourage you to review these principles because they are also relevant for young adolescents as well as young learners; we will not cover these principles again in this chapter.

Key Areas of Adolescent Development

There are five key areas of development related to adolescents—intellectual, physical, social, emotional and psychological, and moral. In whatever context teachers of adolescent learners may find themselves, these developmental factors are at work, and they are at work whether teachers are teaching content, language, or integrating language and content.

Intellectual Development

Characteristics of Learners

In Chapter 5, we outlined the stages in cognitive development (Piaget, 1963) and discussed the characteristics of learners at each stage. Adolescent learners are transitioning from the concrete thinking stage to the abstract thinking stage. Abstract thinking is characterized by developing one's ability to analyze one's own and others' thinking and to think about abstract ideas, such as diversity, compassion, and loyalty. Adolescents are trying to learn how to reflect on and reason about their real-life experiences that have a bearing on abstract concepts and ideas. The ability to think abstractly is manifested by students in different ways, such as the difference between being able to visualize solutions to math problems in one's head and manipulating an actual object to come to a solution. The transition from concrete to abstract thinking is very irregular and unpredictable. Even though adolescents can think logically and even abstractly in some cases, this ability does not mean that they can routinely be counted on to extrapolate key abstract concepts and apply them to other situations in their own lives.

The intellectual focus for adolescent learners is not on the academic topics themselves but is rather on their relationship to these topics. Adolescent learners are extremely curious and interested in the world around them and engage in numerous intellectual pursuits; however, very few of these pursuits are sustained over a long period of time. Nevertheless, it is possible for topics that learners have abandoned to be revisited later on. Adolescents engage intellectually by thinking about themselves in relationship to topics and in asking questions such as the following: Why does this matter to me? What can I do to change the situation? What are others thinking? If I do this, what will they think of me? Because adolescent learners naturally engage in intellectual pursuits in this way, teachers should consider asking such questions of their adolescent learners even if it seems that the questions are diverting them from a serious pursuit of academic content.

Teacher Support

Teachers can support adolescent learners in their intellectual development in the following ways:

- Provide opportunities for students to work together collaboratively. Adolescents have an interest in working with their peers, so group work for adolescents is important for intellectual development.
- Help students connect the abstract concepts they are studying to their real lives by providing time for personal reflection.
- Help students apply their knowledge and skills to worthwhile real-life tasks.
- Differentiate instruction[2] so that adolescent learners have different options for learning new information (both content and language) and expressing what they have learned (Tomlinson, 2001).
- Create classroom tasks that focus on helping learners develop complex thinking skills (see Chapters 10 and 13 in this volume for a discussion of higher-order thinking skills and managing demands on cognition).
- Give learners opportunities to make choices in their learning and to pursue tasks that are interesting to them.
- Talk to learners one-to-one and schedule short, regular student-teacher meetings to find out what they are doing and thinking.
- Teachers can serve as powerful role models by modeling academic tasks that will be useful tools for them outside of the classroom, such as reading critically, reading for pleasure, writing, and self-questioning.

Physical Development

Characteristics of Learners

The physical development in adolescent learners is characterized by rapid and irregular growth. Because growth is so rapid, learners often feel awkward and uncoordinated as if they have not had time to adjust to the physical changes in their bodies. These physical changes also make learners feel self-conscious about their appearance; consequently, adolescent learners have the belief that everyone is looking at them when they stand in front of a class or walk past a peer group in a hallway. They also have the feeling that they are different from everyone else; therefore, they take great pains to blend in and look like everyone else. As it turns out, looking like everyone else during adolescence is almost an impossible task because the range of physical appearances makes it highly unlikely with some people growing in height very quickly but at different times, while others grow only an inch or two. Female adolescents tend to mature earlier than males both in terms of their physical appearance and level of maturity. Females are frequently taller than males for a few years. In addition, male voices change abruptly, with some male voices deepening early in adolescence while others change much later and do so gradually, making male adolescent voices "break" and sound intermittently like both male and female voices. This situation further complicates self-consciousness in males and threatens even the closest male relationships.

The restlessness and fatigue that adolescent learners experience due to hormonal changes were aptly characterized in the vignette above by the author's description of adolescent learner behaviors in the classroom and the impression she got of the teacher's efforts to *"control the undercurrent of adolescent energy."* Adolescent learners need physical activity because of the increase in energy they feel. The author of the vignette also captured the developing sexual awareness of adolescents as she characterized how they were constantly bumping into others in the hallway and pinching and poking their peers in the classroom. In addition, most adolescents do not get sufficient sleep and sleep deprivation over time also contributes to adolescents' inability to function in school.

It is also important for teachers of adolescent learners to understand the capabilities and limitations of the adolescent brain. Brain processes that support cognitive control of behavior are not yet mature in adolescents. The prefrontal cortex that is responsible for the functions that underlie planning and voluntary behavior is distinctively different in adolescents. Adolescents show similar capabilities to adults in some situations; however, when something unexpected occurs, adolescents are not able to tap into other brain regions to manage the cognitive overload. This results in an overtaxing of the prefrontal cortex; thereby, undermining the executive function it serves for planning behaviors and making choices. Full maturation of the executive function occurs in the late teens and even into the early 20s (Sabbagh, 2006).

Teacher Support

Changes in physical development are challenging for adolescent learners, and teachers can support adolescent learners in making adjustments to these changes in the following ways:

- Teachers must understand the physical changes that adolescents are experiencing and then respect these changes. The teacher in the vignette above demonstrated respect for her adolescent learners by showing both patience and respect for them in the classroom. In addition, she developed specific classroom management strategies to engage them intellectually in the learning.
- Instructional methods that give students opportunities to work together and to move around work best with adolescent learners, such as the group work on rocks in the vignette.
- Some teachers have success in allowing for open and honest discussions about issues related to physical development, puberty, and sexuality. Learners often need adults who can discuss the physical changes they are experiencing openly and candidly, in contexts where these discussions would be culturally appropriate.
- Adolescent learners need opportunities for scheduled physical fitness each day. Schools that support adolescents with some physical fitness activity or programming are better at meeting the needs of this age group. If you work in a school without such a program, try to think of ways to incorporate movement and interaction in your classrooms.

Social Development

Characteristics of Learners

If you have ever thought that adolescent learners are generally egocentric and totally concerned with what others think about them, you are certainly not mistaken; they are. The focus on self is a hallmark of the adolescent developmental process at work, and needing to belong to and be accepted by a group is the strongest defining feature of adolescence. Adolescent learners are beginning to think about themselves as individuals in relationship to society. They are expanding their ideas and trying to figure out what they believe in and value. Peers have a powerful influence on the development of the beliefs and attitudes of adolescent learners. When peer beliefs and attitudes differ from the values of adult family members or other adults in their lives, such as teachers, conflict often arises. These conflicting influences often result in feelings of rebelliousness, insecurity, and confusion. Sometimes these conflicting influences play out in disruptive behavior in school. An important part of growing up is anticipating how others will respond to one's actions. The learning curve is a steep one for most adolescent learners. In addition, language learners who are different from the dominant group in terms of primary language, social class, race, ethnicity, gender, or sexual orientation, such as in Inner Circle contexts, find the challenge an even greater one.

Adolescents are seeking group identity and acceptance by their peers, and this focus is very much a constant for adolescent learners. The ways in which adolescents talk and act are part of their search for a social position with their peers. They like fads and are very interested in pop culture. Adolescents experience a tension between wanting safety and freedom. They want to avoid embarrassment with their attention-seeking behaviors, but they also want to experiment with their newly found freedom. Modeling behavior after older learners is one method that many adolescent learners employ in managing this tension.

Teacher Support

Teachers can provide opportunities to support learners in their social development in the following ways:

- Take time to learn about the issues facing their adolescent learners and demonstrate empathy.
- Serve as powerful role models by modeling acceptance of others, working collaboratively with others, and talking through difficult problems to reach a solution.
- Provide opportunities for cooperative and individual work.
- Establish clear expectations for social interaction in the classroom (e.g., use soft voices, stay with your group, use respectful behavior).
- Require students to apply their knowledge and skills to the social issues of concern.
- Teach students the language needed to function democratically in groups.

Emotional and Psychological Development

Characteristics of Learners

For adolescent learners in any context, life is an emotional roller coaster. The author in the vignette above aptly captured this notion about life as an adolescent when she wrote, "It seems like it's one extreme or the other; either they are bouncing off of the walls with energy, or they are bored." These are not uncommon observations of adolescent learners. Adolescents are easily excited about learning and about topics they are studying. This is evidenced by their overly ambitious projects and presentations that often include skits, costumes, handouts, PowerPoint presentations, and extensive realia. However, when it comes time to present in front of their peers, anxiety sets in and often turns into physical illness. Adolescents can be joking and good humored one minute and angry or frustrated the next. This constant emotional roller coaster means that learners often do not know where to position themselves, and the full range of emotions they experience can be frightening. Because adolescent learners believe that they are the only ones to experience these intense feelings, they feel isolated and alone. By taking the time to listen to students, teachers can help them become aware of the fact that they are not alone and that adolescent learners everywhere share similar feelings and experiences. When teachers begin to personalize learning, adolescent learners feel safer and less concerned about their physical changes and group acceptance.

Teacher Support

Teachers can support the emotional and psychological development of adolescent learners in the following ways:

- Create opportunities for small group discussions so that students can share their ideas and beliefs with each other. They may find out that they feel exactly the same as their peers.
- Provide opportunities for students to write and reflect as a part of their learning experiences.
- Offer sincere positive feedback when it is appropriate.
- Create opportunities for students to work together on tutoring and mentoring activities if they so desire.
- Invite guests and experts from the community to visit class, so learners can interact with other adults.
- Help students set and achieve their personal goals.

Moral Development

Characteristics of Learners

Adolescent moral development can be characterized as idealistic and is based on the ideals of the culture in which they reside. During adolescence learners must somehow move from a concern about self to a concern for others. They get excited about making change and making a difference; nevertheless, they underestimate how difficult it is to make change, and they are often impatient with how slowly change happens in reality.

They are also moving away from accepting at face value the moral judgments of the adults in their lives as they try to form their own independent personal values and begin to see the complexity of the human experience. Adult role models who will listen, be trustworthy, and offer advice are essential in helping adolescents make this transition.

Adolescents are quick to judge other people, especially their peers, but they acknowledge their own faults very slowly; nevertheless, when they have all of the facts at hand, they are capable of having a profound compassion for others.

Teacher Support

Teachers can support adolescent learners in their moral development in the following ways:

- Engage students in the community by involving community leaders and other adults in authentic projects.
- Teach students culturally appropriate ways to resolve conflicts in order to solve real–life problems, and teach the language necessary to make the process work.
- Create learning experiences for students that are complex and involve problems that they might encounter in real life.

Tasks: Explore

Work with a partner or a small group. Think of one specific classroom task or activity that you might use with adolescent language learners to promote either their intellectual, physical, social, emotional and psychological, or moral development appropriate for the context in which you work or plan to work. Then, explain how and why this meets the specific developmental needs of adolescent learners in the context that you targeted.

Literacy Needs of L2 Adolescent Learners

The literacy performance of adolescent second language learners is a topic that researchers and educators have often overlooked in Inner Circle countries (Garcia & Godina, 2004). In the U.S., dropout statistics are high for this group of learners, thereby highlighting the importance of developing effective literacy programs to address their needs. A balanced literacy curriculum requires instruction in both reading and writing.

Second Language Oral Proficiency and Second Language Literacy

The relationship between oral proficiency and second language literacy in terms of sequence of instruction is mostly an Inner Circle country issue and related to instructional design practices (e.g., structured immersion) that are often motivated by lack of resources rather than evidence from research. In most Outer and Expanding Circle countries, adolescent learners in English classrooms are literate before commencing study in a foreign language. It is beyond the scope of this chapter to provide an overview of the research on L2 literacy for all contexts; therefore, we have chosen to focus mostly on literacy issues as they relate to Inner Circle countries. Nevertheless, where appropriate, we extend the discussion of L2 literacy to include Outer and Expanding Circle countries as well.

For a complete review of L2 literacy development issues in second language learners in Inner Circle countries, see August and Shanahan (2006) and the report of the National Literacy Panel on Language Minority Children and Youth. The work of Geva (2006) focuses on the development of L2 literacy in relationship to second language oral proficiency. L2 literacy specialists (Peregoy & Boyle, 2010; Linse, 2005) recommend a sequence for skill development wherein oral language development precedes literacy development. Because oral language proficiency is one of the many components that influence the development of literacy, we include a short discussion of this research here. These recommendations are consistent with the approach to L2 literacy development we suggest in Chapter 5 of this volume on young learners and in this chapter for young adolescent learners with low-level oral language proficiency skills. Oral language proficiency conceptualized in terms of grammatical knowledge and vocabulary is not a robust predictor of word-level reading skills in English. Aspects of phonological processing (e.g., phonemic awareness and letter naming) are more robust; however, there are L2 learners (in both Inner and Outer Circle countries) with strong L1 literacy skills who demonstrate advanced reading comprehension skills in the L2 (as measured by oral cloze and sentence memory) but still demonstrate low oral language skills.

L2 Reading Instruction for Adolescent Learners

English language learners can benefit from sound reading instruction even before they are proficient in English, as long as the instruction is consistent with learners' language proficiency (Geva, 2000; Linan–Thompson & Vaughn, 2007). The studies that have been done on instructional reading programs for adolescent learners suggest that L2 learners who were successful English readers used high-level reading strategies (e.g., making inferences from the text, using context clues, asking questions) and that lower-level L2 readers used low-level strategies (e.g., decoding, restating, identifying unknown vocabulary). L2 readers rarely used strategies that were unique to bilinguals (aside from code mixing and code switching). What remains unclear about the use of reading strategies among L2 learners is whether their use causes high-level reading or whether they are a result of high-level reading. Do L2 learners read well because they use high-level reading strategies or do they use high-level reading strategies because they read well? These questions seem to suggest that L2 adolescent learners need a balanced reading program with explicit skill instruction to develop both low-level and high-level reading strategies (i.e., phonological awareness [to include phonemic awareness], phonics and word study, fluency, vocabulary instruction, and text comprehension), as well as access to a wide range of texts on different topics (Guthrie, 2008), in different genres (Christie, 2002), and time to focus on reading (Krashen, 2004).

L2 Writing Instruction for Adolescent Learners

Garcia (1999) suggested a starting point for L2 writing instruction. She pointed out the importance of finding out what students can do in their native language and building on that expertise in teaching L2 literacy skills. Valdés (1999) analyzed the writing performance of three middle school Latino students who had started school in the United States with no English. Valdés expressed concerns about the heavy structural focus in some English classes, suggesting that the overuse of "guided composition strategies" and "controlled composition techniques" may result in more accurate writing, but may seriously limit students' self-expression and their ability to develop a personal voice in their writing. She questioned whether L2 learners could develop the academic writing skills necessary for higher education in an Inner Circle country with these types of writing exercises. However, learners do need explicit instruction in the schematic structure and typical linguistic structures found in different genres (Christie and Misson, 1998). A number of countries have taken this approach to developing literacy in English, including Australia, Hong Kong, and Singapore. Sometimes such curriculum innovation, however, is thwarted because of the power of national examinations (see, for example, Adamson & Davison, 2008).

Obviously, teachers must be sensitive to language proficiency levels, but the point is that "guided compositions" and "controlled composition techniques" should not be the only writing activities that learners experience. These activities, however, may be perfectly appropriate for lower proficiency-level students in Outer and Expanding Circle countries where learners are not competing with native speakers in content-area classes. More controlled writing at lower proficiency levels can be used to build confidence in English language writing skills in adolescent learners and can serve as precursors for less controlled and more personal kinds of writing, as well as more analytic and academic writing tasks.

Several experts in ESL have advocated a process literacy approach (Peregoy & Boyle, 2010; Pérez & Torres-Guzmán, 2002) that uses writing from multiple drafts, integrated reading and writing activities, peer interactions, inquiry-based projects, and open-ended activities, to name a few, in order to bridge the gap between controlled writing exercises and academic writing tasks. Some of these are unfamiliar instructional practices for many contexts where the tradition has been for controlled practice. However, it is important to recognize that moving to a process literacy approach with adolescent learners allows teachers to meet many of the intellectual and social developmental needs of adolescent learners, but it also requires that learners develop a tolerance for language ambiguity and that they learn to become comfortable with a less than complete understanding of the texts they are using. Second language teachers walk a fine line between limiting language development by selecting too many controlled activities or assigning materials that are beyond the comprehension of many learners. Neither is a perfect solution to the L2 adolescent literacy crisis that many Inner Circle countries are experiencing or to teachers' individual dilemmas about how to develop high-level writing skills in their learners regardless of the context. To compound the issue further, it is important to remember that adolescents will go to great lengths not to display their low-level proficiency skills in writing in front of their peers. In order to avoid embarrassment, adolescent learners will copy materials and/or memorize large portions of the text.

Conclusion

In this chapter we have described both the varying backgrounds of adolescent learners and the contexts in which they learn. In addition, we have outlined five key components of adolescent development by describing the characteristics of learners for each of these components and provided suggestions for teachers in working with adolescent learner development relative to each component. Neither the components nor the suggestions are meant to be context specific. Finally, we turned our attention to L2 literacy development and offered some suggestions for instructional features of programs targeting L2 reading and writing.

Task: Expand

Conduct an Internet search on adolescent learners, young adolescent learners, or adolescent language learners. Visit at least two websites. Be prepared to share with your peers additional research or information you found that might be useful in teaching adolescents in the context in which you teach or plan to teach.

Questions for Discussion

1. Develop specific classroom activities for low-level reading strategies and high-level reading strategies.
2. In your own words, explain what is meant by the term **process literacy approach**. What specific activities would be part of this approach? How might process literacy differ from a controlled writing type of approach? What are the benefits and limitations of each approach? Is there room for an integrated approach in your opinion? What might it look like for adolescent learners?
3. How does group work support adolescent learners?
4. At what stage of cognitive development are most adolescent learners? How is their cognitive development characterized?
5. What do you think is the most important way to engage learners in working with abstract concepts?

Notes

1. Middle schools are usually made up of grades 6, 7, and 8, or grades 7 and 8. These are children aged 11–13.
2. A differentiated classroom provides learners with different ways to learn content, to process the content, and to develop products so that they have chances to demonstrate what they know in different ways. Teachers can differentiate on the basis of learners' interests, readiness, or learning profile.

References

Adamson, B., & Davison, C. (2008). English language teaching in Hong Kong primary schools: Innovation and resistance. In D. E. Murray (Ed.), *Planning change, changing plans: Innovations in second language teaching* (pp. 11–25). Ann Arbor, MI: University of Michigan Press.

August, D., & Shanahan, T. (2006). *Developing literacy in second-language learners: Report of the national literacy panel on language minority children and youth.* Mahwah, NJ: Lawrence Erlbaum Associates, Publishers.

Becker, H. (2001). *Teaching ESL K–12: Views from the classroom.* Boston, MA: Heinle and Heinle.

Christie, F. (2002). The development of abstraction in adolescence in subject English. In M. Schleppergrell & C. Colombi (Eds.), *Developing advanced literacy in first and second languages: Meaning with power* (pp. 45–66). Mahwah, NJ: Lawrence Erlbaum.

Christie, F., & Misson, R. (1998). *Literacy and schooling.* London: Taylor and Francis.

Cummins, J. (1996). *Negotiating identities: Education for empowerment in a diverse society.* Ontario, CA: California Association for Bilingual Education.

Garcia, O. (1999). Educating Latino high school students with little formal schooling. In C. J. Faltis, & P. M. Wolfe (Eds.), *So much to say: Adolescents, bilingualism, and ESL in secondary school* (pp. 42–82). New York: Teachers College Press.

Garcia, E. G., & Godina, H. (2004). Addressing the literacy needs of adolescent English language learners. In T. L. Jetton, & J. A. Dole (Eds.), *Adolescent literacy research and practice* (pp. 304–320). New York: Guilford Press.

Geva, E. (2000). Issues in the assessment of reading disabilities in L2 children: Beliefs and research evidence. *Dyslexia, 6,* 13–28.

Geva, E. (2006). Second-language oral proficiency and second-language literacy. In D. August, & T. Shanahan (Eds.), *Developing literacy in second-language learners: Report of the national literacy panel on language minority children and youth* (pp. 123–143). Mahwah, NJ: Lawrence Erlbaum Associates, Publishers.

Guthrie, J. (2008). *Engaging adolescents in reading.* Thousand Oaks, CA: Corwin Press.

Kachru, B. B. (1986). *The alchemy of English: The spread, functions and models of non-native Englishes.* Oxford: Pergamon Press.

Krashen, S. D. (2004). *The power of reading* (2nd ed.). Westport, CT: Heinemann.

Linan-Thompson, S., & Vaughn, S. (2007). *Research-based methods of reading instruction for English language learners.* Alexandria, VA: Association of Supervision and Curriculum Development.

Linse, C. (2005). *Practical English language teaching: Young learners.* New York: McGraw-Hill International.

Piaget, J. (1963). *The language and thought of the child.* New York: W.W. Norton.

Peregoy, S. F., & Boyle, O. F. (2010). *Reading, writing, and learning in ESL: A resource book for K–12 teachers.* Boston: Pearson.

Pérez, B., & Torres-Guzmán, M. E. (2002). *Learning in two worlds: An integrated Spanish/English biliteracy approach* (3rd ed.). Boston: Allyn & Bacon.

Sabbagh, L. (2006). Teen brain hard at work, no really. *Scientific American Mind, 17,* 21–25.

TESOL ESL Standards for Pre-K–12 Students. (1997). Alexandria, VA: Teachers of English to Speakers of Other Language, Inc.

Tomlinson, C. A. (2001). *How to differentiate instruction in mixed-ability classrooms* (2nd ed.). Alexandria, VA: Association for Supervision and Curriculum Development.

Valdés, G. (1999). Incipient bilingualism and the development of English language writing abilities in the secondary schools. In C. J. Faltis, & P. M. Wolfe (Eds.), *So much to say: Adolescents, bilingualism, and ESL in secondary school* (pp. 138–175). New York: Teachers College Press.

Waggoner, D. (1999). Who are secondary newcomer and linguistically different youth? In C. J. Faltis, & P. M. Wolfe (Eds.), *So much to say: Adolescents, bilingualism, and ESL in secondary school* (pp. 13–42). New York: Teachers College Press.

Chapter 7

Adult Immigrants and Refugees

I am observing Sharon teaching in an adult program in the U.S. The class has a changing enrolment, but on this occasion there are 21 mostly Latino, with some Vietnamese and Chinese learners. In the previous lesson they had learned how to fill in forms with name, address, date of birth, telephone number, and so on. She begins by asking learners to take out their calendars. She's already put the day's day and date on the blackboard. She has a calendar on the overhead projector which she uses every day so that the previous days' dates and weather have been filled in. With the class, she writes in that day's day and date and weather. They then complete their own calendar while she walks around and helps with spelling as necessary.

She then writes the lesson objectives on the board. She reminds them that yesterday they had filled out forms, and today they would build on that to write about other people. She then spends some time revising the form-filling from the previous day to ensure they could remember the vocabulary and structures. As she goes over different words for marital status, she uses dolls of a bride and a groom to indicate single, married, divorced. Then she elicits words for feelings—happy, angry, tired, hungry, thirsty—using pictures. She then pins the pictures on the board and writes the relevant feeling word below. The learners copy into their notebooks. They practise.

Then she introduces a new picture and says she'll ask the class questions about the picture. They give the man a name. One student says he's a priest. The teacher points to the ring on his finger. On the overhead she places a story about the man, with blanks. Throughout the time the teacher is asking them questions, they are able to work with her to fill in the blanks. The story has a few sentences—man's name, marital status, age, and how he felt. The learners negotiate different words for the feeling—some making different suggestions until all agree. They also negotiate his marital status. They do the same for a picture of a woman so that in the end they have two stories.

She then shows them more pictures and asks them which they want to write about until they have chosen five pictures. She pastes the pictures onto different colored boards and pins them on the blackboard. She hands out colored cards to students—the cards have cues, such as age, marital status. Then the learners group by the color of their cards, taking their picture with them. They then write their stories of the person in their picture. Learners are responsible for writing the sentence related to their cue, but the whole group has to agree on the content. When finished, learners could read their story to the class—one person, as a group, or one sentence per person. She asks them what they have learned in the lesson—and places check marks against the objectives on the board. She tells them to bring a picture for tomorrow's class when they will again write stories. [Murray, research notes]

Task: Reflect

1. Why do you think the teacher has the learners keep a calendar?
2. Why did the teacher use a partly completed text on the overhead for learners to work with?
3. Why did she give learners a choice of pictures to write about in the practice part of the lesson?
4. Why did she have learners work in groups to write their stories?
5. Why did she randomly assign the sentence each learner was responsible for?

Introduction

In this chapter we discuss instructing a specific subset of adult learners—those who are recently arrived immigrants or refugees in BANA[1] countries. In Chapter 8 we discuss adults who are international students and immigrants and refugees who are studying for or are in higher education or are long-term residents. In Chapter 9 we discuss adults learning in the workplace, including the characteristics of adult learners that result in andragogy being different from pedagogy (Knowles, 1990). Because adult learners in the Outer and Expanding Circles (see Volume I, Chapter 3) are learning English for work-related uses, we will not discuss adults in these countries in this chapter. We begin the chapter by outlining some of the special characteristics of these learners, ones that differentiate them from other adult learners. Then we describe the different BANA (Britain, Australasia, and North America) contexts where these adults are learning. The remainder of the chapter provides content and activities for use with these learners' experiences and learning preferences.

Characteristics of Adult Immigrants and Refugees

Although adult immigrants and refugees are highly individualistic, there are features resulting from their previous experiences and the experience of settling in another country that they hold in common. We will highlight what they have in common; even though for effective instruction, it is vital for teachers to understand the individuality of their learners.

The Immigration Experience

The decision to immigrate is wrenching, even if it means a better standard of living for the immigrant or their future generations. However, it is usually a carefully considered decision; whereas, refugees are usually fleeing from a situation (called **push factors**), rather than choosing to go to a specific country (called **pull factors**). However, immigration may require formal interviews with officers from the receiving country, explanations of financial information, health checks, English tests, and other disclosures of very personal information to complete strangers. This can be a very humiliating experience, especially for immigrants who held high status or had important professional positions in their home country. Others come to be reunited with family members who previously immigrated so may have been separated from their families for some time.

The Refugee Experience

Refugees have usually spent time in a country of first asylum, often close to the border of their homeland. Most spend months and even years in refugee camps before being accepted by an established refugee resettlement country, such as Australia, Canada, New Zealand, the U.K., or the U.S. Only 10 countries world-wide have been traditional resettlement destinations through the United Nations High Commission for Refugees (UNHCR) third-country resettlement scheme[2]—in addition to the four English-dominant countries, the others are Denmark, Finland, the Netherlands, Norway, Sweden, and Switzerland. Recently, the U.K. and Japan have joined these efforts, but currently resettle very small numbers. However, in addition to this orderly program, hundreds of thousands of refugees seek asylum in other countries—in both the developed and developing world. All five BANA countries are final destinations for many asylum seekers. Asylum seekers arrive in the BANA countries without visas and often turn to smugglers to reach safety. This illegal trafficking of people has complicated the orderly flow of people processed by the UNHCR. More importantly for the asylum seeker, most countries have established barriers to settlement, including detention centers, while at the same time the asylum seeker's family has incurred huge debt to pay the smugglers.[3]

Australia, Canada, and the U.S. also have their own humanitarian schemes, independent of the UNHCR. Through these schemes they resettle additional refugees deemed in need by the respective country. Some humanitarian entrants are government-sponsored, others sponsored privately or by churches. The sponsor assumes responsibility for resettlement costs.

The countries of origin of refugees change constantly, depending on where the most recent conflict or persecution is in the world. Thus, teachers may get used to the characteristics of one group, only to find that a new group has very different characteristics. For example, in Australia, during the 1970s, many southeast Asians were resettled in Australia as a result of the Vietnam War. While many of these were well educated, many were not. They were rural people with no formal education. Then, as a result of the conflicts in the former Yugoslavia, in 1999 Australia gave refuge to those fleeing the violence. A great majority of these were well educated. Most recently, because of the conflicts in Africa, refugees have arrived from Rwanda, Sudan, and various other countries there. Because they have been long-term refugees, often living in camps for decades, they mostly have little formal education. Teachers reported that they needed new tools for working with this new population, even though they had taught southeast Asians with little formal education. They had become used to a Western-educated group with the Kosovo refugees, and furthermore, some African refugees already spoke (but did not write) English, with their own dialect version, Liberian English. Such refugees were resistant to being classified as non-English-speaking. In addition, their cultural values and experiences encouraged them to demand services and resist being told what they needed by others (Murray & Lloyd, 2008). More recently, the BANA countries have received Burmese refugees who have been resident in Thai-Burma border camps for more than a decade. Many are not ethnically Burmese, but are Karen, Karenni, or other ethnic minorities. While they share experiences with other refugees, and the camps are assisted by the UNHCR, non-government organizations (NGOs), and the Royal Thai Government, they have a degree of autonomy and themselves have worked with NGOs to provide education and health services within the camps, including some English instruction. Thus, some of those resettling in BANA countries have developed considerable skills and some English proficiency. They also are very politically-oriented, seeking to bring democracy to Burma (also known as Myanmar).

No matter their origin, all refugees have experienced "severe dislocation and trauma, and often persecution and other violations of their human rights. They have often experienced disrupted education and separation from friends and family" (Murray & Lloyd, 2008). These disruptions affect both their settlement in a third country and their learning, including their learning of English.

The Settlement Experience

Although we have separated out immigrants from refugees, this is not a valid dichotomy since many refugees settle, become citizens, and then sponsor relatives through family reunion immigration programs. Furthermore, some immigrants have similar needs to those of refugees.

Because of interrupted or no schooling, many refugees have little or no literacy in their home language or the language of communication in their home country. It is necessary to differentiate between these two languages because many refugees are from minority groups in their own country and do not speak the national language. Some come from language groups where the language is not written. Yet, they have to settle in countries where literacy is both highly valued and an important skill for negotiating everyday life and especially getting and keeping a job. Some do not understand the importance of literacy because of its lack of use in their home community. However, literacy in English is vital for their successful settlement. Others may be literate, but use different scripts, such as Arabic, Russian, or Chinese. Yet, most of the research on second language acquisition has been conducted on literate learners (Bigelow & Tarone, 2004), while that on literacy development has been on children or native speaker (NS) adults. Exceptions include the work conducted in Australia, primarily using action research as the methodology, and the work in the U.S. of the Center for Adult English Language Acquisition (CAELA). While action research is a very useful investigative tool, extrapolation to broader contexts than that of the particular classroom being researched is not possible. Similarly, much of the work conducted by CAELA is descriptive in nature.

As well as bringing different approaches to literacy, immigrants and refugees who have received some formal education may bring quite different views about learning and teaching (see Volume I, Chapter 4 for details on learner and teacher roles). They may expect a textbook, but only be given handouts in their English course; they may expect to learn through memorization, but be asked to think critically and learn by doing; they may expect the teacher to be responsible for every part of the lesson, but work in groups on tasks and projects. Therefore teaching needs to accommodate these different perspectives.

As well as having limited previous formal education, refugees also face health issues, anxiety, poor concentration, and loss of trust, especially of government because their human rights violations were most often state-sanctioned (Victorian Foundation for Survivors of Torture, 1998). While they understand the importance of learning English, other factors may weigh more heavily, including health, family, and financial support. This often leads to only one member of the family (if more than one member has resettled) learning English, while others take care of young children or work. Furthermore, research has shown that learners who have suffered such dislocation may need courses grounded in concrete experiences, especially ones related to their settlement needs (McPherson, 1997). Many benefit from low-intensity courses and bilingual assistance. A preliterate refugee cannot be given the same curriculum and learning activities as a learner with successful, uninterrupted schooling in their first language (Davison, 2001).

Adults with limited English may be asked to use their own children as interpreters, which radically changes parent-child role relationships. The economic successes immigrants anticipated may not be realized. Even the freedom they expected may bring mixed blessings for some because the host society allows freedoms for women and children that are alien to their cultural values. Some experience discrimination. Some even return to their home countries. Thus, the settlement experience is usually disruptive for most refugees and immigrant adults.

Worldwide Contexts

Because of the subset of adults we are discussing in this chapter, the general educational context is that of adult education, a sector that was initially established to teach high school subjects to adults who had not graduated from high school or to provide general interest subjects, such as French cooking or conversational Spanish. The BANA countries differ markedly in terms of their policies regarding immigration and resettlement of refugees, as well as in their approaches to teaching them English. What most of these countries have in common is an underservicing, a lack of coordinated research on this population and a conflation of literacy with ESL in program delivery. We will briefly identify the salient characteristics of immigration/refugee policy as it relates to ESL programming (including curriculum and assessment) for each country.

Australia

Australia has a 50-plus-year history of encouraging immigration and giving sanctuary to refugees. While ESL programming has varied enormously over that period—from a learner-centered curriculum negotiated between learners and teacher to a competency-based national framework—immigrants and refugees have always been provided with initial English language instruction through the Adult Migrant English Program (AMEP). The AMEP is a branch of the Department of Immigration and Citizenship; thus, the focus is on settlement, and the program does not have to compete for funds with other adult education provision, such as introduction to computers or courses in cardiopulmonary resuscitation (CPR). English language instruction is provided by both private and government sectors through a competitive process. Immigrants and refugees with less than functional English proficiency are entitled to 510 hours of instruction, with many refugees with special needs able to access an additional 100 hours, and with those aged 16–24 with fewer than seven years' schooling able to access an additional 400 hours. Once these hours have been exhausted, learners can continue in English classes in technical and further education (TAFE) or community-based courses.

The AMEP uses a competency-based and text-based curriculum framework, the Certificates in Spoken and Written English (CSWE) (New South Wales Adult Migrant English Services, 2003). The text-based approach is based on systemic-functional grammar, a social theory of language. The framework is then arranged around texts (both written and spoken) that learners need to acquire. Instructional content and methodology for helping learners achieve such acquisition are decided at the center level or classroom. They are not provided in the curriculum framework. However, most AMEP teachers use the teaching learning cycle to present new language and have learners practice it (see Chapter 2, this volume, with Peter's lesson plan).

Still, teachers have considerable freedom in choosing content and methodology within the general framework and cycle. Content might include settlement survival settings, such as *visiting the doctor* or topics of interest to learners, such as *about Australia* (see Chapter 2, this volume, for two examples of AMEP teachers teaching using the CSWE). Several content syllabi have been developed, including *citizenship*. Another set has been specifically developed for youth (16- to 24-year-olds), with topics of interest to them, such as *Your money, Your future: Work and Study* (AMEP Research Centre, 2008).

Competencies are assessed as learning outcomes, with learners needing to produce the components of the text (see Volume I, Chapter 10) within the required time to be assessed as having achieved the outcome. In order to ensure consistency of assessment across the AMEP nationally, test items are moderated and teachers are trained in assessment.

Canada

Like Australia, Canada has long been an immigrant-receiving country and has welcomed refugees. In the 1960s, the federal government adopted a points system (Australia much later did the same) for assessing potential immigrants based on a set of objective criteria. The points per criterion change according to the country's needs. In the 1990s, priorities moved towards immigrants with business or other job-related skills, with language training as a key priority for settlement. This led to the federally administered Language Instruction to Newcomers Canada (LINC). LINC provides up to 900 hours of basic language instruction for newly arrived immigrants, delivered at the provincial level. Providers apply yearly for funding and develop their own curriculum, materials, and content.

At the same time, the federal government began developing the Canadian Language Benchmarks (CLB) (Canadian Language Benchmarks, 1996), a competency-based description of 12 levels of English proficiency. The benchmarks tasks require learners to produce a text rather than discrete linguistic items. It differs from the CSWE because learners can be assessed for partial performance, rather than having to produce the entire text correctly. Like the CSWE, it also includes competencies in learning to learn skills. A specific curriculum tied to the CLB is not mandated, but there are curriculum guidelines and instructional resources. LINC and the AMEP both focus on the lower levels of language proficiency. See the Citizenship and Immigration Canada website (Government of Canada, 2008) for further details.

New Zealand

Traditionally, New Zealand has placed little emphasis on ESOL adult immigrants, largely because most immigrants were English-speaking. The exception was a wave of Pacific Islanders in the 1960s and 1970s—although some of them were also English-speaking. Since their immigration was encouraged to fill low-paying jobs, language proficiency was not considered a high priority. More recently, New Zealand has focused on business immigrants, usually with English skills. New Zealand does have a small intake of refugees. Both immigrants and refugees can take language classes through community-based organizations or on a fee-for-service basis from private language schools. In 2003 the government developed an Adult ESOL Strategy and released a discussion document in 2008 (Ministry of Education, 2008). The strategy includes a vision and some principles and targets for what is needed to help immigrants settle and participate in New Zealand life, including being able to use English.

United Kingdom

Until recently the U.K. had not considered the learning of the national language for adult immigrants and refugees to be the responsibility of the national government. However, two recent initiatives have led to a government focus on these residents. The government introduced both language skills and a citizenship test as requirements for granting citizenship. At the same time, the Department for Education included ESOL in its list of core skills, leading to the Adult ESOL Core Curriculum, aligned with the national standards for adult literacy. The curriculum offers a framework for English language learning, defines the skills, knowledge, and understanding that ESOL learners need to demonstrate their achievement of the national standards, and provides a reference tool for ESOL teachers in a variety of different settings. The focus is on whole texts, not discrete language items. Additionally, they have developed standards for teachers in the sector. The department was split in 2007 and now the adult ESOL sector is within the

Department for Children, Schools and Families. Further information is available on the Department's website (http://publications.teachernet.gov.uk/).

United States

The U.S. also has a long history of encouraging immigrants and giving refuge to those who have had to flee their own countries. In addition to these legally defined ways of entering the country, the U.S. has a very large population of immigrants who have entered through other means—some stayed after their tourist or student visas had expired; others crossed over the borders between Mexico or Canada and the U.S. While the U.S. immigrant population includes people from more than 100 different countries, the majority are Spanish speakers. The U.S. does not have a nationally organized instructional program, such as in Australia and Canada. Instruction is fragmented and organized locally by community-based organizations, community colleges, and adult schools in the K–12 sector. The goal of programs has been to move learners along as quickly as possible so they can participate in the workforce. Programs range from life skills to citizenship classes, to job preparation, to study preparation. The most common framework is competency-based, largely because of one of the approved standardized tests, such as the CASAS Life Skills Test (Comprehensive Adults Student Assessment System, 1996). Many learners in the U.S. take evening classes because they work during the day or day classes because they work nights. The Center for Adult English Language Acquisition (CAELA, 2004), established in 2004 and funded by the federal Department of Education, provides rich resources for teachers of immigrants and refugees. Their primary function is to assist states in teaching immigrants English since such instruction is devolved to state control. The center also conducts research in the area.

Instructing for Learning

TESOL, the international professional association, has developed standards for adult program delivery (TESOL, 2002). The activities and issues we discuss in this section fall within this framework. One of the categories, instruction, has the following standards:

A.   Instructional approaches are varied to meet the needs of adult learners with diverse educational and cultural backgrounds (p. 82).
B.   Instructional activities:

   a.   Adhere to principles of adult learning and language acquisition (p. 81).
   b.   Engage the learners in taking an active role in the learning process (p. 83).
   c.   Focus on the acquisition of communication skills necessary for learners to function within the classroom, outside the classroom, or in other educational programs (p. 84).
   d.   Integrate the four language skills (listening, speaking, reading, and writing), focusing on receptive and productive skills appropriate to learners' needs (p. 85).
   e.   Are varied to address the different learning styles (e.g., aural, oral, visual, kinesthetic) and special learning needs of the learners (p. 86).

f. Incorporate grouping strategies and interactive tasks that facilitate the development of authentic communication skills. These include cooperative learning, information gap activities, role plays, simulations, problem-solving, and problem-posing (p. 87).

g. Take into account the needs of multilevel groups of learners, particularly those with minimal literacy skills in their native language and English (p. 88).

h. Focus on the development of language and culturally appropriate behaviors needed for critical thinking, problem-solving, team participation, and study skills (p. 89).

i. Give learners opportunities to use authentic resources both inside and outside the classroom (p. 90).

j. Give learners opportunities to develop awareness of and competency in the use of appropriate technologies to meet lesson objectives (p. 91).

k. Are culturally sensitive to the learners and integrate language and culture (p. 92).

l. Prepare learners for formal and informal assessment situations, such as test taking, job interviews, and keeping personal learning records (p. 93). Teachers of English to Speakers of Other Languages, Inc. (2002). Standards for Adult Education ESL Programs. Alexandria, VA: Author. Reprinted with permission.

Task: Explore

Reread the vignette at the beginning of this chapter. To what extent does this excerpt from a lesson with adult immigrants and refugees follow the guidelines in the TESOL standards?

In many centers, the skills of listening, speaking, reading, and writing are taught separately; in other contexts they are integrated. For convenience, we will discuss content, activities, and issues around literacy and oral language, although we would promote a more integrated approach. Furthermore, as discussed above, many of these learners need formal instruction in learning to learn skills. We begin with learning to learn.

Learning to Learn (see also Volume I, Chapter 13)

We mentioned above that learners may have had limited previous schooling or schooling in a different tradition with different expectations of teachers and learners. As a result they may find the classroom confusing, of little educational value, or even that the teacher is lazy or inexperienced. Therefore it's important for teachers to provide explicit instruction in learning strategies and learning expectations in their new country. We provide some examples of such activities below.

Teacher and Learner Roles

In addition to a discussion about different roles, teachers can have learners complete a grid as in Table 7.1 about what they consider to be their respective tasks in the classroom. Teachers can complete the same grid and show learners how their views differ. Over time, the teacher can refer back to the grid and see how learner perspectives have changed. Teachers can also use the grid when doing one of the activities, to remind learners why they are giving the responsibility over to the learners.

Organizing Learning

Those who have not had formal education and those who are used to following a textbook are unfamiliar with how to organize their learning. Those used to formal teacher-centered approaches may expect frequent tests to tell them they are successful. Teachers therefore need to help adult learners to understand the goals of a lesson, how to organize their materials, and how to evaluate what they have learned.

As Sharon did in the lesson described in the vignette, teachers can write the lesson goals/objectives on the blackboard and then, at the end of the lesson, go through the list with learners, checking off what they have and have not learned. Mini-lists can also be used prior to and after group or pair work or discussion.

Sharon's class kept a calendar with the day, date, and weather. But, they also keep a binder in which they wrote the day, date, the learning objectives, and any vocabulary or other language they learned during the lesson. She also has them file their handouts by the date used so that at the end of the course, they have their own personal textbook. She has them use a colored or tabbed divider at the beginning of each week so they can easily find material. More advanced learners can add a reflection at the end of each lesson. For preliterate or beginning learners, teachers often use a checklist for them to complete at the end of the lesson, as in Table 7.2.

To help learners adapt to educational (and work) expectations in their new country, teachers can have learners keep their own attendance sheets and teach them how to write absence notes, requiring that they produce such a note after an absence.

Other teachers have learners keep a separate dictionary in which they enter new words. This is an especially useful activity for beginning literacy learners. The

Table 7.1 Teacher and Learner Tasks: Who is Responsible?

Task	Teacher	Learners
Choosing content for a lesson		
Correcting grammar errors		
Keeping discipline		
Checking homework is done		
Grading homework		
Assessing learning		
Managing class time		
Making learners come to class on time		
Correcting punctuation		

Table 7.2 Checklist to Reflect on Lesson

Day: _____

Date: _____

	☺ *Very good*	*Good*	*OK*	*Not good*	☹ *Bad*
How I feel about my learning today					
How I feel about my participation in class today					
How I feel about class activities today					

This figure is adapted with the permission of the Commonwealth of Australia from one in Yates, L., & Devi, S. (2006). *Teaching strategies—3: Different cultures of learning.* Sydney: AMEP Research Centre.

teacher can have the students write the letter of the alphabet on each page and then, when new words are written in the class, guide them to the page and how to write the word and possibly its meaning (this depends on the language level of the learners). This can help learners begin to understand the notion of a dictionary and how the alphabet is used to find words and their meanings.

Literacy

As we discussed in Volume I, Chapter 9, literacy is not only the decoding and encoding of a written script, it is also a socioculturally embedded practice, dependent on understandings of the language, culture, and other texts (those that are similar and those that are different). Therefore, special strategies need to be employed when helping most adult learners develop English literacy.

Even at the decoding and encoding level, learners may encounter difficulties. As mentioned above, adult immigrants and refugees may have minimal literacy in their home language, be literate in a non-Roman alphabet or in a nonalphabetic script. Even learners literate in languages that use a Roman alphabet, such as Spanish, may have difficulty in English because, unlike Spanish, English does not have one-to-one letter–sound correspondence. Additionally, English poses stress difficulties for learners from languages that have only monosyllabic words, equal stress on each syllable, or no reduced forms (see Volume I, Chapter 6). Recommendations include:

- With beginning literate learners or those with scripts such as Arabic that write both above and below the line, use paper with three lines so they can practise writing between the lines for capital and noncapital letters. Some refugees with no formal schooling may have difficulty holding a pen and need teachers to physically hold their hands. Transparent paper can be used so learners can write over already written letters. Also air writing can be helpful because the movements are large and don't require the fine motor control and hand–eye coordination that writing on paper requires. In air writing, the teacher has her back to the class and "draws" the letter with large strokes in the air, with the learners copying and then doing it in unison. Or, teachers can have them fashion letters in play dough or write in sand, all of which does not require fine motor skill.

- Avoid using written handouts to support oral language development with learners who have minimal literacy. While it supports the learning of those who are literate, it confuses those who are not. Where possible, use visuals instead.
- With all learners, teach English letter–sound correspondence, using English words, such as **minimal pairs** (e.g., *cat/mat*), not nonsense words.
- With all learners, explicitly teach **morphophonemic** structures in English, such as the three different pronunciations (/əd/ in *waited*, /t/ in *walked*, and /d/ in *smiled*) of simple past that are written with the same morpheme *-ed*.
- With all learners, explicitly teach word-analysis skills, such as **prefixes** and **suffixes** and **word families**, such as *friend, friendly, friendliness, friendship*. Knowledge of word families quickly helps learners extend their reading vocabulary, as does understanding the meanings of prefixes and suffixes (see Volume I, Chapter 7, for more on word formation). This explicit teaching needs to include parts of speech (see Volume I, Chapter 8, for more on parts of speech) and their roles in English so learners can identify, for example, that a word ending in the morpheme *-ion* is a noun.
- With beginning English learners, use written texts whose context is concrete and familiar to learners.
- With all learners, teach **connectives**, such as *first, then, however*.
- With all learners, preteach vocabulary and any concepts that are unfamiliar before having them read a text (no matter how short).
- Check learner comprehension of a reading text through a variety of activities, depending on their language level:
  - checking pictures
  - true/false
  - short answer
  - cloze exercises
  - having them tell a partner what they have read
  - having them use the information in the text for some other purpose
  - writing a summary (for more advanced learners)
  - critically examining the hidden meanings in texts (especially advertising) with more advanced learners.

- Allow bilingual dictionaries. Although this can lead to incorrect meanings and especially collocations, many learners find the definitions in English–English dictionaries to be beyond their understanding. Dictionary use needs to be explicitly taught.
- Explicitly teach the structure of texts (see Volume I, Chapter 9).
- Accept code-switching between L1 and English as a natural part of learning a new language and of being bilingual. Use L1 to support the acquisition of English as a scaffold, not as something for them to rely on. If the learners have the same L1, consider having a bilingual aide to support instruction (Murray & Wigglesworth, 2005).

Research (Hood & Knightley, 1991; Hvitfield, 1985) has shown that preliterate learners have difficulty comprehending the drawings often used in textbooks, work-sheets, and even assessments, such as CASAS. These two-dimensional drawings are often ambiguous, cultural, or outside learners' previous experience. Work with low-literacy learners in Australia has therefore used photographs, rather than drawings in worksheets and textbooks. Readers have been developed using photos only. These photos need to be simple, concrete, and, where possible, tied to a DVD that learners can view and relate to. Figures 4.1 and 4.2 in Chapter 4, this volume, illustrate how this can be done.

Oral Language

Some of the strategies suggested here are also ones that involve literacy learning. Learners who come from highly oral cultures will have experienced interactive oral story-telling, singing, and rhyme and rhythm. Therefore, they "may benefit from classroom learning that includes opportunities for:

- repetition and memorization;
- rhythmic activities, such as clapping, chanting, poetry, and singing; and
- 'imaginative' texts, such as stories and poetry" (Achren & Williams, 2006, p. 1)
- use of art or drawing (Bassano & Christison, 1995).

There is controversy over the teaching of vocabulary, with some researchers advocating teaching it in **semantic sets**, that is, in groups of words semantically related (e.g., *colors, days of the week, food, illness*). Folse (2004), however, has shown that teaching groups like this can cause learner confusion, e.g., between the pronunciation and spelling of *Tuesday* and *Thursday*. We would recommend always teaching vocabulary in context and having learners use new vocabulary in a variety of contexts. Where possible, teach the high frequency words first (Nation, 2000).

As already indicated, teaching methods in BANA countries may be quite alien and even intimidating to some immigrants and refugees. Their cultural patterns of class participation may be quite different. Some learners are from cultures where displays of knowledge are unacceptable; others may be from cultures where giving wrong answers means loss of face; others may be from cultures where teachers teach and learners sit and repeat; others may have learned a language through translation. Although teachers may want to introduce communicative approaches to give learners opportunities to speak, they need to do this carefully. Repetition and choral work with the whole class can often help teachers gain the confidence of some of these learners so that they build trust. They can then have one side of the class take one role in a conversation and the other side take the other role. Only when they feel learners are comfortable in the class can they introduce pair, group, or individual work, explaining to learners why they are asking them to perform certain tasks. Research demonstrates that learners benefit from group or pair work, even when the models of English are limited (Smith, Harris, & Reder, 2005). They have opportunities to negotiate meaning, asking for clarification, or repetition, strategies that are useful outside the classroom. Therefore, teachers need to provide clear tasks for learners to achieve in pair work (see Chapter 3, this volume).

Listening materials should reflect the local context in which these learners are living, so teachers may have to develop their own listening activities (see Chapter 4, this volume). It is not as important for learners to speak the local variety, even though many of them will because of the people they interact with. The primary goal of their speaking should be intelligibility, not native-like pronunciation. ESL teachers are not always the best judge of intelligibility because they have been exposed to different learner speech (Yates & Springall, 2008). It can be helpful to have learners keep a record of misunderstandings they have or have a friend or colleague not familiar with their speech patterns come as a visitor to the class. The visitor can present some useful local information for learners, and through question and answer, the teacher can monitor areas where the visitor has difficulty understanding the learners.

Content for both literacy and oral language learning needs to be tied directly to learners' needs—their actual needs, not what teachers assume might be their needs. One of the most common content areas used in adult immigrant/refugee programs has been survival or life skills, such as reading supermarket labels or completing deposit and withdrawal slips at the bank. However, several researchers working with refugee and low-literacy immigrants have found such content to be inappropriate. Welaratna (1992), working with Khmer refugees, found that they did not use banks. They had little money and when they had saved some, extended families pooled the money to purchase a large, jointly owned item, such as a refrigerator or van. Similarly, Weinstein-Shr found Hmong women did not need her lesson on reading supermarket labels because "they bought their meat wholesale from a butcher and grew their own vegetables" (Weinstein-Shr, 1989, p. 15). Further, as Auerbach and Burgess have pointed out, the life skills content contains a "hidden curriculum" that trains refugees/immigrants to be obedient workers, accepting of their low social status (Auerbach & Burgess, 1985). Therefore, content needs to be based on learner needs—whether that be learning to take a citizenship test, preparing for work, acquiring study skills, learning to interact with their children's schools, or knowing how to discuss world events.

Conclusion

In this chapter we have focused on adult learners who are immigrants or refugees who are learning English in adult education settings. Because they are immigrants and refugees, they bring different learner characteristics than do international students. Because they are in an adult setting, they are usually beginning learners of English. This setting also has its own special characteristics, different from those of immigrants and adults already enrolled in postsecondary education. In order to provide appropriate instruction for this population, teachers are required to know about their specific learners, their backgrounds, their needs, and their goals.

The adult ESL sector varies considerably across the BANA countries, but all have the goal of integrating immigrants and refugees into the host community. These learners bring with them experiences of emigrating and settling that require different strategies to those used with international students or business people learning English in these countries. Of particular importance is the psychological impact of emigrating or being a refugee, and for some, the lack of literacy in their home language.

Task: Expand

http://www.migrationpolicy.org

This is the official website for the Migration Policy Institute, which is an independent, nonpartisan think tank that studies the movement of people around the world. It is a useful source for reports on issues affecting immigrants and refugees.

http://unhcr.org

This is the official website of the United Nations High Commission for Refugees. This contains historical and up-to-date information on refugee resettlement.

http://www.culturalorientation.net

This is the website of the Cultural Orientation Resource (COR) Center, at the Center for Applied Linguistics in the U.S. and provides materials about refugee training and settlement in the U.S.

http://www.cal.org

This is the website for the Center for Applied Linguistics in the U.S. This center engages in research on adult learners of English and houses the Center for Adult English Language Acquisition (CAELA), a rich resource for material on this population.

Questions for Discussion

1. How do the different experiences of immigrants and refugees impact their learning and settling in a new country?
2. Why is it important for immigrants and refugees to acquire English literacy?
3. What strategies can teachers use to help preliterate adults acquire literacy in English?
4. Why do you think that SLA research has not been conducted with this population?

Notes

1. BANA refers to Britain, Australasia, and North America (that is, Britain, Australia, New Zealand, Canada, and the United States). See Volume I, Chapter 2, for more information on this concept.
2. This resettlement is called third country because the asylum seeker has already fled their homeland and sought asylum elsewhere. However, this first country of asylum is unable (or unwilling) to offer a durable solution or the refugee has fears of persecution in the country.
3. We don't have space to discuss all these issues in full, but the immigration and refugee landscape is incredibly complex. For more information, see "Task: Expand" at the end of the chapter.

References

Achren, L., & Williams, A. (2006). *Fact sheet: Learners with low literacy in the AMEP*. Sydney: AMEP Research Centre.

AMEP Research Centre. (2008). *Get wise*. Sydney: AMEP Research Centre.

Auerbach, E. R., & Burgess, D. (1985). The hidden curriculum of survival ESL. *TESOL Quarterly, 19*(3), 475–495.

Bassano, S. K., & Christison, M. A. (1995). *Drawing out: Creative, personalized, whole language activities from grades 5—adult*. Burlingame, CA: Alta Book Center Publishers.

Bigelow, M., & Tarone, E. (2004). The role of native language literacy in second language acquisition: Doesn't who we study determine what we know? *TESOL Quarterly, 39*(1), 689–700.

CAELA. (2004). About CAELA. Retrieved from http://www.cal.org/caela/about_caela/press.html

Canadian Language Benchmarks. (1996). *English as a second language for adults; English as a second language for literacy learners*. Ottawa: Ministry of Supplies and Services.

Comprehensive Adults Student Assessment System. (1996). *CASAS Life Skills Test*. San Diego: Author.

Davison, C. (2001). ESL in Australian schools: From the margins to the mainstream. In B. Mohan, C. Leung, & C. Davison (Eds.), *English as a second language in the mainstream: Teaching, learning and identity* (pp. 11–29). Harlow: Pearson Education Ltd.

Folse, K. S. (2004). *Vocabulary myths: Applying second language research to classroom teaching*. Ann Arbor, MI: University of Michigan Press.

Government of Canada. (2008). Language assessment. Retrieved from http://www.goingtocanada.gc.ca/CIC/display-afficher.do?id=0000000000066&lang=eng

Hood, S., & Knightley, S. (1991). *A longitudinal study of low literacy students*. Darlinghurst, NSW: NSW AMES.

Hvitfield, C. (1985). Picture perception and interpretation among preliterate adults. *Passages, 1*(1).

Knowles, M. (1990). *The adult learner: A neglected species*. Houston, TX: Gulf Publishing.

McPherson, P. (1997). *Investigating learner outcomes for clients with special needs in the Adult Migrant English Program*. Sydney: NCELTR.

Ministry of Education. (2008). Strategy for Adult ESOL. Retrieved from http://www.minedu.govt.nz/NZEducation/EducationPolicies/TertiaryEducation/PolicyAndStrategy/StrategyForAdultESOL.aspx

Murray, D. E., & Lloyd, R. (2008). *Uptake of AMEP provision by youth from Africa: Opportunities and barriers*. Sydney: NCELTR.

Murray, D. E., & Wigglesworth, G. (Eds.). (2005). *First language support in adult ESL in Australia*. Sydney: NCELTR.

Nation, I. M. P. (2000). Learning vocabulary in lexical sets: Dangers and guidelines. *TESOL Journal, 9*(2), 6–10.

New South Wales Adult Migrant English Services. (2003). *Certificates in Spoken and Written English* (4th ed.). Sydney: NSW AMES.

Smith, C., Harris, K., & Reder, S. (2005). *Applying research findings to instruction for adult English language learners: CAELA Brief*. Washington, D.C.: Center for Applied Linguistics.

TESOL. (2002). Standards for Adult Education ESL Programs. Retrieved from http://www.tesol.org/s_tesol/sec_document.asp?CID=364&DID=1839

Victorian Foundation for Survivors of Torture. (1998). *Rebuilding shattered lives*. Melbourne: VFST.

Weinstein-Shr, G. (1989). *Literacy and social process: A community in transition*. Unpublished manuscript, Philadelphia: Temple University, College of Education.

Welaratna, U. (1992). A Khmer perspective: Connections between Khmer students' behaviors, history, and culture. In D. E. Murray (Ed.), *Diversity as resource: Redefining cultural literacy* (pp. 135–147). Alexandria, VA: TESOL.

Yates, L. S., & Springall, J. (2008). *Assessing intelligibility*. Sydney: AMEP Research Centre.

Chapter 8

Postsecondary Adult Learners

VIGNETTE

I'm having a very hard time teaching my ESL 105 class (expository writing), and I'm wondering if you could visit my class and if we could please talk. I heard that you taught ESL writing for many years and that you might have some ideas. I think I'm a good writer, but that fact does not seem to help me in teaching academic writing to these international students. I just don't know how to help them. I haven't taught writing to ESL students before, but I've taught other ESL classes at the community college (and loved it!) before I started my M.A. degree. My students are studying in engineering, business, chemistry, history, biology, some other areas of science, but I cannot remember which ones. They are mostly Asians, but I have three Hispanic students who actually graduated from high school here and who tested into my class from the Writing Program—four students from Europe and two Arabic speakers. They all seem to have different needs when it comes to writing and their writing is all over the place. In general, the sample essays that I collected from them were full of errors and so poorly organized. I feel completely overwhelmed in trying to respond, so I haven't done anything with the papers. The students keep asking me about them because they want them back before their next essay is due. I just don't know where to begin. Some grad students who have taught the course before gave me the syllabus and some materials, and there is a book. But, these syllabi are mostly based around the exercises in the book. Oh yes, a number of students don't think the exercises I have them do in the book are helpful and have told me so (both in and after class—another problem). I wouldn't say they have a bad attitude really; I think they just want to improve their writing abilities, and I don't seem to be helping them. Can you please meet with me and help me soon? I'll be in the lab all morning and will try to come back to find you. Also, my phone number is below, and I have a mailbox in the Department. [Personal correspondence, 2009]

Task: Reflect

1. If you were the person to whom the note in the vignette was directed, what specific advice would you give to this teacher in order to help him

move forward in solving the problems he is experiencing in his L2 academic writing class?

2. What do you think are some reasons for these problems? Do you think such problems are common in teaching L2 writing? How could some of the problems have been avoided or at least mediated?

3. Describe the probable context this vignette is taken from. Do you think such a situation could occur in other contexts?

Introduction

There are numerous postsecondary learners studying English in Inner Circle countries. Some postsecondary learner populations are discussed in other chapters (see Chapter 9 on workplace literacy and Chapter 7 on immigrants and refugees). In this chapter, we will focus our attention on academic postsecondary learners who have been admitted to and are studying in institutions of higher education in Inner Circle countries or who are studying at English medium universities or are receiving discipline-specific curricula delivered in English in Outer and Expanding Circle countries. Postsecondary learners study English for both occupational and academic purposes, meaning that some learners see themselves as needing English for their nonacademic-related jobs while others see themselves needing English to work in academia or publish their research in scholarly journals.

The population of postsecondary adults studying English is expanding worldwide. According to the Institute for International Education (IIE) and its *Open Doors* publication in 2007, there were 582,984 international students studying in the United States (www.opendoors.iienetwork.org). This number is up by 10% from the previous year with Asia being the largest source region and India, China, and Korea becoming the countries sending the largest number of students. International students bring about $14.5 billion to the U.S. in tuition, fees, and living expenses. Over 66% of students receive funding from sources outside of the United States. Other Inner Circle countries are experiencing similar increases in numbers of postsecondary students. In 2008, there were 543,898 international students studying in Australia (www.studies.australia.com), 130,000 in Canada (www.cic.gc.ca), and 460,000 in the U.K. (www.i-studentadvisor.com), with over 83,000 international students studying in London alone (www.londonmet.ac.uk).

English language teaching (ELT) programs that address the needs of academic postsecondary learners fall within the domain of English for specific purposes (ESP) (Lackstrom, Selinker, & Trimble, 1970) or English for academic purposes (EAP), referring to English programs for postsecondary learners housed in formal academic settings (see also Chapter 9, this volume). Technically, EAP can be further subdivided into English for general academic purposes (EGAP) and English for specific academic purposes (ESAP), with the scope being the principal difference between the two types of programs (Carkin, 2005). In the vignette above, the novice EAP writing instructor was most likely teaching EGAP since the course he was teaching was designed for academic postsecondary students from many different disciplines and focused on general features of academic writing. ESAP courses are directed to students in specific disciplines, such as engineering or chemistry, or students with specific needs, such as publishing research in academic journals or writing research proposals for dissertations. We recognize that postsecondary learners may be at different levels of English proficiency and some learners may benefit from a basic and general English curriculum, especially within Outer and Expanding Circle countries where the requirements for admission to the university or a specific discipline within the university may or may not be tied to English proficiency, or general English is a required part of the curriculum for all students, regardless of discipline; nevertheless, we focus this chapter on the needs of postsecondary learners who must acquire academic language specific to their discipline because this population is not dealt with elsewhere in this volume, and the way in which issues related to a general English curriculum have been covered in this volume and in Volume I do not exclude adult postsecondary learners (see Chapters 1–4 in this volume, for example).

As a discipline, EAP came into existence in the 1960s. The early work of Halliday, McIntosh, and Strevens (1964) provides the rationale underlying the particular language needs of different academic disciplines relative to English, such as discipline-specific registers (i.e., vocabulary, syntax) and genres (i.e., text structures and particular registers).

This focus on learning academic language through academic tasks, texts, and content is the basis for claims that EAP instruction represents a highly pragmatic approach to learning, encompassing needs analyses, evaluation, academic skills, disciplinary content, and tasks in support of student learning in tertiary educational contexts (Halliday, et al., 1964, p. 85).

EAP is different from English for general purposes because it involves a needs assessment to determine the particular features of language, such as vocabulary, organizational structures, varieties of English, or discoursal patterns found in formal postsecondary learning environments; consequently, EAP does not rely on a preset or predetermined curriculum external to the context and may vary greatly across contexts. To this end, EAP has been investigated in a number of different ways by interviewing university faculty (Bridgeman & Carlson, 1984; Horowitz, 1986) and students (Christison & Krahnke, 1986; Leki & Carson, 1994) and examining academic texts (Biber, Conrad, Reppen, Byrd, & Helt, 2002) and academic writing tasks (Hale, et al., 1996).

Characteristics of Learners

EAP learners vary by country, culture, institution, and academic goals (Dudley-Evans & St. John, 1998). Many postsecondary learners are young adults from countries throughout the world who are seeking undergraduate degrees from universities in Inner Circle countries, such as the international students in the vignette above. Most of them are using their own or family financial resources. Other postsecondary learners are pursuing graduate degrees. While many of these young adults use their own or family resources, many of them also have scholarships or research and teaching assistantships that cover tuition and provide a stipend. They are generally of a higher socioeconomic status and have proven their scholarly abilities sufficiently at the undergraduate level to enter graduate school and compete with both NS and NNES (non-native English speaking) applicants for admission. Other postsecondary learners are studying in English-medium universities in countries where there are multiple native languages and English has official recognition in education, such as in Zimbabwe and Singapore. Learners in these contexts have a long history of English study but generally use their mother tongue for daily communication and for other nondiscipline-specific study. A third group of postsecondary learners study in countries where specific disciplines or subject areas are taught in English, such as medicine, engineering, chemistry, and other science subjects, while the remainder of the curriculum is taught in the native language. This situation is true of a number of Arabic and European countries. EAP learners also exist in post-secondary contexts in countries where the native language is the primary language of instruction, but learners are required to read research found only in English. This is a familiar context in many postsecondary schools throughout most of South America (Carkin, 2005).

Learners studying in these different contexts have very different English profiles and have different proficiency levels relative to the four skills, and, in addition, they interface with English in different ways. For example, English learners in Singapore who have been studying in English for most of their lives, read academic texts and research in English, write their research papers in English, as well as listen to lectures and discuss them in English. English learners in South America in postsecondary contexts may need to develop their skills in reading English but would write their research papers, listen to lectures, and discuss them in their native language. Because English study varies in different contexts, the research tradition in EAP places a strong emphasis on needs analysis (see Chapter 1 in this volume for additional information on needs and stakeholder analyses).

Task: Explore

Work with a partner or in a small group. Briefly describe each of the EAP contexts identified above and make a list of between three and four different countries that would fit into each of the contexts. In which of these different contexts do you teach or might you see yourself teaching in the future?

Instructing for Learning

Academic Literacy

The prominent use of language for literary purposes, such as poetry, short stories, plays, novels, and other types of creative writing in postsecondary contexts is quite distinct from EAP with its descriptive goals (Swales, 2001) that revolve around the particular skills and levels of expertise known as **academic literacies** or **competencies**. Johns (1997) argues for the plural use of academic literacy because of the wide range of purposes associated with literacy in different academic traditions and the ways in which academic skills are influenced by each other and by the strategies learners use for understanding the social discourse in which academic language is produced. Other EAP researchers construct their view of academic literacy in the traditional terms—the reading and writing demands of the university and the formal study of language. Still other researchers suggest that while the formal study of academic language is important, they also recognize that academic literacy is acquired when language is viewed by learners as a vehicle for understanding.

Academic language is different from the language used in everyday social settings and communicative encounters. It is noted for being decontextualized and explicit (compared to everyday social language), often requiring the use of technical terms. In addition, academic language is embedded in a complex set of relations that require learners to acquire background in the specific sociocultural context in order to make sense of both text and discourse. Second language learners in all postsecondary contexts must develop academic competencies and second language academic literacy instructors must be concerned with how such competencies develop.

L2 Academic Writing

L2 Academic Competencies

In a sense, writers are at a communicative disadvantage since they cannot exploit all of the devices that are available to listeners and speakers in order to assure understanding. Writers are unable to make use of facial expressions or changes in pitch, stress, and tone of voice. They cannot make use of repetitions, clarifications, and hesitations. A writer has to figure out how to make up for these disadvantages, and it is no easy task for writers in either a first or second language. In addition to the general challenges writers face, academic writers have an additional set of requirements or competencies.

Hedge (1988) outlines at least five different competencies that postsecondary adult learners must employ. First, writers must have a high level of organizational competence so that ideas and information make sense to the reader (i.e., the use of rhetorical features such as topic sentences, supporting details, and thesis statements). Second, there must be a high level of accuracy in the writing, especially related to the technical aspects of the subject matter, so that there is little ambiguity in meaning. Third, the writer must control complex grammatical structures so that information can be properly focused and emphasized. Fourth, the writer must have control over technical vocabulary, and finally, the writer must combine all of these competencies to create a style that is appropriate for the intended readers in the specific socio-cultural context. These five competencies—organizational, accuracy, grammatical structures, technical vocabulary, and style—are essential for learner success.

L2 writing teachers struggle in helping learners develop these academic writing competencies. In the vignette above, the novice writing teacher had difficulties helping his learners develop academic writing competencies; yet, the learners recognized the need for these competencies and that the skills they had developed to date were not sufficient. Their frustration resided in the fact that few of the classroom writing tasks seemed to move them towards their desired goal.

Kaplan (1983) identified four of the most common types of writing tasks for the second language classroom:

1. Writing without composing, such as filling in the blanks in writing exercises, completing forms, writing transcriptions of words or sentences.
2. Writing for informational purposes, such as taking notes, summarizing, outlining, and writing short reports.

3. Writing for personal purposes, such as journals, diaries, memos, and notes.
4. Writing for imaginative purposes, such as writing poems or stories.

Although L2 writing teachers recognize that L2 writing tasks are hierarchical in nature and that some of the L2 writing tasks in Kaplan's list are necessary in emerging L2 writing skill development, it is important to remember that these tasks are not sufficient for learners to develop the academic competencies that EAP students need.

ACTFL (American Council for the Teaching of Foreign Languages) (1985) developed descriptions of L2 writing proficiency according to content, function, and accuracy for different levels of language proficiency; however, even at the highest level of proficiency (i.e., advanced-plus[1]) this taxonomy does not take into account either the complicated cognitive operations, such as determining the meaning that is to be conveyed, the genre to be used, the style of the prose, the purpose of the text, and the appropriate amount of detail (Clark & Clark, 1977) needed to demonstrate high-level skill development in academic literacy.

Task: Explore

Work with a partner or in a small group. Consider the five academic competencies for L2 academic writing proposed by Hedge (1988)—organizational, accuracy, grammatical structures, technical vocabulary, and style—and discussed in this chapter. Select one of the competencies and create a specific classroom task for L2 writers in your context to focus on skill development for that competency.

Approaches to L2 Composition

There have been many different approaches to teaching L2 academic writing. In this short chapter, we look at three different approaches to L2 writing and the theoretical concepts that underpin these approaches. Because it has been our experience that L2 academic writing teachers draw heavily on these different approaches in teaching L2 writing, we believe this overview to be useful.

PROCESS APPROACHES

The process-oriented approach to L2 writing is a reflection of the research in L1 composition. In process approaches, sometimes referred to as expressivist views, the focus is on the process that L2 writers must go through in order to create and produce a product. Teachers advocating for this approach are nondirective. They focus on facilitating classroom activities to promote fluency and encourage self-discovery through activities such as journal writing and personal essays, through which learners can "write freely and uncritically so that [they] can get down as many words as possible" (Elbow, 1973). The approach emphasizes personal and expressive writing, but for L2 writers, this approach is often at the expense of specific skills needed by academically bound L2 students who have limited exposure to the kinds of writing required in various university contexts (Hinkel, 2002; Reid, 1984).

In the process writing movement, it has been the cognitivists (i.e., writing as problem-solving) who have had the most effect on L2 academic writing. This group has focused on the higher-order thinking skills associated with problem-solving. The research (Hayes & Flower, 1983; Spack, 1984; Zamel, 1983) was concerned with the mental processes L2 writers use in the composing process. Process approaches focus on prewriting activities and encourage multiple drafts of papers and revision at both the macro (organizational) and micro (sentence-level error) levels (Johns, 1986). Writing is not seen "as linear or formulaic but rather individual and recursive" (Johns, 1994, p. 26). The goal for this type of process writing is to produce competent L2 writers who have an understanding of their own writing process and have developed a repertoire of strategies to use in that process (Flower, 1985). Yet, it is very important that teachers recognize that providing language learners with explicit instruction and specific activities for working with academic language is important and often necessary in order to help them have the requisite skills to join the desired discourse community (Delpit, 1988). In addition, Generation 1.5 learners may not have been taught these skills as young adults in secondary school (see Volume 1, Chapter 3, for additional information on Generation 1.5 learners).

INTERACTIVE APPROACHES

The interactive approach to writing is based on the work of Bakhtin (1973) and his idea that the writer is involved in a dialog with his or her audience. In this approach to writing, both the writer and the reader take responsibility for coherent text. English is generally thought to be a writer-responsible language because the person who is primarily responsible for the communication is the writer. Other cultures rely on different assumptions about writing and the relationship between the writer and the reader. For example in Japan, it is the responsibility of the reader to understand what the author intended to say (Hinds, 1987). L2 writing teachers who take an interactive approach to L2 writing work with their learners by taking the part of the reader in order to help learners create topics, develop organizational features, focus on transitions, and make arguments clear to their readers.

SOCIAL CONSTRUCTIONIST VIEW

In a social constructionist view of L2 writing, the written product is considered a social act that occurs within and for a specific context and audience (Coe, 1987). In this approach to L2 writing, the language, focus, and form of the text are determined by the discourse community; hence, L2 writing teachers who adhere to a social constructivist view must not only focus on helping their learners develop academic writing competencies, they must also help their learners understand the discourse community for whom they are writing. For L2 writing teachers who are not part of the same discourse community as their learners or who teach learners from potentially different discourse communities (e.g., the novice teacher in the vignette above) adhering to such an approach in its purest form can prove to be difficult unless a close collaboration can be achieved with a teacher or professor from the specific discourse community.

According to Swales (1990), a discourse community has 1) a broadly agreed-upon set of common public goals, 2) mechanisms for communication among members (e.g., meetings, journals, newsletters), 3) participatory mechanisms (i.e., how members of the community respond and give feedback to each other), 4) one or more genres to further its aims, 5) specific vocabulary, and 6) a threshold level of members with a suitable degree of relevant content and discoursal expertise.

Teaching Considerations

In designing and planning for academic writing tasks, L2 writing teachers may find the following list proposed by Palmer (1985) a helpful guide:

1. Graphical or visual skills, such as conventions of spelling, punctuation, capitalization, and the format for specific text types as in letters, memos, lists, notes, reports, proposals, journal articles, etc.
2. Grammatical abilities, such as using a variety of sentence patterns and constructions.
3. Expressive or stylistic skills, such as using appropriate registers and styles depending on the purpose of the writing and anticipated response from the discourse community.
4. Rhetorical skills, such as the ability to use cohesive devices such as connectives, reference words, and lexical variety.
5. Organizational skills, such as the arrangement of information into paragraphs and taking into account the types of ideas and how they should be interrelated to produce a unified whole (see also Volume I, Chapter 9, for further discussion of the features of written text). Research has shown that learners can write more and more accurately when they are familiar with the content, even if content familiarity was in the L1.

Task: Explore

Work with a partner or a small group. Examine a few lessons from an L2 writing textbook in English. Classify the activities for writing using Kaplan's taxonomy and the list proposed by Palmer above.

The Reading–Writing Connections

We consider Johns' (1997) notion of academic literacies by exploring the reading and writing connection. Reading can be seen as a source of language input, influencing the development of writing abilities. Studies of the relationship between reading and writing offer four interrelated hypotheses to explain the relationship (Eisterhold, 1994). These interrelated hypotheses are described in terms of the direction in which the input is transferring from one modality (i.e., reading or writing) to the other.

DIRECTIONAL HYPOTHESIS

According to this hypothesis, connection between reading and writing is directional. For example, being able to recognize a rhetorical pattern such as cause and effect in a reading passage would presumably allow the reader to eventually reproduce the pattern in writing. In the directional model, the transfer of information proceeds in only one direction—reading to writing. The claim with the directional model is that reading influences writing, but that writing is not particularly useful to reading. The model receives support from the research (Eckhoff, 1983; Stotsky, 1983). It is important to recognize that most of the research that supports this hypothesis focuses on transfer when it is supported by instruction (Belanger, 1987); transfer is not automatic.

NONDIRECTIONAL HYPOTHESIS

The second hypothesis in favor of a link between reading and writing is known as the nondirectional hypothesis. This hypothesis suggests that reading and writing derive from a single underlying proficiency. Unlike the directional model, transfer can occur in either direction. The argument is that improved ability with one modality can lead to increased abilities in the other. For example, Hiebert, Englert, and Brennan (1983) found that there was a relationship between recognition of a text structure and the ability to produce the text structure (i.e., a reading–writing connection) for all text structures except description. In addition, they found that writing performance was a better predictor of reading achievement (i.e., writing–reading connection) than the ability to recognize details in reading (i.e., the reading measure used in the study).

BI-DIRECTIONAL HYPOTHESIS

The third hypothesis is the most complex of the three. This hypothesis suggests that reading and writing are interactive and interdependent. There are multiple relations and what is learned at one level of language proficiency may be qualitatively different from what is learned at another level and affected in different ways. For example, as learners become more proficient, the nature of the reading and writing relationship may change. For grade 2 (ages 6–7), the relationship between reading and writing was based on the ability to recognize and spell words. For grade 5 (ages 10–11), the variables determining the relationship had changed to organizational structure and diversity of vocabulary (Shanahan, 1984).

INTERDEPENDENCE HYPOTHESIS

Cummins's interdependence hypothesis (1981) makes a strong case for transfer but does not specify direction. This hypothesis states the following:

> To the extent that instruction in Lx (i.e., Language X) is effective in promoting proficiency in Lx, transfer of this proficiency to Ly will occur provided there is adequate exposure to Ly (either in school or environment) and adequate motivation to learn Ly. (p. 29)

Like the nondirectional hypothesis outlined above, the interdependence hypothesis proposes an underlying proficiency that makes it possible for learners to transfer literacy-related skills from one language to another; consequently, developing literacy skills in a second or subsequent language will be affected by the literacy skills developed in a first language. For postsecondary learners who are already literate and have acquired academic language proficiency in their native languages, the acquisition of literacy in English will be affected by L1 academic literacy.[2] The interdependence hypothesis adds the additional variables of length and intensity of exposure and motivation as variables that could affect the relationship.

Each of the above hypotheses offers an important perspective on the reading and writing connection. Although L2 research has been conducted relative to these hypotheses, three of the four hypotheses (i.e., all but the interdependence hypothesis) were constructed from a first language base and do not adequately consider the complexities involved in academic writing for second language learners, particularly those who are already literate in at least one other language, their native language (Eisterhold, 1994). Rather than providing a definitive answer on the reading–writing connection, it seems that each hypothesis contributes to an emerging perspective, suggesting that there is a connection between L2 reading and writing, particularly when explicit skill instruction is part of the equation.

L2 Academic Reading

In Chapter 5 in this volume, we introduced the idea that reading is a bottom-up process that involves decoding written symbols, starting from the smallest units (e.g., letters, syllables, and words) and moving to the larger units (e.g., clauses, sentences, paragraphs, or essays) and also a top-down process in which the reader brings to the task an array of information, ideas, and beliefs about the text. A third perspective on reading, and the one that we adhere to in this chapter for postsecondary academic learners, is that reading is an interactive process in which readers use both bottom-up and top-down processes to comprehend text. Meaning is created through the interaction of text and reader. Successful readers use a variety of strategies in reading that involve both bottom-up and top-down processes (Hosenfeld, Arnold, Kirchoffer, Laciura, & Wilson, 1981), for example skipping unnecessary words, guessing contextually, identifying words according to grammatical category, using side glosses, using content from preceding and following sections of the text to evaluate guesses in meaning, and using illustrations and other visuals.

Working with Academic Text

One prominent challenge that postsecondary academic learners face is that L2 academic reading involves working with a broad range of **text types** and that each text type has its distinctive topic and structure, placing a heavy cognitive and language demand on L2 readers and requiring that learners read strategically and employ different types of strategies in reading. However, even strategic readers can face difficulties with academic texts because unfamiliar text structures or difficult text structures can cause L2 readers to revert to poor reading strategies. Background knowledge and cultural schemata also play a role in understanding text. L2 readers read faster, and recall more accurately, texts that have familiar structures or contexts.

Academic postsecondary learners need to work with a full range of academic texts for their anticipated discourse community (Davies, 1982, 1983). In order to prepare learners, some researchers suggest using a conceptual frame (Fillmore, 1976) or a set of topic-types (Davies, 1982, 1983; Johns & Davies, 1983). It is possible for EAP texts to cover an unlimited number of topics; however, these unlimited topics fit into a limited number of topic types or topic structures.

For example, the following topics appear on the surface to be unrelated: a suspension bridge, a flowering plant, a skeleton, a blast furnace. Nevertheless, in a general sense they are all about the same thing: a physical structure of one sort of another. Furthermore, in practice, descriptions of such physical structures consistently provide information which falls in the following categories:

1.   the parts of the structure,
2.   the properties or attributes of the parts,
3.   the location of the parts,
4.   the function of the parts.

(Johns & Davies, 1983, p. 5)

Texts that describe physical structures, no matter what the topic is, not only give information that falls into the four categories above, but (virtually) they give no other information.

Johns and Davies (1983) offer 12 topic structures—physical structure, process, characteristics, mechanism, theory, principle, force, instruction, social structure, state/situation, adaptation, and system/production—each with its own set of structure constituents and each given in a type of formula. For example, physical structures are made up of the following constituents:

physical structure = part → location + property + function

Constituents to the left of the arrow are obligatory, and constituents to the right of the arrow are optional; + indicates *and*, not ordered. Johns and Davies have defined the obligatory and optional constituents for each of the 12 topic structures listed above. Together, these topic structures are useful for managing the wide range of topics that postsecondary academic readers encounter. This is one example of how researchers in EAP are helping learners develop efficient strategies for working with varied texts. The variety of texts that learners encounter is challenging because the texts learners work with, the tasks they are assigned or required to complete, and goals they have are constantly changing.

Reading Strategically

It takes time and focused practice for academic language learners to become strategic readers, and most curricula and reading materials do not recognize these facts (Grabe & Stoller, 2002). Nevertheless, teachers should try to integrate strategy use and discussions about strategies in every lesson. This involves introducing and modeling the strategy and raising student awareness of the strategies by encouraging their use and guiding learner reflections. These strategies include recognizing the type of text (e.g., narrative, information, persuasive), the type of text structure

Table 8.1 Strategies for L2 Learners in Working with Academic Texts

---

1. Recognizing text type
2. Recognizing types of text structures
3. Familiarity with topic structures
4. Connecting information in the text to background knowledge
5. Making predictions
6. Summarizing content
7. Referencing text for key information
8. Searching for details
9. Determining the meaning of unknown words from context
10. Analyzing morphological components of unknown words
11. Posing questions
12. Answering questions that have been posed
13. Connecting pieces of the text
14. Using discourse markers to see textual relationships
15. Critiquing the text
16. Judging how well the objectives were met
17. Reflecting on what has been learned

(e.g., story schema or expository prose), and the type of topic structure. In addition, readers must be able to connect texts to background knowledge (Carrell, 1983), make predictions, summarize the content, reference information that is textually implicit, determine the meaning of unknown words from the context, and analyze the morphological components of unknown words. Grabe and Stoller (2002) expand on this list of strategies to include posing questions about the text and finding answers to posed questions, connecting one part of the text to another, using discourse markers to see textual relationships, critiquing the text, judging how well the objectives have been met, and reflecting on what has been learned. Table 8.1 presents a summary of the suggested L2 reading strategies for working with academic texts.

Conclusion

We have focused this chapter specifically on the needs of postsecondary learners in formal academic contexts. In the first part of this chapter we looked at issues related to the development of academic literacy and focused on L2 academic writing, including different approaches to L2 writing and the challenges teachers encounter in implementing these different approaches. Next, we considered the reading–writing connections and reviewed hypotheses that might account for possible transfer of skills between modalities. Finally, we looked at L2 reading, specifically working with varied academic texts and strategies for L2 readers.

Task: Expand

Grabe, W., & Stoller, F. L. (2002). *Teaching and researching reading.* New York: Pearson Education.

Teaching and Researching Reading is designed to help language professionals understand the complex nature of reading. This volume builds connections from research on reading, to sound instructional practices and action research possibilities. Offering an overview of reading theory, it summarizes the main ideas and issues in first and second language contexts and covers the key research studies. Grabe and Stoller explicitly link this research to teaching practice.

Ferris, D. (2009). *Response to student writing: Implications for second language students.* Mahwah, NJ: Lawrence Erlbaum.

This book surveys the research on teacher response to L2 writing and discusses how the findings translate into classroom principles and practice. Ferris offers numerous suggestions for responding to student writing that are based on the research reviewed.

Questions for Discussion

1. Use the information provided in this chapter to prepare a list of suggestions for beginning EAP teachers on how to organize L2 writing tasks for their learners.
2. Choose an authentic EAP writing task and prepare a lesson using the process approach to writing—prewriting, writing, and postwriting activities.
3. Based on the information given in this chapter, prepare a list of suggestions for the beginning teacher of postsecondary adult learners.

Notes

1. ACTFL Proficiency Levels for Writing. *Advanced-plus:* able to write about a variety of topics with significant precision and in detail. Can write most social and informal business correspondences. Can describe and narrate personal experiences fully but has difficulty supporting points of view in written discourse. Can write about the concrete aspects of topics relating to particular interests and special fields of competence. Often shows remarkable fluency and ease of expression, but under time constraints and pressure writing may be inaccurate. Generally strong in either grammar or vocabulary, but not in both. Weakness and unevenness in one of the foregoing, in spelling, or character writing formation may result in occasional miscommunication. Some misuse of vocabulary may still be evident. Style may still be obviously foreign (pp. 15–24).
2. Cummins's interdependence hypothesis also explains why minority language children with low-level literacy skills in their L1 often have such a difficult time acquiring literacy skills in their L2.

References

American Council for the Teaching of Foreign Languages (ACTFL) (1985). Retrieved from www.sil.org/lingualinks/languagelearning/OtherResources/ACTFLProficiencyGuidelines/contents.htm. Originally published as *ACTFL Proficiency Guidelines.* Revised 1985. Hastings-on-Hudson, NY: ACTFL Materials Center.

Bakhtin, M. M. (1973). *Marxism and the philosophy of language.* (L. Matejka & I. R. Titunik, Trans.). New York: Seminar Press.

Belanger, J. (1987). Theory and research into reading and writing connections: A critical review. *Reading-Canada-Lecture, 5,* 10–18.

Biber, D., Conrad, S., Reppen, R., Byrd, P., & Helt, M. (2002). Speaking and writing in the university: A multidimensional comparison. *TESOL Quarterly, 36*, 9–48.

Bridgeman, B., & Carlson, S. (1984). Survey of academic writing tasks. *Written Communication, 1*, 247–280.

Carkin, S. (2005). English for academic purposes. In E. Hinkel (Ed.), *Handbook on research in second language teaching and learning* (pp. 85–98). Mahwah, NJ: Lawrence Erlbaum Associates.

Carrell, P. L. (1983). Some issues in the role of schemata or background knowledge in second language comprehension. *Reading in a Foreign Language, 1*, 81–92.

Christison, M. A., & Krahnke, K. (1986). Student perceptions of academic language study. *TESOL Quarterly, 20*, 61–82.

Clark, H. H., & Clark, E. V. (1977). *Psychology and language*. New York: Harcourt Brace Jovanovich.

Coe, R. M. (1987). An apology for form: Or, who took the form out of process? *College English, 49*, 13–28.

Cummins, J. (1981). The role of primary language development in promoting educational success for language minority students. In California State Department of Education Sacramento (Ed.), *Schooling and language minority students: A theoretical framework* (pp. 3–49). Los Angeles, CA: Evaluation, Dissemination and Assessment Center, California State University.

Davies, F. I. (1982). Fostering independent reading through group discussion. *Teachers Resource Book Level* 13. Reading 360. London: Ginn.

Davies, F. I. (1983). Towards a methodology for identifying information structures based on topic-type: a classroom-based approach to the analysis of texts in specific subject areas. In J. M. Ulijn, & A. K. Pugh (Eds.), *Reading for professional purposes: Methods and materials in teaching languages.* Leuven, Belgium: ACCO.

Delpit, L. D. (1988). The silenced dialogue: Power and pedagogy in educating other people's children. *Harvard Educational Review, 58*, 43–61.

Dudley-Evans, T., & St. John, M. (1998). *Developments in ESP*. Cambridge: Cambridge University Press.

Eckhoff, B. (1983). How reading affects children's writing. *Language Arts, 60*, 607–616.

Eisterhold, J. C. (1994). Reading-writing connections: Toward a description of second language learners (pp. 88–101). In B. Kroll (Ed.), *Second language writing: Research insights for the classroom.* Cambridge: Cambridge University Press.

Elbow, P. (1973). *Writing without teachers*. New York: Oxford University Press.

Ferris, D. (2009). *Response to student writing: Implications for second language students.* Mahwah, NJ: Lawrence Erlbaum.

Fillmore, C. J. (1976). Frame semantics and the nature of language. In *Annals of the New York Academy of Sciences: Conference on the Origin and Development of Language and Speech, 280*, 20–32.

Flower, L. (1985). *Problem-solving strategies for writing.* (3rd ed.). San Diego, CA: Harcourt Brace Jovanovich.

Grabe, W., & Stoller, F. L. (2002). *Teaching and researching reading.* New York: Pearson Education.

Hale, G., Taylor, C., Bridgeman, B., Carson, J., Kroll, B., & Kantor, R. (1996). *A study of writing tasks assigned in academic degree programs.* Research Report 54. Princeton, NJ: Educational Testing Service.

Halliday, M., McIntosh, A., & Strevens, P. (1964). *The linguistic sciences and language teaching.* London: Longman.

Hayes, J. R., & Flower, L. (1983). Uncovering cognitive processes in writing: An introduction to protocol analysis. In P. Mosenthal, L. Tamar, & S. A. Walmsley (Eds.), *Research in writing* (pp. 206–220). New York: Longman.

Hedge, T. (1988). *Writing.* Oxford: Oxford University Press.

Hiebert, E. H., Englert, C. S., & Brennan, S. (1983). Awareness of text structure in recognition and production of expository discourse. *Journal of Reading Behavior, 15*, 63–79.

Hinds, J. (1987). Reader versus writer responsibility: A new typology. In U. Connor, & R. B.

Kaplan (Eds.), *Writing across language: Analysis of L2 text* (pp. 141–152). Reading, MA: Addison-Wesley.

Hinkel, E. (2002). *Second language writers' texts: Linguistic and rhetorical features*. Mahwah, NJ: Lawrence Erlbaum Associates.

Horowitz, D. (1986). What professors actually require: Academic tasks for the ESL classroom. *TESOL Quarterly, 20*, 445–462.

Hosenfeld, C., Arnold, V., Kirchoffer, J., Laciura, J., & Wilson, J. (1981). Second language learning: A curricular sequence for teaching reading strategies. *Foreign Language Annals, 14*, 415–422.

Institute for International Education (IIE). *Open Doors 2007*. Retrieved from (www.opendoors.iienetwork.org).

Johns, A. M. (1986). Coherence and academic writing: Some definitions and suggestions for teaching. *TESOL Quarterly, 20*, 247–266.

Johns, A. M. (1994). L1 composition theories: Implications for developing theories of L2 composition. In B. Kroll (Ed.), *Second language writing: Research insights for the classroom* (pp. 24–36). Cambridge: Cambridge University Press.

Johns, A. (1997). *Text, role, and context: Developing academic literacies*. Cambridge: Cambridge University Press.

Johns, T., & Davies, F. I. (1983). Text as a vehicle for information: The classroom use of written text in teaching reading in a foreign language. *Reading in a Foreign Language, 1*, 1–19.

Kaplan, R. B. (1983). An introduction to the study of written texts: The "discourse compact." In R. B. Kaplan, A. d'Angelejan, J. R. Cowan, B. B. Kachru, & G. R. Tucker (Eds.), *Annual review of applied linguistics: 1982* (pp. 138–151). New York: Newbury House.

Lackstrom, J., Selinker, L., & Trimble, L. (1970). Grammar and technical English. In R. Lugton (Ed.), *English as a second language: Current issues* (pp. 101–133). Philadelphia: Center for Curriculum Development.

Leki, I., & Carson, J. (1994). Students' perception of EAP writing instruction and writing needs across the disciplines. *TESOL Quarterly, 28*, 81–101.

Palmer, D. (1985). Writing skills. In A. Matthew, M. Spratt, & I. Dangerfield (Eds.), *At the chalkface: Practical techniques in language teaching* (pp. 69–72). London: Edward Arnold.

Reid, J. (1984). Comments on Vivian Zamel's The composing processes of advanced ESL students: Six case studies. *TESOL Quarterly, 81*, 149–153.

Shanahan, T. (1984). Nature of the reading-writing relation: An exploratory multivariate analysis. *Journal of Educational Psychology, 76*, 466–477.

Spack, R. (1984). Invention strategies and the ESL college composition student. *TESOL Quarterly, 18*, 649–670.

Stotsky, S. (1983). *Relating reading and writing: Developing a transactional theory of the writing process*. Bloomington, IN: Indiana University School of Education.

Swales, J. (1990). *Genre analysis: English in academic research settings*. Cambridge: Cambridge University Press.

Swales, J. (2001). EAP-related linguistic research: An intellectual history. In J. Flowerdew, & M. Peacock (Eds.), *Research perspective on English for academic purposes* (pp. 42–54). Cambridge: Cambridge University Press.

Zamel, V. (1983). The composing processes of advanced ESL students: Six case studies. *TESOL Quarterly, 17*, 165–187.

Chapter 9

Workplace Literacy

VIGNETTE

A large supermarket chain has contracted with one of our local adult community centers to provide English as a second language classes for their employees. Marta is teaching in the break room. There are tables and chairs, which give the space a classroom-like atmosphere, and a portable white board has been moved to the front of the room. There is also a sink, microwave, refrigerator, coat racks, lockers, couches, chair, and drink machines. Newspapers and magazines are strung about. Although it appears to be a well-used and busy break room, the manager has assured Marta that other employees will not be in and out during the time that she is teaching. She teaches one group of learners twice a week, but they are of mixed levels relative to English language proficiency. I am observing Marta's class of 12 adult learners.

When I arrive, the students are clustered in three groups around two large tables. They are interacting and working with small pieces of paper. Marta explains to me that she has divided them into groups based on the jobs that they are doing in the store. Four women work in the produce section, two women in fabrics, and five are cashiers. One man stocks shelves and returns "lost items[1]." He is working with the produce group. Students are working with vocabulary specific to their jobs by matching words and pictures. Marta walks around working with each group.

It occurrs to me that Marta has spent considerable time creating materials for this group of students, and I hope that she is getting some compensation for this. She has taken photos of produce, labeled pictures, and recorded the words, so the produce group is involved in a three-way matching—listening to the recorded word, finding the matching picture, and then matching the picture to the written word. The cashiers are also working with materials that Marta has prepared because I can see pictures of their workstations.

After about 30 minutes, Marta introduces new material in the form of a dialog and store maps. All of the students are working together on this activity. The dialog is based on a customer asking for something. Students use the maps of the store to reply to the customer. Each phrase or line of the dialog is introduced and practised. Then, the teacher plays the role of the customer—"Excuse me, can you tell me where I can find . . ."—and different students are called on to use their maps and reply—"Yes, you can find it on Aisle 11." She recycles vocabulary from the previous activity for some of the lower-level students. The class ends before students have a chance to do a role-play, but Marta explains to me that they will continue with the activity next time. [Christison, research notes, 2001]

Task: Reflect

1. To what extent do you think the break room was conducive to language learning and teaching?
2. Why do you think that Marta took authentic photos to use in the class?
3. Why do you think she worked with the whole class on the dialog?
4. How do you think students felt when they were called on to respond to the "customer" question?

Introduction

Because English is the international *lingua franca,* many adults around the world, whether in Inner Circle, Outer Circle, or Expanding Circle countries may learn English to prepare for getting a job or for on-the-job training. Workplace literacy as a designator is different from the other instructional settings we have provided in Part 2 of this volume because it defines the place of learning or the goal of learning, rather than the learner. Most literature on workplace literacy constrains discussion to programs that take place on the work site and often to reading and writing. Cunningham Florez (1998) and Burt and Mathews-Ayndinli (2007) make a useful distinction between workplace instruction and workforce preparation, which we will follow here. We use the term workplace literacy as the overarching term to refer to both. We choose this because the language content and cultural skills involved include all the aspects of literacy we discussed in Chapter 9, Volume 1. Literacy here does not refer only to written material, but to the ability of workers to interact and navigate successfully in the culture of a workplace where English is a primary means of communication. In the vignette above, these learners need to understand the layout of the supermarket, as well as be able to identify which items are on which aisle.

In New Zealand, workplace literacy has been defined as "the skills needed for effective performance in today's workplaces including: speaking, listening, maths, using technology, reading, writing, problem solving, and critical thinking" (Workbase, n.d., p. 4). Then is listed a number of literacy tasks required in the workplace:

- following production schedules
- understanding health and safety requirements
- estimating quantity and weight

- reading and recording product codes
- finding a solution if a problem occurs (p. 4).

The Skills for Life strategy in the U.K., which includes both native English speakers and nonnative English speakers, refers to workplace instruction as work-based.

Workplace literacy could be considered an aspect of English for specific purposes (ESP) and content-based instruction (CBI). It is CBI because the workplace discourse determines the content. Workplace instruction can be considered a form of ESP because it can be based on linguistic analyses and discourse communities (Johns, 1992), and it is also used in EFL settings, where ESP has mostly been applied (Johns, 1992; Master, 1997). Although ESP has a long tradition of both research and instruction, there is a sense in which all ELT should be ESP, responding to particular learners with particular needs. It has traditionally, however, been used primarily for specific content areas such as science, technology (EST), and academic purposes (EAP), as discussed in Chapter 8.

The Need for Workplace Literacy

In BANA countries, increasingly the workplace includes large numbers of workers for whom English is not the first language; yet research shows that proficiency in the national language has a positive effect on workplace participation and earnings, with language proficiency being even more important for those working in skilled occupations (Burnley, Murphy, & Fagan, 1997; Chiswick, Lee, & Miller, 2003). Additionally, literacy (in the sense of reading and writing) has been identified as vital for advanced work (Greenberg, Macias, Rhodes, & Chan, 2001; National Institute of Literacy, 2000).

Yet, in the BANA countries the numbers of workers with limited English proficiency entering the workforce are increasing. In the U.S. "the number of such individuals has grown dramatically over the past decade—accounting for nearly half of all workforce growth" between 1990 and 2001 (Spruck Wrigley, Richer, Martinson, Kubo, & Strawn, 2003, p. 1) so that the 2000 census found that they constituted 12% of the workforce and their salaries were lower than those for native-born workers. Many have low levels of English and literacy and lack education credentials. Consequently, if they have work, it is for low wages. Many researchers and others have argued that the U.S., along with other countries, encourages immigration to fill unskilled positions that the native-born do not want (McKay, 1993). This secondary labor market, such as farm labor, pays workers a nonliving wage, lacks safe working conditions, and provides no health benefits or job security. As well as filling undesirable jobs, the secondary job market also provides a buffer for periods of economic downturn, where these workers are easily fired.

In Canada, immigrants account for more than 70% of the growth in the labor force (Fleming, 2009). These immigrants are increasingly coming from countries where the L1 is neither English nor French, with 43% having minimal proficiency in either official language. As a result, "Canadian government funding of literacy programs has increasingly reflected an emphasis on targeted job-related foci" (p. 38). Additionally, Canada has established a national agency (Foreign Credentials

Referral Office) to evaluate professional qualifications gained outside Canada and provide pathways for such professionals to acquire Canadian credentials.

In the U.K., a 1999 report identified 25% of the population as having difficulties with literacy and numeracy, not all of whom were ESOL speakers (Moser, 1999). In response to this report, the Skills for Life strategy was introduced in 2001, with the goal of improving the literacy, language, and numeracy of groups that were at risk of exclusion from workforce and civic participation. ESOL learners were identified as one group at risk. As well as these national economic needs, individual learners have their own motivations for participating in workplace or vocational training. These reasons include:

- finding work
- seeking promotion
- taking on voluntary roles, such as in the union
- keeping up with new levels of work skills, such as ICT
- helping their children
- overcoming embarrassment
- regaining confidence
- integrating into their local community and to communicate on behalf of that community
- improving access to public services in the U.K. such as transport and health care (Warner & Vorhaus, 2008).

In the Outer and Expanding Circles, the need for workers with English skills is also increasing because of the use of English as the international language of business, education, politics, science and technology, and administration. Local companies often need English-fluent staff who can interact with other companies around the world for import and export. International companies increasingly use English as the medium of communication across the company. Companies in BANA countries are outsourcing work such as call centers to Outer Circle and Expanding Circle countries. India and the Philippines in particular have become hubs for U.S. business process outsourcing (BPO) and, although they have English speakers, they need additional skills training to be successful in the call center environment (Lockwood, 2007). Of particular importance are the "soft" skills, which include communication skills, teamwork, and problem-solving, as opposed to the "hard" skills of particular technical expertise. For those working for U.S. companies and interacting with customers in the U.S., they need communicative skills such as politeness markers in U.S. English, and an understanding of U.S. cultural values.

Task: Reflect

What experiences have you had interacting with (other) NNS speakers of English in nonsocial contexts? What were the characteristics of those interactions? Were there instances of miscommunication? What was the basis of the miscommunication? When the communication went smoothly, what contributed to the quality of the interaction?

The Adult Learner

Because learners in either workforce preparation or workplace programs are adults, teachers need to work within the framework of andragogy, not pedagogy. Andragogy was clearly explored by Knowles (1990), who identified characteristics of adult learners, ones that differentiate them from younger learners. Adults:

- are self-directed in their learning
- are reservoirs of experience that serve as resources for their learning
- are practical, problem-solving-oriented learners
- want their learning to be immediately applicable to their lives
- want to know why something needs to be learned.

These principles need to be the basis of developing work-related programs and in instruction for adult learners. The process for designing and evaluating such programs is the same as we discuss in Chapters 1–3, 12, and 14 in this volume. Here we provide some specifics concerning their application to the work context.

Conduct a Needs Analysis

In the case of work-related programs, it is essential for curriculum designers to investigate the specific skills required by the workplace or that occupation learners are training for. "Task analyses are generally used in curriculum development as educators observe and record their observations of the discrete steps included in workplace tasks such as setting up the salad bar for a cafeteria or making change for a customer at the cash register" (Burt & Saccomano, 1995 p. 2). Often workplace literacy providers are asked to solve a specific workplace problem, but when a thorough needs analysis is conducted they find that there is a mismatch between the perceptions of the causes of the problem and the actual causes. The misperceptions can be on the part of management, but also the instructor may have misperceptions if workers are not consulted along with management. We relate an example below (p. 141).

Develop a Curriculum

The curriculum should be based on the tasks and skills learners need to be successful in their workplace or chosen occupation. Situations should be work-related, such as, *asking a supervisor or manager for sick leave, polite requests for help from a co-worker, serving a customer.* Furthermore, they should be as job-specific as possible. So, for example, in a course for flight attendants on an international airline, *serving a customer* should cover the range of *requests made by passengers and other crew.* In a course for nurses, *polite requests for help from a co-worker* should cover *asking doctors, office staff, janitors, and other nurses for help.* Stakeholders such as management and unions need to be consulted and participate in the curriculum development process.

Plan Instruction

As far as possible, actual workplace realia should be used, such as *job application forms, occupational and health signs, reporting documents, vacation application forms, manuals, safety procedures*. In the vignette above, Marta went to great lengths to develop realia for the different work functions of the learners in her class.

Plan Strategies and Activities

Strategies and activities should build on what learners already know, and teachers need to explicitly inform learners of the value of the particular activities. For example, some learners with minimal or no literacy in their home language or English may feel that the jobs they can take do not require literacy. However, almost all positions in the 21st century require literacy skills. If learners are unable to read the safety signs and notices, they can be in danger. They are likely to be severely disadvantaged if they are unable to complete forms.

Evaluate the Program

The program should be evaluated while being taught (**formative**) and after the course has ended (**summative**) (see Chapters 12 and 14, this volume). Since the purpose of workplace literacy programs is to help learners be successful in their work, it is essential to include postcourse performance data in the evaluation. All stakeholders should be consulted. This can include interviews or focus groups with learners once they are at work; interviews, focus groups, or questionnaires to supervisors and managers; interviews, focus groups, or questionnaires to unions. Where possible, actual workplace observation can provide rich data on how the program has helped learners be more successful.

Workforce Preparation Programs

Workforce preparation occurs primarily in BANA countries and refers to programs to help learners be successful in the workplace by teaching specific vocational skills, or employability skills that are offered through colleges or community-based organizations. While these programs could have been included in Chapter 7, this volume, because they service immigrants and refugees, we include them here because they are strongly tied to workforce language and nonlanguage skills development. Spruck Wrigley et al. (2003, p. 1) argue that "few programs focus on providing the nexus of language, cultural, and specific job skills that are key to helping low-income adults with limited English skills increase their wages and economic status—and to helping our nation's economy grow." The focus for best practice programs therefore shifts from getting any job to developing potential for building a career. We provide principles and examples of programs that endeavor to provide such a focus.

Vocational Programs

Vocational programs involve teaching the necessary skills for specific jobs. These programs are often conducted in technical and further education institutions, and may include communication skills. However, they do not necessarily include second language instruction. There are innovative programs that do include such language instruction, usually taught by an ESL professional, in collaboration with a vocational instructor who teaches the work-related content and skills, which is similar to the adjunct content-based instruction model. We provide a detailed example in order to help readers get a flavor of the types of programs offered in BANA countries. One course we studied involved an IT course that led to an initial certificate in IT and a language course that also had a certificate outcome for learners (Murray, 2006). The IT course included software, hardware, and communication in the workplace and took place over 18 weeks of full-time study. The language component was two 10-week modules each consisting of one week with 20 hours of instruction (at the beginning of each module), two hours per week for six weeks, then five hours per week for the remaining three weeks. The language teacher attended the IT classes and used those as a spring-board for identifying language content. In one class we observed, the language teacher used a call center dialog for listening comprehension so that learners could practise the technical vocabulary and also telephone skills. She had them listen not just for content, but also for affective factors such as politeness. She also reviewed the IT class they had had that morning, having them summarize what they had learned, and scaffolding their knowledge and language to express that knowledge.

Within the vocational sector, certification often requires assessment of communication skills, but this is not focused on the second language population, but on native speakers. Both Australian and Canadian vocational systems provide detailed competencies for different vocational skills nationally. For example, the Canadian Centre for Language Benchmarks suggests that oral communication skills for assemblers and inspectors in electrical appliance, apparatus and equipment manufacturing include:

1. listening to announcements made by the lead hand, foreperson or operations manager to receive information,
2. interacting with their lead hand or supervisor to receive parts lists, discuss quality, problems and advise them when they are leaving their workstation,
3. interacting with suppliers to obtain information on the availability of parts or to explain rejection reports,
4. communicating with co-workers during the course of the shift to exchange information and troubleshoot assembly problems,
5. communicating with employees at all levels of the company during production meetings to discuss work processes and quality problems, and
6. presenting proposed solutions to problems and suggestions for improving work processes to lead hands or supervisors (Centre for Canadian Language Benchmarks, 2006).

In Australia, the training package for office-based positions in the tourism industry identifies the following communication skills:

• communicating with colleagues, supervisors and suppliers or agents to assist with the coordination of customer's tourism experience,
• interpreting verbal and written information on tourism product conditions and customer requirements, and
• providing clear and accurate verbal and written information to customers and

suppliers or agents in a culturally appropriate manner to ensure a positive tourism experience (National Training Information Service, 2008).

Within the vocational sector successful programs often include workplace placements. For example, in one of our research projects, learners were taking a course in English for the Health Care Services, which included a work experience placement. Most learners had chosen aged care, largely because it is a burgeoning industry and jobs are plentiful. Others saw it and the course as a step towards gaining nursing qualifications.

Some providers of vocational programs collaborate with local employers on curriculum development. These employers may donate equipment to the provider, release staff to provide training, and have student groups visit their workplaces. Some also provide work experience or jobs (McKay, 2007).

Professional Qualifications

Many immigrants bring with them high skills or qualifications from their own country, but find it difficult to have those qualifications validated in their new country. This can be because of their English proficiency or the bureaucratic barriers to endorsement of their overseas certification. Therefore many need to take classes to pass qualifying exams for their profession. Such courses are very specific. Sometimes professionals have to take a job in the same general field, but not at the professional level for which they trained. For example, in one of our research projects, a Sudanese woman, who had a nursing diploma from Sudan, was extremely frustrated because after five years in Australia she was still assessed as not having sufficient written English to pass the nursing courses. Instead, she was working in aged care, where she had been highly praised by her employers, while taking English for the Health Care Services to try to both improve her English and acquire the language specific to healthcare.

One program in Canada trains internationally trained accountants. The program includes English language skills, adapting and improving their accounting skills to meet Canadian standards, training for the Certified Management Accountant (CMA) entrance exam, a requirement for practising in Canada. This program is a collaboration between a community college and the CMA organization in Alberta (E&I Calgary Region Employment, 2009).

Employability Skills

In response to perceived literacy and numeracy difficulties among workers, and concerns about not being competitive in the global marketplace, many countries have sought to define what their workers need to be successfully employed. In addition to English, a number of other skills have been identified. These go by a variety of names, such as job-readiness, generic skills, soft skills, and include a variety of competencies regarded as key by employers. The Canadian Office of Literacy and Essential Skills lists reading, document use, numeracy, writing, oral communication, working with others, thinking, computer use, and continuous learning (Office of Literacy and Essential Skills, 2007). The Australian Chamber of Commerce and Industry and Business Council of Australia (ACCI/BCA) list communication skills, teamwork skills, problem-solving skills, initiative and enterprise skills, planning and organizing skills, self-management skills, learning skills, technology skills, and personal attributes (Australian Chamber of Commerce and Industry and Business Council of Australia, 2002). In the U.S., the federal government contracted business and education leaders to form the SCANS Commission (Secretary [of Labor]'s Commission on Achieving Necessary Skills). Their report (U.S. Department of Labor, 1991) listed five workplace competencies and three foundation skills as essential for workplace performance by all workers, whether second language learners or native-English speakers. The competencies are resource management, information management, social interaction, systems behavior and performance skills, and technology utilization. The underlying foundational skills are basic skills, higher order intellectual skills, and motivational or character traits. In the U.K., the skills were divided into key skills and wider key skills. The key skills are effective communication, application of numbers, and use of information technology. The wider key skills are working with others, improving own learning and performance, and problem-solving (Leitch, 2006).

Although worded differently, there is considerable overlap among the lists. Only the Australian and U.S. lists include personal traits such as motivation and honesty. The ACCI/BCA personal attributes are: ability to deal with pressure, adaptability, balanced attitude to work and home, commitment, common sense, enthusiasm, honesty, loyalty, positive self-esteem, reliability, sense of humor. How one might teach such attributes is not explored and some of them are culturally biased, not measurable and therefore open to interpretation by employers. For example, not all cultures would expect loyalty to their employer or a sense of humor.

Task: Explore

Interview two to three friends who work in noneducational settings, preferably where English is used. Base your open-ended interview on the following general questions:

1. What is the role of English in this setting:

    a. between management and workers,
    b. between workers,
    c. between workers and customers, and
    d. between workers and suppliers?

2. What is the role of reading/writing, e.g., safety signs, reports, company emails, newsletters, vacation request forms, training manuals?
3. How have literacy demands in the workplace changed over the last five or more years? What language(s) are these in?
4. What skills training programs does the company provide? Where? Who pays?

Workplace Instruction

Workplace instruction usually takes place in the workplace and is closely tied to the need of the particular employer or profession. These programs occur around the world, not only in BANA countries. However, there is a subtle difference between the basis of those in the Inner Circle and those in Outer and Expanding Circles. In Inner Circle countries, programs seek to integrate immigrants into the local workforce. In other contexts, the programs prepare their workforce for global markets. In both cases, workers themselves are interested in gaining skills for future advancement in the workplace (current or future). Because workplace programs are designed to meet local needs, they can include the manufacturing industries, service industries, professions, and the public sector. Learners can be in management or at the lowest levels of employment. We provide an overview of some programs around the world, then discuss the issues involved in designing and implementing workplace instruction, and conclude with commonalities among programs that have been successful. Another example of a workplace program was provided in the vignette.

Sample Programs

In Thailand, a national government-sponsored center offers programs in areas of economic need for the country. Because of the recent growth of plastic and other surgery for tourists wanting a cheaper, but safe, alternative from that available in their own country, courses include those for doctors, nurses, and dentists. Because of tourism and a large spa industry, courses include those for receptionists at health spa businesses, massage therapists, and tour guides. Some of these courses are delivered face-to-face and others online.

Also in Thailand, an extensive program was designed for staff of the national airline, Thai Airways International. Courses go from pre-intermediate through to advanced, with some general workforce courses such as English for effective communication, to those for specific jobs within the functional areas, such as technical English, aviation English, and business English. Of particular note in this program was the training of Thai Airways staff as trainers. They received extensive training in teaching methodology, and in language teaching methodology in particular.[2]

In the U.S., Horvath (1998) documents a program she developed for employees at an ice-cream additive producer company, who worked as forklift operators, machine operators on the production line, packers, quality controllers, and custodians. She found that these learners responded positively to repetition, a form of learning they had practised many times in developing the hard skills of their respective jobs. One worker without literacy skills had memorized the 6-digit stock number of the various ingredients in the recipes so that her efforts to teach him to read the words of the ingredients were met with resistance. There was therefore a mismatch between his actual needs and the perceptions of his needs by the instructor.

The Candy Institute/Food Chicago is a consortium of food processing companies, government, and community organizations. They have provided funding for employees to take job-related ESL courses. Many of the workers had minimal schooling in their home language, but they were successful in large-scale assessments at the end of the course. Additionally, the company had a 30% increase in productivity following the training (AFL–CIO Working for America Institute, 2004).

In Hong Kong, a different type of program was developed for a specific profession. Offord-Gray and Aldred (1998) describe the principles they used in designing a written business communications course for accountants, either practising accountants or those who had accounting qualifications but were not in the workforce. Earlier research (Forey & Nunan, 2002) had shown that junior accountants were not necessarily familiar with the types of texts required in the workplace. The principles they developed based on extensive linguistic analysis were:

1. Teaching and learning materials:

    a. should reflect the needs as perceived by the discourse community,
    b. need to be based on knowledge of what is regarded as effective written communication in the discourse community (p. 82), and
    c. need to reflect the communicative purposes for which the discourse community produces written texts (p. 80).

2. The forms and functions that characterize the internal linguistic structure of the texts need to be made explicit in the course materials (p. 81).
3. The course materials need to go beyond making the language explicit but provide a means by which learners can engage in a process of reconstruction (p. 82).
4. Teaching and learning materials need to engage the learners in a process of developing skills for evaluating their own writing and becoming independent learners in the workplace.
5. The methodology and content of the teaching and learning materials need to be sensitive to learners' previous learning experience (p. 83).

Issues

"[W]orkplace classes always face a double dilemma. Whose interests do they serve and who pays?" (Read & Mackay, 1984, p. 67). Consequently, several issues arise in such programs—curriculum content, instructors, scheduling and funding, and outcomes.

Curriculum Content

Although all the literature recommends a needs analysis determined through a work-task needs analysis, workers and employees may have quite different views about what they need. Employers are usually more interested in specific, work-related skills, while employees are also interested in improving their general English skills.

Table 9.1 What Employers and Employees Want

What employers want	What employees want
Language related to workplace tasks	Language related to personal lives and work
Language needed to communicate with co-workers	Language for communication with co-workers and the world outside work
Content related to the workplace	Content of general interest

Grognet (1996) (Crocker, Sherman, Dlott, & Tibbetts, 2000) lists a number of categories for inclusion in the curriculum:

- workplace communications
- following directions and instructions
- job-specific terminology
- crosscultural factors
- company organization and culture
- upgrading and training.

Instructors

One of the major concerns in ESP, whether workplace or other special content areas, is who should instruct. Usually staff with the technical knowledge do not have the language teaching skills, while the ESL teacher does not have the content area knowledge. One model is to provide professional development in teaching to the professionals, as in the Thai Airways example discussed above. Yet another is the ESL instructor who had previously acquired the content skills through work in the area. For example, one of us (Murray) worked in a center that had a policy of hiring some trained ESL teachers who had expertise in another content area, such as accounting or IT, who could develop curricula and instruct in specific workplace contexts. To be able to develop and teach tailor-made courses that match the requirements of the job or profession, instructors need skills in a range of areas:

- language
- culture and intercultural training
- andragogy
- curriculum and materials design
- assessment
- soft skills training
- business consulting.

Scheduling and Funding

Funding is an issue for both employers and employees. Conducting a needs analysis and evaluating a program as we have suggested is expensive and many employers, with little background in education, fail to see the value in using extensive data. They are mostly more used to training programs that show immediate benefit in the workplace, for example, teaching keyboarding skills or use of a specific machine, and that require little in the way of needs analysis or evaluation. They are especially unfamiliar with how long it takes to acquire language. However, many successful programs have been developed with joint funding from companies, unions, and government.

As well as being conscious of funding issues, developers need to ensure that class scheduling meets both learner and employer needs. While some employers are willing to allow classes during work time, many will only provide space. As we demonstrated in the vignette above, sometimes even the space is limited in its use for instruction. Meanwhile, workers have demands on their time outside of work, such as family responsibilities. Therefore scheduling requires delicate negotiating skills on the part of the course developer.

Outcomes

Just as there is tension between different stakeholders in designing the curriculum, there is tension in terms of evaluating outcomes. Management might consider the learner gains insufficient for the resources they provided, while learners and instructors feel they have made enormous progress. One of the difficulties is measuring the outcomes in the evaluation process. The number of workplace accidents can be measured and, if they have declined, can be attributed to workers having developed the literacy skills to read the safety notices and so on. However, many of the other workplace essential skills such as motivation, attitude, or critical thinking are much harder to measure. Indeed, workers may acquire sufficient skills and self-confidence to leave low-paying positions and seek higher-paying ones. This is a measure of success for learner and program, but not for the previous employer.

Factors for Successful Programs

Research on workplace programs has found that they need to consider not only the vocational and language needs of the learners, but also the wider social and economic context. Peirce, Harper, and Burnaby (1993), for example, found that workers dropped out of a workplace program in Levi Strauss because of supervisor resistance, fears about performance and income on the part of the workers, domestic and social pressures on the workers. Others have recommended greater participation in course development by both employees and employers, and classes held during the working day, with at least partial funding by the employer (Valeo, 1998). A U.K. study found that the key factors for successful programs were commitment and involvement by all levels of management, along with union involvement.

Conclusion

In this chapter, we have discussed both workforce preparation programs and workplace programs, situating both in the field of adult learning and teaching (andragogy). The variety of programs available is extremely broad, but some basic principles of program design and instructor/developer skills are common across the sector. These programs occur across all regions of the world as English is being used as the language of international communication.

Task: Expand

AFL-CIO Working for America Institute. (2004). *Getting to work: A report on how workers with limited English skills can prepare for good jobs*. Washington, D.C.: AFL-CIO Working for America Institute.

This report provides a variety of examples of both workforce preparation and workplace programs in the U.S., many organized through and funded by companies, unions, and government working together.

Canadian Labour and Business Centre. (2004). *Towards understanding business, labour and sector council needs and challenges related to enhanced language training.* Ottawa: Canadian Labour and Business Centre.

This report provides an excellent overview of workplace literacy programs in Canada.

http://www.cal.org

This is the website for the Center for Applied Linguistics in the U.S. This center engages in research on adult learners of English and houses the Center for Adult English Language Acquisition (CAELA), a rich resource for materials on workplace literacy.

Questions for Discussion

1. How does workplace literacy differ from literacy for personal needs? Think of examples of literacy use in your own workplace. Compare your list with a colleague's.
2. Training programs in BANA countries often include communication skills. Why do these not include skills for those with limited English proficiency? How do their needs differ from those of native speakers?
3. How do you think workplace programs in BANA countries might differ from those in the Outer and Expanding Circles? Why?
4. What are the essential skills for developers of workplace literacy programs? Share your ideas with a colleague.

Notes

1. Customers pick up items to buy, change their minds, and discard the items anywhere throughout the store. It is almost a full-time job to retrieve items and return them to their correct place.
2. Personal communication with Assistant Professor Permsuk Wisnuwong, Founder of Language and Culture Institute, Thai Airways International.

References

AFL-CIO Working for America Institute. (2004). *Getting to work: A report on how workers with limited English skills can prepare for good jobs.* Washington, D.C.: AFL-CIO Working for America Institute.

Australian Chamber of Commerce and Industry and Business Council of Australia. (2002). *Employability skills.* Canberra: Department of Education, Science and Training.

Burnley, I. H., Murphy, P., & Fagan, R. (1997). *Immigration and Australian cities.* Sydney: Federation Press.

Burt, M., & Mathews-Ayndinli, J. (2007). *Workplace instruction and workforce preparation for adult immigrants.* Washington, D.C.: Center for Applied Linguistics.

Burt, M., & Saccomano, M. (1995). *Evaluating workplace ESL instructional programs.* Washington, D.C.: Center for Adult English Language Acquisition.

Centre for Canadian Language Benchmarks. (2006). *On the job: Essential skills of oral communication.* Retrieved from http://www.nald.ca/library/learning/cclb/oral/oral.pdf

Chiswick, B. R., Lee, Y., & Miller, P. W. (2003). Schooling, literacy, numeracy and labour market success. *The Economic Record, 79*(245), 165–181.

Cunningham Florez, M. (1998). *Concepts and terms in adult ESL* [electronic version]. Retrieved from http://www.cal.org/caela/esl_resources/digests/termsQA.html

E&I Calgary Region Employment. (2009). *Immigrant training and employment programs and services.* Retrieved from http://employment.alberta.ca/documents/RRM/RRM-CG_etcs_immigrant.pdf

Fleming, D. (2009). The sea we swim in: Literacy, ESL and Canadian nation-building. *Literacies, 10,* 34–40.

Forey, G., & Nunan, D. (2002). The role of language and culture in the workplace. In C. Barron, N. Bruce, & D. Nunan (Eds.), *Knowledge and discourse: Towards an ecology of language* (pp. 204–220). Harlow: Longman.

Greenberg, E., Macias, R. F., Rhodes, D., & Chan, T. (2001). *English literacy and language minorities in the United States (Statistical Analysis Report No. NCES 2001464).* Retrieved from http://nces.ed.gov/pubsearch/pubsinto.asp?pubid=2001464

Grognet, A. G. (1996). *Planning, implementing and evaluating workplace ESL programs.* Washington, DC: Center for Applied Linguistics, Project in Adult Immigrant Education.

Horvath, I. (1998). Employee skills and attitudes utilized in workplace ESL training. *The Internet TESL Journal, 4*(9).

Johns, A. (1992). What is the relationship between content-based instruction and English for specific purposes? *The CATESOL Journal, 5*(1), 71–75.

Knowles, M. (1990). *The adult learner: A neglected species.* Houston: Gulf Publishing.

Leitch, S. (2006). *The Leitch review of skills: Prosperity for all in the global economy – world class skills.* Norwich: HMSO.

Lockwood, J. (2007). An interdisciplinary approach to teaching adults English in the workplace. In J. Cummins & C. Davison (Eds.), *International handbook on English language teaching* (pp. 403–420). New York: Springer.

Master, P. (1997). ESP teacher education in the U.S.A. In R. Howard & G. Brown (Eds.), *Teacher education for LSP* (pp. 22–40). Clevedon, U.K.: Multilingual Matters.

McKay, A. (2007). *An investigation of strategies and programs that assist refugees and migrants into employment. A report to the Winston Churchill Trust of Australia.* Unpublished manuscript.

McKay, S. L. (1993). *Agendas for second language literacy.* Cambridge: Cambridge University Press.

Moser, S. C. (1999). *A fresh start: Improving literacy and numeracy.* London: DfEE.

Murray, D. E. (2006). *Developing vocationally specific content for the CSWE.* Paper presented at the AMEP National Conference, Perth, Australia.

National Institute of Literacy. (2000). *Equipped for the future content standards: What adults need to know and be able to do in the 21st century.* Washington, D.C.: Author.

National Training Information Service. (2008). *Tourism, hospitality and events training package.* Retrieved from http://www.ntis.gov.au/Default.aspx?/trainingpackage/SIT07/qualification/SIT10307/rules

Office of Literacy and Essential Skills. (2007). *Workplace skills: Essential skills* [electronic version]. Retrieved from http://www.nald.ca/fulltext/sticht/31jan05/31jan05.pdf

Offord-Gray, C., & Aldred, D. (1998). A principled approach to ESP course design. *Hong Kong Journal of Applied Linguistics, 3*(1), 77–86.

Peirce, B. N., Harper, H., & Burnaby, B. (1993). Workplace ESL at Levi Strauss: "Dropouts" speak out. *TESL Canada Journal, 10*(2), 9–30.

Read, C., & Mackay, R. (1984). *Illiteracy among adult immigrants in Canada.* Educational Resource Information Center: Number 291 875.

Spruck Wrigley, H., Richer, E., Martinson, K., Kubo, H., & Strawn, J. (2003). *The language of opportunity: Expanding employment prospects for adults with limited English skills.* Washington, D.C.: Center for Law and Social Policy.

U.S. Department of Labor. (1991). *What work requires of schools: A SCANS report for America 2000.* Washington, D.C.: U.S. Department of Labor. (ERIC No. ED 332 054).

Valeo, A. (1998). A case study of employee participation in a workplace ESL program. *TESL Canada Journal, 16*(1), 75–87.

Warner, J. R., & Vorhaus, J. (2008). *The learner study: The impact of the skills for life strategy on adult literacy, language and numeracy learners.* London: National Research and Development Centre for Adult Literacy and Numeracy.

Workbase. (n.d.). *An economic imperative: How to maintain competitiveness in a rapidly changing world?* Retrieved from http://www.workbase.org.nz/Resource.aspx?ID=214

Chapter 10

Integrating Language and Content

VIGNETTE

For the past year I have been working on a collaborative project with my own university in the United States and a private university for science and technology in the Middle East. The university I am working with indicates on their website that they offer the courses in the various disciplines in English. The faculty members come from backgrounds in architecture, chemistry, engineering, computer science, mathematics, dentistry, and pharmacy. There is no faculty or department of education or English language, and the individual faculty members have had no formal training in teaching. In addition, most of the faculty members and their students are native speakers of Arabic.

I have been working with about 23 faculty members from five different faculties. Twenty-two of the 23 professors are native speakers of Arabic with varying levels of English language proficiency. All of them have advanced degrees and most have PhDs; some of them were educated in the Middle East, but the majority of the professors have had educational experiences as graduate students in the U.S., Europe, and the U.K. The professors have completed a 38-hour course with me on effective teaching, and I am now visiting classes and following up with individual coaching sessions. The professors are enthusiastic about their teaching, and I am learning so much about the challenges these professors face as they teach their content area subjects in English to university level L1 speakers of Arabic with varying levels of proficiency. [Research notes. Christison 10/16/09].

Task: Reflect

The writer of the vignette above indicated that she was learning so much about the challenges that the professors faced as they attempted to integrate language and content in their classrooms. Work with a partner or in a small group of three. Generate at least three responses to each of the following questions:

• What challenges do you think the university faces in providing a curriculum in English in this context?

- What challenges do you think the individual faculty members face in providing a curriculum in English in their classes?
- What challenges might the learners in these classes face?

Introduction

In this section, we have talked about instructing for learning with five specific groups of learners—young learners (Chapter 5), adolescent learners (Chapter 6), immigrant and refugee adult learners (Chapter 7), postsecondary adults (Chapter 8), and adult learners in workplace environments (Chapter 9). Unlike the previous five chapters in this section, this chapter is not structured around one specific population of learners but instead is structured around learners in each of the groups. Programs that integrate language and content have been used with all types of learners in many different contexts.

We begin this chapter by describing different types of learners and different contexts where the learning of content and language takes place. We also introduce some types of programs that have been successful in these contexts. Finally, we discuss features of a teaching model for the integration of content and language, including the teacher variable.

There is an extensive body of research from diverse fields that supports either directly or indirectly the integration of language and content (Grabe & Stoller, 1997; see also Chapters 1 and 3, this volume). These research fields include second language acquisition research (Krashen, 1985; Swain, 1993; Lantolf, 1994; Cummins, 1992), cooperative learning (Slavin, 1995), learning strategy instruction (Marzano, Pickering, & Pollock, 2001), and extensive exposure to written text (Krashen, 2004; Walmsley, 1994). In addition, there are studies related to program outcomes that provide additional support (Christian, 1995; Echevarria, Vogt, & Short, 2008).

Characteristics of Learners and Contexts

Contexts for Young and Adolescent Learners

As discussed in Chapter 5 in this volume, context mediates how both teachers and programs determine what content to teach and how to integrate language and content. In BANA (Britain, Australasia, and North America) countries, the context for most young and adolescent language learners is in public schools; consequently, the content is generally determined by a core curriculum. Private schools for young learners in these same countries are also responsible for teaching a core curriculum. In these contexts the integration of language and content is not a curricular choice made by the teacher, program, or school, but a requirement external to the program or school. Regardless of language background, all learners must demonstrate competencies in the same core content curriculum.

In some Outer and Expanding Circle countries, young and adolescent learners are generally in one of two contexts. In some countries, the ministries of education mandate English instruction in primary grades. However, the English instruction is often not tied to a core content curriculum. Instead the English language instruction typically focuses on English itself—teaching the four skills, developing general

English vocabulary, and learning about language structure in English. Although this is slowly changing, it is still the predominant situation as we see it. As previously mentioned in Chapter 5, private English language teaching centers are starting programs for young and adolescent learners, and a number of programs have decided to use an integrated language and content approach (see CLIL reference in Chapter 3); however, the decision in private language centers has been motivated by a curricular choice rather than a mandated requirement. However, as the influence of English as a global language is strengthened, some governments, such as Malaysia, require that some K–12 subjects be taught in English. In order to be competitive, private language centers must also comply.

Contexts for Adult Learners

Immigrants and Refugees

Context mediates the selection of content in programs for adult immigrants and refugees. In Chapter 7 on immigrants and refugee adult learners, we noted that in BANA and Inner Circle countries in the context of adult education, the content of language instruction is often tied to life skills (e.g., content related to health issues or the schooling of their children) and the skills required for getting a job. In BANA countries, government funding is available for immigrants and refugees for a limited amount of time; consequently, English language programs for adult immigrants and refugees must focus on language that helps them to function in society as quickly as possible and get a job within the time frame established by the sponsoring country. The selection of content is not mandated in the same way as it is in public school but neither is it a curricular choice governed by teachers or programs.

Postsecondary Learners

In Chapter 8 we learned about adults who are interested in pursuing postsecondary education in Inner Circle countries. These learners are principally adults who move to another country specifically for postsecondary education, but they may also be immigrants or refugees or children of immigrants or refugees. In order to improve their academic English skills, many of them attend English language teaching programs (see Chapter 8 in this volume for a description of these types of programs) for short periods of time. Most of these programs are associated with institutions of higher education (both privately owned and operated, and university owned and operated), although there are some privately owned English language teaching programs that also serve this purpose. These programs have a great deal of autonomy when it comes to selecting content. Many English language programs that target this population are quite traditional in their approach to language teaching with a focus on developing the four skills and improving knowledge of English structure. Other programs offer specific content-based courses, such as English for business or engineering, that focus on developing English language skills while learning content specific to a discipline. The choice is determined by the program and sometimes even by the instructor.

With the spread of English as an international language and its importance in the fields of science and technology for the dissemination of research, as well as the abundance of published materials in English available for instructional purposes, more universities worldwide are moving towards offering discipline-specific courses in English to their young adult learners. Many international universities are finding themselves in the position of the university in the vignette above, asking professors to teach courses in English rather than their mother tongue. The argument supporting this curricular change is directed towards preparing graduates for future jobs that will almost certainly involve an international clientele. The change is not without consequences for all stakeholders. For example, not all young adult learners in these classes may have the requisite skills to understand lectures in English. In addition, the professors may not have the requisite academic English language skills that would allow them to move comfortably towards delivering all of the instruction in English; therefore, the quality of instruction may suffer. Universities opting to take this risk may be placing the quality of their overall curriculum in a precarious position, at least for a short time. Others believe that the move away from native language instruction diminishes the importance of mother tongue languages and makes a statement that reflects negatively on national character and the status of the native language (see Chapter 2, Volume 1, on the hegemony of English).

Young Adults in Secondary Schools

In a number of countries in Europe (for example, The Netherlands), secondary school students can choose to study a second language in content language integrated learning (CLIL) programs (see discussion below). Students in these programs receive subject matter courses, such as history, geography, and math, in the second language. Other subjects are taught in the native language. Young adult learners in these programs either select the programs by personal choice or qualify for the program based on exams and are then able to select the program by personal choice.

Workplace Learners

Learners in workplace ESL/EFL programs are focused on learning the language they need to do and keep their jobs. Some companies provide workplace programs for both entry-level and mid-management positions depending on the company, so learner profiles vary greatly from young single adult learners to older learners who are married and have children. Because workplace ESL/EFL programs are focused on the specific needs of the workplace, they begin with a needs analysis to determine the context-specific vocabulary and language needed to do the job, such as effective language use with other employees and customers (see Chapter 9). Workplace learners have often been out of school for some time, some may have had very few classroom experiences.

Task: Explore

Work with a partner. Generate a list of possible content concepts that could be taught in two of the contexts described above.

Models and Programs for Integrating Language and Content

The integration of language and content is a concern for teachers working in many different contexts. In each context, teachers are concerned about developing models for second language instruction that are embedded in the context and make an effort to use discourse from the real world in the classroom. Many practitioners believe that a general English curriculum cannot prepare learners for the demanding linguistic, rhetorical, and contextual challenges of the real world (Johns, 1997).

There are a number of other terms used to describe the integration of language and content. Below is a list of some common terms associated with specific programs or contexts; the list is not meant to be exhaustive.

Content-Based Instruction (CBI)

We use the term content-based instruction (CBI) as an umbrella term to refer to all types of programs that make a dual commitment to content and language objectives. The term has been widely used to describe programs for both adults and children, as well as programs for different groups of learners in Inner, Outer, and Expanding Circle countries (Crandall, 1993; Stoller, 2004). The term applies to programs taught by both content-area specialists who are not language teachers and language teachers who are acquiring content-area expertise, and has been used in different contexts for over 40 years (Cantoni-Harvey, 1987; Grabe & Stoller, 1997; Christison & Bassano, 1992, 1997; Bassano & Christison, 1992) to refer to the integration of language and content. In addition, it is not associated with any particular "designer" or researcher. Although we will use the term CBI in this chapter, in the sense described above, we also recognize that not all researchers and authors have used CBI in this way.

Content and Language Integrated Learning (CLIL)

Content and language integrated learning (CLIL) is a recent movement for integrating language and content. It is a term commonly used in Europe and the U.K. (see the example of Germany discussed in Volume I, Chapter 3). In general, it involves learning in a curricular subject through the medium of a nonnative language, such as studying history or geography in English in Spain or France. The European Commission (www.ec.europa.eu/education/language-teaching/doc236_en.htm) states that CLIL has been found to be effective in all sectors of education from primary through to adult and higher education. This finding is not surprising and mirrors results for content and language integration elsewhere. Teachers working with CLIL are specialists in their own discipline who are proficient speakers of the target language (in this case, English).

Workplace Literacy

A number of different acronyms have been used to describe programs that integrate language and content in the workplace environments (see Chapter 9, this volume).

In the U.S. the term VESL (vocational English as a second language) has been used (Wong, 1997). Australians employ the term English for the workplace (EWP).

English for Specific Purposes (ESP)

English for specific purposes (ESP) is a term that has been widely used for the past three decades in international contexts to describe courses for adults who have needs that are immediate and identifiable, such as writing or reading in university discipline-specific contexts or workplace contexts. ESP specialists work closely with experts in different disciplines to make certain that they know what learners will be required to do and how to design activities to assist learners in interacting with content in context-appropriate ways. Language becomes "a vehicle for communication" and not just a "linguistic object" (Johns & Davies, 1983) that learners use in isolation. In ESL settings, EAP (English for academic purposes) is the term often used in place of ESP (see Chapter 9 for a discussion about ESP contexts).

Sheltered Instruction

In U.S. public school settings the term sheltered instruction (also known as structured immersion, SDAIE [specially designed academic instruction in English], CELT [content-based English language teaching], and mainstreaming[1]) has been used to describe instructional models that attempt to integrate language and content in content-area classrooms that must address the content and language learning needs of both first and second language (L2) speakers (Echevarria & Graves, 2007). The primary goal of sheltered instruction is to make grade-level academic subject matter comprehensible for all learners.

One of the most widely used models for sheltered instruction is SIOP (sheltered instructional observation protocol) that identifies 30 teacher indicators associated with positive outcomes for learners (Echevarria, Short, & Powers, 2006; Echevarria, et al., 2008). It is divided into eight components—lesson preparation, building background, comprehensible input, strategies, interaction, practice/application, lesson delivery, and review/assessment. It is currently being used in all 50 states in the United States and in several countries. Although originally designed as a protocol for classroom observation (Guarino, Echevarria, Short, Schick, Forbes, & Rueda, 2001), teachers now use SIOP in planning instruction and in lesson delivery (see www.siopinstitute.net).

The Cognitive Academic Language Learning Approach (CALLA) was developed as a sheltered instructional model to meet the academic needs of K–12 learners in U.S. public schools (Chamot & O'Malley, 1994). The CALLA model includes three components—topics from the major content subjects, the development of academic language skills, and explicit instruction in learning strategies for both content and language acquisition.

Options for the Delivery of Instruction

Given the ever-increasing numbers of English language learners worldwide, it is reasonable to assume that in some contexts, such as in public schools, L2 language specialists alone cannot meet the needs for content and language for all learners in all content areas. Relative to the teacher variable, there are three approaches that can be considered in order to effectively integrate language and content.

The L2 Specialist

In the first approach, the L2 specialist teaches the CBI courses. The advantage of this approach is that the L2 specialist already has expertise in how to teach language and is already sensitive to the language needs of the learners. The disadvantage is that the L2 specialist may have no background in the content area. Developing expertise at the level needed for secondary and university education in content areas may not be realistic unless the language teacher has previously developed expertise in a content area.

Content Specialist

In the second approach, the content-area specialist teaches the CBI course (such as in the CLIL model). The obvious advantage of this approach is that the course is taught by someone with content-area expertise. The disadvantage is that the content-area specialist may know very little about second language acquisition and may not have developed teacher language awareness (see Volume I, Part 2), making it difficult for the instructor to know how to provide the necessary modifications in instruction to make content and language comprehensible for L2 learners. Proficiency in the target language does not guarantee that instructors have teacher language awareness. Learning a second or foreign language is a complex endeavor affected by a variety of factors.

Collaborative Effort

The third approach involves both content and second language specialists in a collaborative effort. Some programs have had success with this type of approach (Gee, 1997; Johns & Dudley Evans, 1991). This type of collaboration seems to be both desirable and necessary; yet, despite the instructional desirability of such an approach, there are often reasons why it is not implemented. For example, programs often lack the financial resources or flexibility in personnel to assign two instructors or professors to cover one course.

Task: Explore

Select one of the contexts identified above under the chapter heading "Characteristics of learners and contexts." What advice would you give to content and language specialists about collaborating in this context to create a course that included L2 learners? Be specific. Share your suggestions with another group.

Instructing for Learning

Although many English language teaching programs in many different contexts promote the integration of language and content, there is no single methodology supported by the field. The focus for all of the programs is making content and language comprehensible for language learners. It is beyond the scope of this short chapter to list all of the techniques that teachers might use to make this happen. Instead, we have identified six characteristics that are common to most contexts and models of instruction. We review these features below because they seem to represent the beginnings of an instructional design model for the integration of language and content.

Identifying Content Concepts

In each content area (whether it is physics or adult life skills), teachers must first be concerned about determining the content knowledge that learners must master if they are working within an integrated content and language paradigm. Planning for the integration of language and content does not begin at the level of a lesson, but rather at the level of content for a unit or course. The most important questions that teachers must answer are the following: What information should students know at the end of a course or unit? What important questions should they be able to answer? In terms of planning, this is where teachers who integrate language and content begin. We suggest creating a conceptual framework or flow chart with the content concepts at the top level, subtopics that support the content concepts at the second level, and lessons that support the subtopics at the third level (see Figure 10.1). The bi-directional arrows indicate connections that must be established between concepts, subtopics, and lessons.

When content concepts have been determined in a hierarchical manner as in Figure 10.1, the essential details associated with individual lessons can be created, thereby making the best use of instructional time and assuring that concepts are sequenced and connected accordingly (see Chapters 2 and 3, this volume).

Writing Clear Objectives

Once content concepts have been identified (in the hierarchical manner suggested in Figure 10.1) and important questions have been framed, teachers determine what learners will do in order to demonstrate their understanding of the content concepts. These understandings are written as performance objectives for content concepts because the focus is on student performance—what they will actually do to demonstrate their knowledge of the content concepts. In Chapter 3 in this volume, we discussed performance objectives and outlined the four main components that are necessary for writing effective performance objectives. We review these components in an abbreviated form here. Performance objectives include identifying: 1) what students will be able to do (e.g., the thinking skills—identify, list, categorize, tell, etc.), 2) what they are expected to learn (i.e., the content concept), 3) how they will demonstrate what they have learned (i.e., what strategies they will use), and 4) what the conditions for practice will be (e.g., grouping strategies, time allocated, type of input, or type of response). Using these four

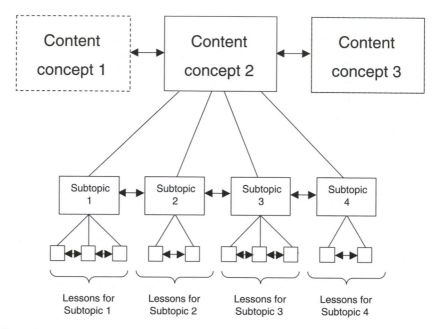

Figure 10.1 A Conceptual Framework for Identifying Content Concepts.

components in order, we arrive at the following sample content objective from a CBI history lesson.

> *LWBAT[2] explain the main causes of the U.S. Civil War by completing a search and find worksheet individually with a text in class.*

Deriving Language from Content

Most content specialists have difficulty in identifying and creating language objectives. In the planning process, language objectives cannot be determined in advance of content and then mapped onto it because the content one chooses determines the language that learners will need. Language objectives must be derived from content objectives. In our experience in working with content specialists, those who have experienced the most success in writing language objectives wrote them once content objectives had been established and appropriate texts (construed broadly here to include all types of text, including media, and not simply textbooks) had been chosen. The most important questions that teachers must answer about language are the following: What language must learners master in order to work with the content concepts in the lesson? What vocabulary, language structures, and academic function words and genres do they need?

Many teachers have found it useful to think about language concepts in two different categories—**content-obligatory language** and **content-compatible language**. Content-obligatory language is the language that must be learned in order to understand the content concepts. Content-compatible language is language that supports the students in learning the content but is not critical to understanding the content concepts.

Managing Demands of Cognition

Skutnabb-Kangas and Toukomaa (1976) first made the distinction between "surface fluency" and "conceptual-linguistic knowledge" in a second language. Cummins (1979, 1980) later formalized these terms as basic interpersonal skills (BICS) and cognitive academic language proficiency (CALP). Shuy (1981) expressed the distinction between the two types of language proficiency using the iceberg metaphor in which he elaborated on the linguistic distinctions between BICS and CALP with the formal aspects of language (e.g., pronunciation, grammar, and vocabulary) "visible" above the surface and functional and semantic meaning residing at deeper levels below the surface. Chamot (1981) elaborated on the cognitive aspects of this model in terms of Bloom's Taxonomy (Bloom, 1956; Bloom & Krathwohl, 1977) with the lower-order thinking skills above the surface (knowledge, comprehension, and application) and the higher-order thinking skills residing at deeper cognitive levels below the surface (analysis, synthesis, and evaluation). The metaphor is useful in elaborating on the relationship between second language acquisition and academic development. Inventories of thinking skills, such as Bloom's Taxonomy, are useful to both language and content specialists in managing demands on cognition as they select tasks and activities for the classroom (see the four components for writing objectives above). When the thinking required is more sophisticated and cognitively challenging, teachers select familiar or less complicated strategies or provide support in other ways, such as increasing the use of visuals and realia, drawing on learners' past experiences, rephrasing and repeating important concepts, and increasing the number of examples. When the language is difficult, teachers should think about initially selecting thinking skills that are cognitively less demanding.

Teaching Strategies for Learning

Strategy instruction is typical of almost all programs that integrate language and content. Learners become more skilled at monitoring their own learning when they are taught and work with specific strategies for learning. Strategies for learning have been configured in many different ways (see Volume 1, Chapter 13) in L2 teaching. Whatever strategies are selected should focus on assisting learners in working with both content and language. How teachers work with the strategies is as important as what strategies they choose. In language and content integrated classrooms, strategy instruction proceeds in the following manner.

Modeling

Teachers identify the strategy, model how to use it, and explain when to use it. Last, but not least, teachers explain why to use it and how using the strategy will help learners.

Gradual Release Practice

In this practice model, teachers promote interaction among students and gradually release control of learning to the students (see the Graduate Release Learning Model in Chapter 3). Teachers provide guided practice until learners are able to demonstrate they can use the strategy alone or with a peer.

Independent Practice

Teachers create opportunities for students to practice the learning strategies without assistance from the teacher or peers. The anticipated outcome is that the learning strategies practised in this way will eventually become automatic skills.

Checking for Understanding

Checking for understanding of content and language must be an important part of every lesson (see Chapter 12, this volume) and is a defining feature of successful models for integrating language and content.

It has been our experience in working with both content and language specialists that identifying content concepts, writing clear objectives, deriving language from content, managing demands on cognition, teaching strategies for learning, and checking for understanding are the defining features of second and foreign language programs for integrating language and content that promote positive outcomes for their students.

Conclusion

In this chapter we identified the characteristics of the contexts in which programs that integrate language and content function, as well as the types of learners these programs serve—young and adolescent learners and adults (immigrants and refugees, postsecondary learners, young adults in secondary schools, and workplace learners). We also reviewed the most prominent models or programs for integrating language and content, such as CBI, CLIL, VESL, ESP, and sheltered instruction to include SIOP and CALLA, and reviewed the options for the delivery of instruction in such models. We then offered our own views on the features of instructional design that affect instruction, including identifying content concepts, writing objectives, managing demands on cognition, and promoting interaction.

Task: Expand

Explore at least one of the following websites and find an activity or a suggestion not covered in this chapter to share with a partner or a small group.

www.ec.europa.eu/education/languages
www.teachingenglish.org.uk
www.clil.copendium.com
www.onestopenglish.com/section.asp?docid=144587
www.tesol.org

www.everythingesl.net/inservices/internet_resources.php
www.siopinstitute.net
www.cal.org/siop/

Questions for Discussion

1. Use Figure 10.1 to help you create a conceptual framework for a unit you teach or might wish to teach in the future.
2. Identify a lesson in your conceptual framework on which to focus. What content-obligatory language would you need to teach?
3. Work independently or with a partner; write a content objective for a lesson in your conceptual model. Then, think of what language students would need to work with the content. Write a language objective. Share your objectives with another person or group.
4. What strategy or strategies would you use to teach the content?

Notes

1. We use the term mainstreaming here to refer to placing L2 students in classrooms designed for L1 speakers of English. In other contexts mainstreaming is a term used only in connection with special education students.
2. LWBAT = learners will be able to

References

Bassano, S. K., & Christison, M. A. (1992). *Life sciences: Content and learning strategies*. White Plains, NY: Longman Publishers.

Bloom, B. S. (1956). *Taxonomy of educational objectives, Handbook I: The cognitive domain*. New York: David McKay Co Inc.

Bloom, B., & Krathwohl, D. (1977). *Taxonomy of educational objectives: Handbook I: Cognitive domain*. White Plains, NY: Longman.

Cantoni-Harvey, G. (Ed.). (1987). *Content area instruction: Approaches and strategies*. Reading, MA: Addison-Wesley Publishing Company.

Chamot, A. U. (1981). *Applications of second language acquisition research to the bilingual classroom*. Washington, D.C.: National Clearinghouse for Bilingual Education.

Chamot, A. U., & O'Malley, J. M. (1994). *The CALLA Handbook: Implementing the Cognitive Academic Language Learning Approach*. Reading, MA: Addison-Wesley Publishing Company.

Christian, D. (Ed.). (1995). *Directory of two-way bilingual programs in the United States*. Washington, D.C.: Center for Applied Linguistics.

Christison, M. A., & Bassano, S. K. (1997). *Social studies: Content and learning strategies*. White Plains, NY: Longman Publishers.

Christison, M. A., & Bassano, S. K. (1992). *Earth and physical sciences: Content and learning strategies*. White Plains, NY: Longman Publishers.

Crandall, J. (1993). Content-centered learning in the United States. *Annual Review of Applied Linguistics, 13*, 111–126.

Cummins, J. (1979). Cognitive academic language proficiency, linguistic interdependence, the optimum age question and some other matters. *Working Papers on Bilingualism, 19*, 121–129.

Cummins, J. (1980). The exit and entry fallacy of bilingual education. *NABE Journal, 4*, 25–29.

Cummins, J. (1992). Language proficiency, bilingualism, and academic achievement. In

P. Richard-Amato, & M. A. Snow (Eds.). *The multicultural classroom: Readings for content-area teachers* (pp. 16–26). New York: Longman Publishers.

Echevarria, J., & Graves, A. (2007). *Sheltered content instruction*. New York: Pearson Education.

Echevarria, J., Short, D., & Powers, K. (2006). School reform and standards-based education: An instructional model for English-language learners. *Journal of Educational Research, 99*, 195–210.

Echevarria, J., Vogt, M. E., & Short, D. (2008). *Making content comprehensible for English language learners: The SIOP® Model* (3rd ed.). New York: Pearson Education, Inc.

Gee, Y. (1997). ESL and content teachers: Working effectively in adjunct courses. In M. A. Snow, & D. M. Brinton (Eds.), *The content-based classroom: Perspectives on integrating language and content* (pp. 324–330). White Plains, NY: Addison-Wesley Longman Publishers.

Grabe, W., & Stoller, F. L. (1997). Content-based instruction: Research foundations. In M. A. Snow, & D. Brinton (Eds.), *The content-based classroom* (pp. 5–21). White Plains, NY: Longman Publishers.

Guarino, A. J., Echevarria, J., Short, D., Schick, J. E., Forbes, S., & Rueda, R. (2001). The sheltered instruction observation protocol: Reliability and validity assessment. *Journal of Research in Education, 11*, 138–140.

Johns, A. M. (1997). English for specific purposes and content-based instruction: What is the relationship? In M. A. Snow, & D. M. Brinton (Eds.), *The content-based classroom: Perspectives on integrating language and content* (pp. 363–366). White Plains, NY: Addison-Wesley Longman Publishers.

Johns, A. M., & Dudley-Evans, T. (1991). English for specific purposes: International scope, specific in purpose. *TESOL Quarterly, 25*, 297–314.

Johns, T. E., & Davies, F., (1983). Text as a vehicle for communication: The classroom use of written texts in teaching reading in a foreign language. *Reading in a Foreign Language, 1*, 1–19.

Krashen, S. D. (1985). *The input hypothesis: Issues and implications*. New York: Longman Publishers.

Krashen, S. D. (2004). *The power of reading* (2nd ed.). Westport, CT: Heinemann.

Lantolf, J. (1994). Sociocultural theory and second language learning. *Modern Language Journal, 78*, 1.

Marzano, R. J., Pickering, D., & Pollock, J. (2001). *Classroom instruction that works*. Alexandria, VA: Association for Supervision and Curriculum Development.

Shuy, R. (1981). Conditions affecting language learning and maintenance among Hispanics in the United States. *NABE Journal, 6*, 1–18.

Skutnabb-Kangas, T., & Toukomaa, P. (1976). *Teaching migrant children's mother tongue and learning the language of the host country in the context of the socio-cultural situation of migrant family*. Helsinki: The Finnish National Commission for UNESCO.

Slavin, R. E. (1995). *Cooperative learning* (2nd ed.). Boston: Allyn and Bacon.

Stoller, F. L. (2004). Content-based instruction: Perspectives on curriculum planning. *Annual Review of Applied Linguistics, 24*, 261–283.

Swain, M. (1993). The output hypothesis: Just speaking and writing aren't enough. *The Canadian Modern Language Review, 50*, 158–164.

Walmsley, S. A. (1994). *Children exploring their world: Theme teaching in the elementary school*. Portsmouth, NH: Heinemann.

Wong, K. (1997). VESL and content-based instruction: What do they have in common? In M. A. Snow, & D. M. Brinton (Eds.), *The content-based classroom: Perspectives on integrating language and content* (pp. 359–362). White Plains, NY: Addison-Wesley Longman Publishers.

Chapter 11

Exploring One's Own Instruction

VIGNETTE

Cindy and I were both teaching in an intensive English program at a university in the U.S. Students in this program have already been accepted into masters and doctoral programs and are taking an English for Academic Purposes course to prepare for their study in the U.S. Cindy expressed concern that the students in her writing class "haven't asked many questions. They sort of let me do the talking." She hypothesized that it might be cultural because some of the students were from East Asia or they came from a different kind of educational system. The class of 11 included Central/South Americans, an Iranian, an Israeli, Japanese, and Chinese. She further elaborated her perceptions, "They sort of expect you to lecture to them, evaluate how they're doing . . . rather than coming to you with questions." At her request, I observed a couple of her classes, and later met briefly with the students. We also audiotaped the lessons. On viewing the transcripts of the lesson, we found that all students did in fact instigate questions. However, they did not respond when she asked, "Do you have any questions?", which she did several times each lesson. In many cases, students actually interrupted the teacher to pose a question, usually for clarification as in the following where she had been explaining the conventions for writing abstracts:

Cindy: *. . . (several utterances) I would encourage you to try to stick to the one-page limit, one typewritten page of course, not handwritten and that wouldn't necessarily*

Student: *. . . that's for papers, not for dissertation?*

When I met with the students, they offered various reasons why they didn't ask questions. Some said they preferred to go to office hours and ask individually, rather than in class. Others said they were learning new things and still didn't know enough to ask questions. Still others said that in their culture they didn't ask questions like American students do, just to be competitive. They were also concerned about making errors in English or asking stupid questions. One said first you ask a classmate, then the teaching assistant, and only last the professor.

However, as our analysis of classroom interaction showed, students did ask a variety of questions. Cindy's perception was based on the several times she asked if they had questions and got no response. We analyzed those examples further and found that perhaps Cindy had not allowed sufficient time for students to think and respond. So, she then monitored her own language. One technique she tried was to leave a longer time for students to respond. [Murray research notes]

Task: Reflect

1. The students provided several reasons why they didn't ask questions. Can you think of other reasons?
2. To what extent do you think Cindy's perceptions of East Asians as "not asking questions" affected her ability to hear their actual questions?
3. How do you feel about asking questions in a classroom? What is your preferred way of getting clarification or getting answers to questions you have about the material?
4. What other techniques could Cindy try?

Introduction

In Volume I, Chapter 14, we explored the importance of lifelong professional development. One of the key activities that assists teachers in developing their professional practice is an exploration of their own classrooms. In this chapter we provide tools teachers can use to explore their beliefs and perceptions about teaching and learning, and for observing their own classrooms.

Teacher Beliefs and Perceptions

In Volume I, Chapter 4, we discussed the effect of both teacher and learner perceptions on classroom behaviors and, ultimately, on learning itself. Here we will build on that information and provide tools for teachers to explore their own beliefs and perceptions.

Investigating Teacher Beliefs

One of the most important sources of teachers' beliefs is their own experience as learners. In the absence of other information, teachers teach how they were taught and even the most experienced, reflective teacher falls back on these techniques when they are tired or stressed. When teachers think about how many hours teachers have spent as students—in K–12, then undergraduate courses, they far outnumber the number of hours of teaching practice in a teacher education program. Kennedy (1990) has in fact estimated that the former is around 3,060 days, while the latter only around 75 days. Teachers are also influenced by their own experience as teachers, by institutional practices, by research, by professional development events, and curriculum orientations. These beliefs include language and English in particular, about learning, about teaching, and about their particular learners. We provide the following teacher belief inventory for teachers to examine their own beliefs. We recommend that teachers keep their responses and take the inventory several times over the course of their career. It is instructive to take the inventory when some aspect of the context changes, such as different learners, a different class level, a different country, or a different curriculum.

Task: Explore

Complete the following inventory. On a five-point scale, say if you agree or disagree with the statement.

1 = *Strongly disagree*
2 = *Disagree*
3 = *Neutral*
4 = *Agree*
5 = *Strongly agree*

Once you have responded to the questions, for each one, think about why you hold that belief. Was it how you were taught? Have you read research about this? Have you observed this in your own teaching?

Teacher belief inventory

1. Children learn a foreign language more easily than adults.

    1   2   3   4   5

2. Some languages are easier to learn than others.

    1   2   3   4   5

3. People from my country are good at learning languages.

    1   2   3   4   5

4. Perfect pronunciation is important.

    1   2   3   4   5

5. I should always correct student errors in English.

    1   2   3   4   5

6. I should teach speaking before I teach writing.

    1   2   3   4   5

7. To learn English, students need to memorize and repeat a lot.

    1   2   3   4   5

8. To learn English, students need to speak to people in English.

    1   2   3   4   5

9. We should only use English during English lessons.

    1   2   3   4   5

10. Grammar is the most important part of English.

    1   2   3   4   5

11. It is easier to learn English if you have already learned other languages.

    1   2   3   4   5

12. Reading and writing in English are easier than listening and speaking.

    1   2   3   4   5

13. Vocabulary is the most difficult part of English to learn.

    1   2   3   4   5

14. Everyone can learn to speak a foreign language.

    1   2   3   4   5

15. English is an easy language to learn.

    1   2   3   4   5

16. Teachers should be in control of the lesson.

    1   2   3   4   5

17. We should not discuss controversial issues in class.

    1   2   3   4   5

18. Students can learn from their peers and should be forced to work in groups.

    1   2   3   4   5

19. I should be an expert and know all the answers.

    1   2   3   4   5

20. Students do not need to learn about culture in the language classroom.

    1   2   3   4   5

Teacher Perceptions

In the vignette at the beginning of this chapter, we showed the value for Cindy in examining her own perceptions and also see and analyze the actual classroom interaction. In the next sections, we discuss ways to observe and analyze one's own class. Often teachers' perceptions are affected by their beliefs and attitudes. However, because teachers make decisions based on their understandings, articulating those understandings is as important as analyzing actual classroom data. Teachers have used a number of ways of recording their understandings. In Volume 1, Chapter 14, we referred to diary studies and learning logs. A diary study is a first-person account of teaching. The teacher documents classroom experiences in a personal journal. Usually, these entries are made regularly and then analyzed for recurring patterns. However, teachers can also record experiences when they perceive a particular issue in their classroom. In Cindy's case in the vignette, instead of recording it in a personal journal, she discussed it with a trusted peer. We use the term trusted peer deliberately, because this process is quite different from peer interviews or observations conducted for evaluation purposes. The goal in this instance was for Cindy to explore her perceptions of this particular class and then see whether they matched actual classroom data and student perceptions.

A learning log is similar to a diary study, but focuses on what the teacher has learned from a professional development activity or by observing a classroom. Again, the goal is to capture teacher perceptions so they can be compared with actual classroom data. For both a journal and log, it is important to capture perceptions as soon as possible after the event.

Many teachers use a free-form to write up their entries. However, to help teachers reflect on their perceptions of what happened in a lesson we provide a list of questions to think about and guide the entries. Some of these questions refer to classroom behaviors discussed later in the chapter and so you might want to come back to this list at the end of the chapter.

Reflection questions

1. What was your objective? Did you achieve it?
2. What content did you teach? How did the learners react to the content?
3. What materials did you use? Were they effective? How do you know?
4. What activities did you use? Were they effective? How do you know?
5. What classroom interaction was there? Did you use groups? Pair work? Teacher-fronted? Were learners active participants? How successful was the interaction?
6. Were there any "teachable moments"? How did you capitalize on them?
7. How did you balance between challenging learners and supporting them?
8. Did anything unexpected and unplanned happen? How did you deal with it?
9. What did **you** enjoy most? What did the **learners** enjoy most?
10. If you were to teach this lesson again, what would you do differently? Why?

As an alternative to responding to the questions, we provide a reflection form (See Table 11.1). This form helps the teacher focus on what worked and what didn't and, as a result, how to improve practice for better learner outcomes.

Sometimes, teachers find it difficult to maintain a journal or complete a reflection form consistently and soon after the lesson because they may have to move from one class to another; learners stay behind and ask questions, or there are other duties to perform. A quick technique for recording perceptions is to answer these three questions immediately at the end of the lesson:

1. What did you like most about this lesson?
2. What did you like least about this lesson?
3. What did you learn about your teaching/learners?

Similarly, teachers can get feedback from learners by asking them three simple questions. We have learners write their answers on a slip of paper and turn them in anonymously. This information then helps in planning the next lesson and the rest of the unit:

1. What did you like most about this lesson?
2. What did you like least about this lesson?
3. What did you learn today?

Table 11.1 Teaching Reflection

Teaching reflection

Class:_____   Lesson:_____

Date:_____

Goals:
>   What were my objectives for this class session?

>   _____

>   What did I want to work on in my teaching during this session?

>   _____

My reaction to the class:
>   How would I evaluate the class overall?

>   _____

>   poor   excellent

>   Did I accomplish all of my goals?

>   _____

>   not accomplished   all accomplished

>   How much student learning took place?

>   _____

>   little   a lot

>   How did I feel as I left the class or finished the activity?

>   _____

>   dissatisfied   pleased

>   What do these feelings tell me about what happened in the class?

>   _____

>   _____

>   What made the lesson good or not so good (in my perception)?

>   _____

>   _____

>   What could I do to improve the lesson? How would I change the lesson if I could do it over?

>   I would_____

>   I would_____

>   I would_____

>   What new action(s) will I try in my next lesson in order to achieve my goals?

>   _____

>   _____

>   _____

>   What did I do better this time than ever before?

>   _____

>   _____

>   _____

Observing Classrooms

In Volume I, Chapter 14, we provided a number of ways for teachers to work together on their professional development. Here, we build on those tools. While this chapter focuses on exploring one's own practice, teachers can work with a trusted peer, as in the vignette, to assist them in this exploration. Therefore the tools we discuss here can either be used by a teacher alone or a trusted peer.

In order to explore one's own practice, teachers need to observe their own classrooms objectively, analyze their observations, and reflect on their practice. Therefore it is important for teachers to have actual data, in addition to their own understandings of their practice. In this way, they can compare their own perceptions with the data. We therefore recommend that teachers audiotape or videotape some of their lessons. The advantage of a videotape is that it captures the nonverbal behaviors, such as how learners are grouped or paired, how they respond and how equipment is used, such as blackboard work. The disadvantage is that video recorders are quite intrusive in the classroom. However, we have found that once the novelty wears off, both learners and teacher quickly forget the video recorder is there. To obtain effective recordings most teachers find it takes some experimenting before they find the best fit for their particular context. In many settings, teachers need to get informed consent from learners or their parents before they can record a lesson. This varies by country and institution.

Below we provide two different observation tools, with slightly different emphases. Additionally, more specific tools are in the section below on classroom interaction. These can be used by a trusted peer or by the teacher when observing a videotape of a lesson. The first tool (Table 11.2) is in fact quite similar to the lesson planning guidelines we provided in Chapter 2 in this volume and can be a useful tool to compare a lesson plan with what actually happened. It can also be used by a trusted peer.

The guidelines in Table 11.2 are quite general, but require the observer (or teacher) to write details in prose. We also provide an observation form (Table 11.3) that only requires checkmarks, which may be easier to use or used as a supplement to the one in Table 11.2. There are more comments about learners than teachers because, as we discussed in Chapter 1 in this volume, learner outcomes need to be the focus of classroom instruction.

Analyzing Classroom Interaction

In order to understand what is happening in the classroom, teachers need to analyze interaction, between learners and between teacher and learners. While they don't need to become linguistic researchers, they do need to have the tools to explore such interaction because the quality of such interaction profoundly affects learning (Ellis, 1985). We will provide tools from a number of perspectives: teacher action zone, teacher instructional talk, scaffolding, and teacher research.

Teacher Action Zone

In a teacher-fronted classroom, Adams and Biddle (1970) consistently found a triangular **action zone** with the base at the front row. The zone is not only the

Table 11.2 Lesson Observation Guidelines

Lesson Observation Guidelines

Teacher: (first and last name)
Date/Time: (day, date, and time)
School/Room: (school, building, and room)
Level/Subject: (level/subject area)
Student body: (number, age, gender, and ethnicity of the students)
Book: (what book or computer program the students are using, if any)
Seating: (what the seating arrangement is)
Materials: (e.g., handouts, blackboard, audiotape, video, CALL)
Prior lesson(s): (What content—both language and topic content—was learned in the previous lesson(s) that will be built on in this lesson?)

Objective(s) of the lesson:
  (Objectives should be specific—what students will know and be able to do as a result of the lesson)

Rationale or relevance of the objective(s):
  (Why is this objective important for the students?)
  (What evidence is there that students need work in this area?)

Approach or philosophy:
  (Is the lesson driven by any particular approach?)
  (What can you say about the teacher's apparent philosophy about what should occur in the classroom? When observing, even if the teacher doesn't state an approach/philosophy, her approach should be transparent to students and you as observer.)

Procedure:
  (Housekeeping tasks: announcements, attendance, homework collection, etc.)

  Introduction or staging: (approx. number of minutes)
  (How does the teacher frame the activity and present or elicit information needed to work towards the objective(s)? Be sure to focus on student learning, not just teacher presentation.)

  Presentation: (approx. number of minutes)
  (What materials or activities does the teacher use to present the new content? How do students respond, e.g., listening, reading, questioning?)

  Practice: (approx. number of minutes)
  (What activities/tasks are undertaken to give students practice in attaining the objective(s)? What learning takes place during these activities?)

  Evaluation:
  (How do both teacher and students know that progress is being made toward the objective(s)? Is evaluation ongoing throughout the lesson? How does the teacher respond to student feedback?)

Summary or wrap-up: (approx. number of minutes)
  (How does the teacher review or pull together the main points at the end of the lesson?)

Homework and information about the next class:
  (Is there a follow-up assignment? Is there some indication of what will happen in the next class?)

Table 11.3 Lesson Observation/Reflection Form

Lesson Observation/Reflection Form			
Teacher:_____	Observer:_____		
Date:_____	Class:_____		
	Excellent	*Good*	*Needs improvement*
Teacher's knowledge of subject matter			
Teacher's speech			
Teacher's presentation of subject matter			
Teacher's practice of subject matter			
Teacher's choice of materials			
Teacher's rapport with students			
Learners' interest			
Learners' participation			
Learners' feeling of ease in classroom			
Learners' performance			
Learners' understanding of lesson			
Learners' use of L2 in class			
Other:			
Comments:			
Alternatives, suggestions, or recommendations:			

result of proximity to the teacher, but is where the teacher's gaze is directed. The action zone constitutes where the teacher's main attention lies and it is the students in this zone who receive most teacher attention. For most teachers, this is quite unconscious, but it has a major impact on learner participation and therefore learner behavior and learning. Research has shown that students who sit in the periphery usually have low self-esteem and are trying to distance themselves from the teacher, whom they feel threatens them (Dykman & Reis, 1979). Their research also shows that when such students are moved into the action zone, their self-esteem is raised as they are called on more by the teacher and so participate more.

Therefore, as well as the reflection and observation tools provided above, teachers find it very useful to complete an action diagram of classroom teacher–learner interaction. This is best done from viewing a videotape or asking a trusted peer to observe the interaction. This can then be compared with the teacher's perceptions of how she interacts with learners. In Figure 11.1, we illustrate with a sample classroom diagram. Although this classroom has traditional row and columns for student seating, the technique can be used with any student seating arrangement. As the legend indicates, there are three different arrow directions/shapes for the three different types of interaction in the classroom: teacher to student, student to teacher, and student to student. The observer marks each interaction. Repeat interactions between the same people can be noted by numbers on the arrow line or by slash marks on the arrow line. In the example in Figure 11.1, the teacher's action zone is towards the front and left-hand side. For most teachers, such preferences are unconscious and, when shown a video, they are surprised.

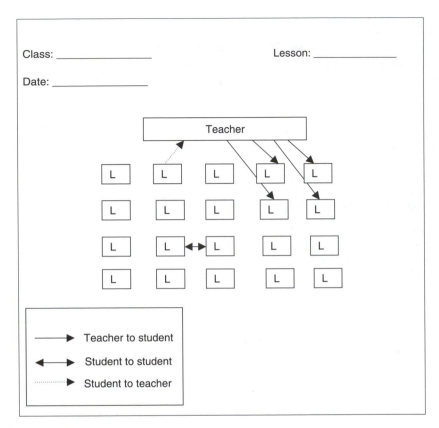

Figure 11.1 Classroom Action Zone.

Teacher–Learner Exchange

As mentioned in Chapter 12 in this volume, the most common interaction in the classroom is **initiation–response–feedback (IRF)**, first identified by Sinclair and Coulthard (1975). However, IRF covers a continuum of exchanges from recitation and display to "a way of scaffolding instruction, a way of developing cognitive structures in the zone of proximal development, or a way of assisting learners to express themselves with maximum clarity" (Van Lier, 2001, p. 96). Below, we provide a range of exchanges to illustrate (scaffolding is covered in more detail in the next section).

The class in Text 1 is working on a unit on eating healthy food and the teacher is showing a chart with different food items in the healthy food triangle.

Text 1

Teacher:	*What is this called? (point to an apple)*
Students (in chorus):	*An apple*
Teacher:	*Yes. An apple. What's this? (pointing to nuts)*
Students:	*Nut*
Teacher:	*They are nuts (with stress of ts)* [Murray, research notes]

In this exchange, the learners are displaying their knowledge of English vocabulary.

The class in Text 2 is working on getting a job and the teacher has told them they're going to look at job qualifications, what would make someone want to hire them. She writes *personal qualities* and *job qualities* on the blackboard.

Text 2

Teacher:	*What personal qualities would impress? What . . .*
Student 1:	*A good worker*
Teacher:	*Yes, a good worker (writes 'good worker' on the blackboard)*
	What else? [Murray, research notes]

In this case the teacher initiates with a question, one student replies and the teacher provides feedback in two ways—verbally saying *yes* and by also writing *good worker* on the blackboard. This exchange requires more thought on the part of the learners than does Text 1 because they have to decide whether their suggestion is personal or job related.

IRF is not the only type of exchange in classrooms, but has been found to be common around the world and in a variety of languages. As in Text 1 above, the teacher's question is a **display question**, because she already knows the answer. This type of question, in which the teacher is trying to elicit student knowledge, is the most common function of the IRF exchange. While this basic pattern is useful for checking background knowledge and their understanding of facts or procedures, it gives learners limited opportunities to use language in other ways, such as asking questions or giving instructions. Text 2 does extend the learners a little as they decide whether their idea is personal or job related. Furthermore, the students' answers might be unexpected. In fact the transcript of this lesson shows that learners offered ideas the teacher had not considered.

In the section below on scaffolding we discuss how teachers encourage learners to use language more creatively, to clarify, support, illustrate, or reformulate their ideas and therefore their language.

The feedback teachers give can take a variety of forms: confirmation, rejection, repetition, reformulation, or elaboration. In both Texts 1 and 2, the teachers confirmed only, before going on to their next question. The transcript in the task below illustrates some of the other feedback forms.

Task: Explore

Examine the transcript below. This advanced writing class is discussing a reading about biased news reporting. Identify the type of feedback the teacher uses in each of her utterances. Think about why she chose the particular type and how effective it appears to be. Discuss your ideas with a colleague.

Text 3

Teacher:	*And he [the writer] has to prove what? What's he going to prove?*
Student 1:	*The article is biased.*

> | Student 2: | Incorrect |
> |---|---|
> | Teacher: | OK. Incorrect. That the news is incorrect. So how do you prove that something's incorrect? |
> | Students 3: | With facts |
> | Teacher: | Yea. Yea. Other facts to contradict and hopefully you've got some way of knowing that your facts are more correct than the facts the author chose and then the next aspect of it is not only the incorrectness or inaccuracy, but what? |
> | Student 3: | Wrong. |
> | Teacher: | Bias, yes, bias or wrong. Now it's a little bit difficult to prove bias, isn't it? How would you prove bias? |
> | Student 4: | Give more facts. |
> | Teacher: | Yes, but then how does one indicate in an article? How do you judge whether an article's biased or not? |
> | Student 5: | You don't take in consideration all the facts. So you only choose some of them. |
> | Teacher: | OK. What's that called? |

Teacher Instructional Talk

As we discussed in Chapter 2, this volume, teaching language(s) differs considerably from other content areas because the language of instruction is also the target of instruction. Therefore, it is important for instructional language to be comprehensible to learners. However, as we noted in Chapter 2, often the most authentic target language learners receive as input is instructional language. Therefore, it is vital for teachers not to distort the language in their efforts to make it comprehensible. As we discussed in Volume I, Chapter 3, teachers may also use learners' L1 in the classroom. However, it is important that learners don't come to rely on L1, but that it is used to support the learning of English.

In the section above, we discussed the types of questions teachers ask. Another aspect of teacher instructional language that was key in the vignette is the amount of time teachers allow for learners to respond, that is, **wait time**. Research has found that teachers of content usually wait one second or less for learners to respond, before reformulating or providing the answer themselves. However, if teachers allow three or more seconds, learners become more confident and their participation increases (Rowe, 1986). While this is true in classrooms where learners are using their L1, it is even more likely when they are trying to use another language (Long, Brock, Crookes, Deike, Potter, & Zhang, 1984).

A checklist to help guide you in making adjustments in your teaching appears in Table 11.4.

Task: Expand

Work with a partner. Generate an example of adjusted teacher talk for each of the indicators in Table 11.4.

Table 11.4 Adapting Teacher Talk for English Learners

Description of Adjustment

Slower rate of speech

Place extra stress on important nouns.
Use fewer contractions.
Use more pauses and pause after critical and important information.

Vocabulary

Avoid slang and idiomatic expressions.
Use fewer pronouns or referential forms.
Contextualize and embed definitions into your speech.
Use visual aids or pictures.
Use gestures and body language.

Syntax

Use simple syntax.
Use short sentences.
Avoid complex sentences with lower proficiency-level students.
Repeat or rephrase difficult information.
Use fewer pre-verb modifications and more modification after the verb.
Expand on learners' utterances.

Discourse

Move from closed (yes/no) questions to open (Wh-) questions.
Use simple command forms for instructions.
Put instructions on the overhead, blackboard, or projector.
Allow students to demonstrate their understanding in nonlinguistic ways.

Speech setting

Repeat classroom routines daily.
Repeat task types.

Scaffolding

Wood, Bruner, and Ross (1976) introduced the term scaffolding to describe how tutors guide the development of problem-solving in young children. It has since been widely used to describe how teachers assist learners to complete a task so that the learner recognizes a solution, works with others to complete it, completes it by themselves, and then the teacher confirms this achievement. The concept of scaffolding is based on Vygotsky's (1978) theory of learning as collaborative and interactive: learning takes place when children are challenged by a task beyond their current level of competence, but are provided with task-specific support by a more competent adult or peer. Vygotsky called this gap between what the child can do unaided and can do with support the zone of proximal development (ZPD). "Scaffolding, then, is more than help and instruction because it involves the use of task-specific explicit strategies that help the learner become independent by exploiting their ZPD" (Murray & McPherson, 2006, p. 140).

In research in Australia with second language learners in mainstream content classes, Hammond and Gibbons (2001) identified two types of scaffolding: macro and micro. Macro refers to the type of preplanned selection and sequencing of tasks we discussed in Chapter 2, this volume. Micro, on the other hand, is contingent on what actually happens in the classroom, how teachers take advantage of the teachable moment. Micro scaffolding, then, is the co-construction of learning that occurs through effective classroom interaction.

The following interaction is from an advanced EAP class and in this particular unit students are learning how to read and write abstracts of journal articles in their field and how to write summaries. They have discussed the difference between a summary and abstract just prior to the excerpt below, and the teacher has noted that many people read only the abstract and so it must be comprehensible by itself.

Text 4

Teacher:	*Any other problems or questions that you encountered in trying to write a summary of your article?*
Student 1:	*Do we have to try to explain what we do in the abstract? I mean to make it comprehensible? Usually when you read an abstract you don't understand it. You get only an idea of what the article's about.*
Teacher:	*You may not understand exactly what went on. The methodology, is that what you're talking about or the terminology?*
Student 1:	*Uhm. You understand the terminology but you don't understand how he. . . Sometimes you don't understand where to apply. . .*
Teacher:	*Yes. May not understand the application. You almost always would read the article if you were looking for applications.*
Student 1:	*I had the impression that a good abstract would give me an idea of what is in the article and then, well, let's put it this way. . . If I don't read the article for three or four months I don't have to read the article. I have only to read the abstract.*
Teacher:	*It would remind you. Yes, that would be very helpful.*
Student 1:	*But when I first read the abstract, I almost never understand the article.*
Teacher:	*It may not be clearly done. May be a problem with your field. M., how about your field?*
Student 2:	*Similar problem. Engineer article. They cannot explain in the abstract very clearly I think. I have the same problem.* [Murray, research notes]

In this excerpt, the teacher elicits information from the learners, to discover that abstracts in their fields may be different from those in the social sciences, which she had been using as examples. Through her clarification questions, she assists the learner to more clearly state his opinion about reading abstracts. After this exchange she goes on to suggest that the general principles she has taught about the characteristics of an abstract still hold and they continue discussing how to write an abstract, recognizing that they have different ideas about what being comprehensible is.

In reflecting on their own classrooms, teachers may want to focus on interaction. We therefore provide questions to ask about interaction.

Questions for analyzing interaction

1. How clear are my directions to learners?
2. What kinds of questions do I ask?

3. What is the proportion of learner talk to teacher talk in class?
4. In what ways do learners participate? Is their participation recitation or display or do they clarify, illustrate, reformulate, or express extended opinions? Is it extended discourse or one or two words?
5. What kinds of verbal and nonverbal feedback do I use?
6. How does my feedback vary depending on the learner receiving it?
7. How often do learners interact with classmates?
8. How often do learners initiate discourse?
9. How well do I answer learners' questions? Are my answers more complex linguistically or cognitively than learners can comprehend?
10. Is my pacing too fast or too slow for the majority of students in the class?

Teacher Research

In Volume I, we discussed research tools that have been used to explore classrooms, in particular, ethnography (Chapter 3) and action research (Chapter 14). The tools provided in this chapter can be used in such research.

Task: Reflect

Reread Chapter 3, Volume I. Think about how you could use some of the tools discussed in this chapter to engage in a more extended research of your classroom.

Conclusion

In this chapter, we have provided a range of tools teachers can use to explore and analyze their own classrooms, either by themselves or with a trusted peer. We have also shown how complex classrooms are. Although teachers plan their lessons, learning and discourse are co-constructed in the language classroom. Part of the art of teaching is learning to respond to unexpected situations and scaffold (micro) content for learners through appropriate discourse.

Task: Expand

Freeman, D. (1998). *Doing teacher research: From inquiry to understanding*. Pacific Grove, CA: Heinle and Heinle Publishers.

In this book, Freeman provides an extensive range of teacher research tools, with examples from how they have been used in classrooms. In particular he provides a new perspective on research as being "an orientation toward one's practice." (p. 8)

Richards, J. C., & Lockhart, C. (1994). *Reflective teaching in second language classrooms*. Cambridge: Cambridge University Press.

As the title of this book suggests, the focus is on individual teachers reflecting on their own practice and covers a wide range of aspects of instruction. It includes tools for self-observation and self-reflection.

Wajnryb, R. (1992). *Classroom observation tasks*. Cambridge: Cambridge University Press.

This book, although designed for observers, has a variety of tasks focusing on different aspect of instruction that could be used by teachers observing their own videotaped lesson.

Questions for Discussion

1. How can teachers frame questions so that learners become active participants in their learning?
2. When are the most appropriate occasions to use IRF for recitation or display or for more creative and cognitively demanding learner responses?
3. We have suggested in this chapter and in Volume I, Chapter 14 that teachers need to explore their own practice in order to understand it and make adjustments as necessary. To what extent do you agree? How can teachers find time for such activities?

References

Adams, R. S., & Biddle, B. J. (1970). *Realities of teaching: Explorations with videotape*. New York: Holt, Rinehart, and Winston.

Dykman, B. D., & Reis, H. T. (1979). Personality correlates of classroom seating position. *Journal of Educational Psychology, 71*, 346.

Ellis, R. (1985). *Understanding second language acquisition*. Oxford: Oxford University Press.

Hammond, J., & Gibbons, P. (2001). *Scaffolding teaching and learning in language and literacy education*. Sydney, Australia: PETA.

Kennedy, N. (1990). *Policy issues in teacher education*. East Lansing, MI: National Center for Research on Teacher Education.

Long, M. H., Brock, C., Crookes, G., Deike, C., Potter, L., & Zhang, S. (1984). *The effect of teachers' questioning patterns and wait-time on pupil participation in public high school classes in Hawaii for students of limited English proficiency. Technical Report No. 1*. Honolulu: Center for Second Language Classroom Research, Social Science Research Institute, University of Hawaii at Manoa.

Murray, D. E., & McPherson, P. (2006). Scaffolding instruction for reading the Web. *Language Teaching Research, 10*(2), 131–156.

Rowe, M. (1986). Wait time: Slowing down may be a way of speeding up. *Journal of Teacher Education, 37*, 43–50.

Sinclair, J. M., & Coulthard, M. R. (1975). *Towards an analysis of discourse: The English used by teachers and pupils*. Oxford: Oxford University Press.

Van Lier, L. (2001). Constraints and resources in classroom talk: Issues of equality and symmetry. In C. N. Candlin & N. Mercer (Eds.), *English language teaching in its social context* (pp. 90–107). London: Routledge.

Vygotsky, L. (1978). *Mind in society*. Cambridge, MA: Harvard University Press.

Wood, D., Bruner, J. S., & Ross, G. (1976). The role of tutoring in problem solving. *Journal of Child Psychology and Psychiatry, 17*.

Part III

Assessing for Learning

Part III is entitled *Assessing for Learning* and contains three chapters. Chapter 12 focuses on what teachers need to know about classroom assessments. In this chapter we work with both formative and summative assessments, but we will limit the scope of the discussion for each one. With formative assessments we show teachers how to increase their skills at checking for student understanding by focusing on creative formative assessment practices. We will limit our discussion to strategies that use oral language to assess learning. This is not to say the other skills are not important, but to do justice to each skill would be beyond what could be expected in a single chapter. Where appropriate, we will also suggest ways in which other skills can be assessed using the same materials. With summative assessment, we will limit our discussion to alternative assessment and offer eight alternative assessments that teachers have found to be useful.

Chapter 13 focuses on concepts that teachers need to know about large-scale assessment, including different types of language tests, such as proficiency, achievement, diagnostic, oral language interviews, direct writing samples, and how they are used. In addition, a number of the most common commercial, high-stakes tests in English language are described and reviewed, such as IELTS, TOEIC, and TOEFL. We also cover important issues with high-stakes assessment, including assessment abuse, and how to understand validity claims for such tests.

Chapter 14 expands the concept of assessing for learning beyond the individual language learners themselves to include the assessment of educational units (e.g., courses, programs, departments, schools, districts).

Chapter 12

Formative and Alternative Assessment

VIGNETTE

Teacher: Okay, what do you think are the most important concepts that we have covered today? (The teacher points to a student in the front row who has his hand in the air.) Let's see, Ben. What do you think?

Ben: *I would like live Plains Indians.

Teacher: No, listen again to my question. What do you think are the most (emphasis) important concepts that we have covered today? (Ben looks down and avoids eye contact with the teacher. She looks away and calls on someone else.) Macey.

Macey: (She also looks down, avoids eye contact, and says nothing.)

Teacher: Macey, I'm waiting. What do you think are the most important concepts we have covered in class today?

Macey: (More waiting.) 7 tribes of American Indians.

Teacher: That's true, Macey. There are 7 tribes of Indians that we have covered, but is it the most important concept? No. What are the most important concepts?

Marcus: (volunteers) We covered synonyms.

Teacher: Yes, we covered synonyms, but are they most important? No, what are the most important concepts? It sounds like some students had better study. [Christison, research notes, 2004]

Task: Reflect

Work with a partner or small group. Discuss the following questions based on the vignette.

1. Is this type of questioning an effective means of formative assessment?
2. Explain why or why not.
3. How might this teacher make formative assessment more effective? What changes could she make?
4. What cues are the learners giving her about the effectiveness of this type of formative assessment?

Introduction

Most teachers think about assessment in terms of testing and the different kinds of tests with which they are familiar, such as **proficiency** and **achievement** tests. Achievement tests are associated with instruction and are designed to support teaching by measuring what students learn as a result of teaching. Proficiency tests are generally not associated with instruction but provide indicators of how test-takers will perform on similar tasks in the real world. Tests are assessments, but they are different from other forms of assessment because they require all learners to complete the same specific task(s) in a controlled environment and at the same time. Typical tasks on traditional tests include items, such as short answers, true or false, matching, and multiple choice. All tests are assessments, but not all assessments are tests, as you will see below. An assessment is a systematic way of gathering information for the purposes of making decisions.

Language educators use assessments to make decisions in six different areas of language learning. They are used to:

1. Make decisions relative to screening and identification. For example, in U.S. public schools, different assessments are used to screen students (e.g., to determine if they are limited English-proficient) or to determine the level of services they should receive.
2. Make decisions about placement. In most large EFL centers, students are given assessments that place them into the appropriate level of instruction (e.g., beginning, intermediate, advanced in a three-level program) relative to their language proficiency.
3. Reclassify learners within a program, such as to determine if a student should move from intermediate to advanced level courses or to make a decision about when students should exit a program and should be deemed language proficient.
4. Monitor student progress in order to make decisions about instruction, such as when to move on to new concepts and content or when to recycle and repeat information from previous learning periods.
5. Inform the process of program evaluation (see Chapter 14, this volume). Learner performance on various types of assessments is used to determine overall effectiveness of a given program.
6. Help teachers focus on learner outcomes and take joint responsibility for learner progress.

Task: Explore

Work with a partner. Make a list of all the different assessments (including tests) you have used as a student and as a teacher. Which of these assessments did you think were the most effective? Least effective? Why?

There are two different kinds of assessments available to classroom teachers—**summative** and **formative**—but there are important differences between the two.

An assessment is generally summative if it is given at the end of a learning period, and it is formative if it is ongoing and given during the process of learning. However, there is nothing inherent in an assessment task that makes it summative or formative. For example, we normally associate the use of true or false statements with summative assessment, but we have seen a teacher use a series of true or false statements very effectively as a formative assessment.[1] While most tests are given at the end of a learning period, they do not have to be. A test can be given during a learning period as well, and experienced teachers often use short tests in order to check for understanding. Other tests, such as midterm and final exams, unit tests, and oral proficiency exams, are used at the end of a learning episode.

The main difference between formative and summative assessments has to do with the purpose of the assessment (Fisher & Frey, 2007). The purpose of formative assessment is to improve instruction by helping teachers make determinations about when to move instruction on to new concepts and when to recycle concepts that have previously been covered. Formative assessment helps teachers determine how to revise and modify instruction in order to address difficulties students have in learning the concepts and in acquiring new skills. Formative assessment also provides ongoing feedback to students relative to the achievement of their goals. The purpose of summative assessment is to measure competency, to determine how well students can perform relative to a given concept or skill. Because summative assessment is tied to determining competency, it is given at the end of a learning period.

In addition to differences in purpose, teachers and students use the results differently. Teachers and students use the two types of assessments in different ways. Teachers use formative assessments to plan for and modify instruction, while summative assessment is used for giving grades and making determinations about what has been learned, such as whether students have proficiency in language in order to move levels or to take certain classes. Summative assessments can also be used for planning purposes, but the planning is of a different nature, such as predicting how many teachers would be needed for an upcoming semester based on how many students are projected to pass an exam. Students use summative assessments to gauge their progress towards a specific goal. Teachers use the results of formative assessments to plan and modify instruction, and students use the results to self-monitor or self-assess their understanding of new concepts or development of new skills.

Task: Explore

Use the information in the two preceding paragraphs above and create a graphic organizer that outlines the differences between formative and summative assessment.

In this chapter we will work with both formative and summative assessments, but we will limit the scope of the discussion for each one. With formative assessments, we will limit our discussion to strategies that use oral language to assess learning. This is not to say the other skills are not important, but to do justice to each skill would be beyond what could be expected in a short chapter. Where appropriate, we will also suggest ways in which other skills can be assessed using the same materials.

With summative assessment, we will limit our discussion to alternative assessment—a technical term that we will define at a later point in the chapter.

Formative Assessment

Most classroom teachers who have been teaching for any length of time have had the experience of planning a lesson and providing what they believe to be excellent instruction only to find out later, after giving a chapter or unit test, that very few students understood the concepts that were taught. Several questions enter a teacher's mind at this point: Why aren't students mastering the concepts? Why didn't I recognize the problems that students were having with the material before we were finished working with the materials and concepts and before the test? What can I do to make the changes necessary to remedy this situation? We believe that the answers to these difficult questions lie in developing competence with formative assessment. Teachers must develop skills in assessing students if they are to check for understanding in ways that inform instruction.

Because formative assessment is so closely tied to learning, it is critical that teachers develop skills with formative assessment. We have spent a collective five decades watching teachers. On the basis of these experiences (and, of course, our collective six decades of teaching!), we have both noted that the most common practice of formative assessment is what we call the *general question–no response model*. In other words, teachers say to students, "Do you understand?" Teachers frequently get no response to this question, but they make the assumption that when students don't respond, the no response is equal to students saying, "We have no questions; we understand." Although this model is the most common way for teachers to assess students (Durkin, 1978), it does not provide the teacher or the students with a way to truly check for understanding relative to the concepts being taught; there is no student performance involved, no basis for checking understanding.

Cazden (1988) introduced the field to another common type of teacher questioning process that is based on the work of Sinclair and Coulthard (1975). We have also noticed this type of formative assessment in our observations of teachers; yet, it is more specific than the model we mention above. She calls this model the *initiate–respond–evaluate model*. This model is illustrated in the classroom vignette above in the following way. In this model, the teacher initiates the question and calls on a student to respond. Then, the teacher evaluates the response. With the initiate–respond–evaluate model, there is little focus on the students demonstrating what they know. The focus is often on the teacher. The nature of teacher questioning in this model places students in the unfortunate situation of trying to guess what the teacher is thinking and what the teacher thinks is the "right" answer. In addition, when one student is called upon, there is no way for teachers to assess learning for the entire group or to check for critical thinking. One of the challenges that teachers face in using this model is that it is so easy to make wrong assumptions about learning because the assumptions are often based on the interactions with one student or the vocal minority in a group of students.

In the classroom vignette above, the initiate–respond–evaluate model is highly evident. The teacher asks individual students to identify the most important concepts in the lesson. One young man in the front row believes that he knows the answer and volunteers. However, the most important concept for him is the fact that he has decided which of the tribes he would like to belong to and wants to share this with the teacher. He volunteers this information freely only to have his contribution ignored. His response is not the response the teacher is looking for. By not following up on the student's response, the teacher misses a prime opportunity to engage with the student: Why would the student rather belong to the tribe of Plains Indians? Other students in the class witness the fact the student was not successful in providing the answer the teacher was looking for. A second student is called on to answer the question. This student tries to avoid eye contact with the teacher, but is finally "forced" to answer. This student also finds herself in the same situation as the first student; namely that she is not able to provide the answer the teacher is looking for. Most of the students in the class now look away from the teacher; a third student finds the confidence to volunteer still another possibility only to find that he fails as well. Instead of using the students' answers to focus on student learning, the teacher continued to make them guess what she was thinking. Finally, the teacher became frustrated because the students did not give her the answers she was looking for; she decides the students are at fault. A careful examination of student responses would have told this teacher what the students had actually learned from the instruction.

We believe that at least part of the problem with formative assessment practices rests with teacher education. In the absence of exposure to more effective ways of assessing students, teachers do what was commonly done to them in the process of learning or what they see other, more experienced, teachers do. In this chapter, it is our purpose to introduce you to some specific strategies for formative assessment that can get you away from the two questioning models mentioned above and get you thinking about other ways to check for understanding.

Strategies for Formative Assessment

Strategies for Assessing Learning

Oral language development includes the development of both speaking and listening skills. There is a substantial body of research that supports the importance of oral language for English language learners (Rothenberg & Fisher, 2007; Short & Echevarria, 2004/2005) and oral language development is the foundation of literacy (Fisher & Frey, 2007). Nevertheless, oral language is often not used in ways that are most beneficial for students (e.g., the two questioning models given above). With English language learners, teachers tend to speak more (Lingard, Hayes, & Mills, 2003) while students speak less. However, the ratio of student talk to teacher talk is important since research shows high-achieving students speak more in the classroom than low-achieving students (Cotton, 1989). Consequently, teachers should be cognizant of the ways in which they encourage student talk in the classroom and use student talk in formative assessment.

In addition to speaking less, teachers often focus only on basic skills with English language learners and less on critical thinking (Stipek, 2004). This practice is noted by the fact that content-area teachers with English language learners in their classes often ask questions of English language learners that are less difficult than the ones they ask their monolingual peers (Rothenberg & Fisher, 2007). We have also witnessed EFL teachers ask advanced-level learners only basic factual questions based on their reading of texts when the learners were clearly capable, in terms of language ability, of evaluative responses. The two formative assessment strategies we give you below offer ways to increase student talk, focus on critical thinking, and use questioning strategies that require higher-order thinking.

RETELLING

The first strategy that we introduce you to is retelling. Retelling is a strategy you can use to increase student talk in the classroom and promote critical thinking through the guided analysis of text. It is appropriate for learners who are high beginning to advanced levels; it can be used with most language learners although beginning language learners may need more scaffolding (see Volume 1, Chapter 10, for a detailed explanation of scaffolding) and support in the form of formulas and rubrics. The purpose of retelling is to help students analyze a text and give them an opportunity to use oral language to recreate a text or talk about an experience in their own words. Retelling can be used with both informational and narrative text, but it is easier with narrative text since most students are familiar with narrative in their native languages and may even be used in retelling to talk about a favorite movie or CD with a friend.[2]

When using retelling with language learners, it is important to provide scaffolding, the support students need to carry out the task successfully. The first type of scaffolding is a formula. The formula for retelling with narrative text consists of three key elements: 1) deciding what to keep, 2) what to delete, and 3) what to change from the original. For narrative text, we use these three key elements and focus on four essential components of narrative—characters, setting, problem, and solution. Begin with a narrative text that all of the students have read. Create the retelling together by writing the formula in three columns on the board as in Table 12.1.

Ask the students to tell you what they want to keep, delete, or change from the story with each of the components. Write their ideas on the board or have them write after they have shared orally. They do not need a response for each component under each key element. Once students have worked with the formula as a large group, they can work independently in small groups to create their own retelling of the same narrative text or a different narrative text.

In order to be successful at retelling, lower proficiency level language learners may need some additional scaffolding beyond the simple formula given in Table 12.1. We have found simple rubrics to be a helpful addition. We define rubrics as explicit summaries of the criteria used for assessing student work, plus a description of the levels of potential achievement for each criterion. If students see a rubric when they are given an assignment, they have a clear idea of what the instructor expects. The same criteria are applied to each student's work (see Table 12.2).

Table 12.1 Formula for Retelling

What to keep	What to delete	What to change
Characters:	Characters:	Characters:
Setting:	Setting:	Setting:
Problem:	Problem:	Problem:
Solution:	Solution:	Solution:

Table 12.2 Rubric for Retelling with Narratives

Components of Narrative Text	Needs improvement (0)	Meets the standard (1)	Exceeds the standard (2)
Character	My retelling does not name or describe the characters correctly. My listeners are confused.	My retelling names the characters correctly but does not tell the listeners much about the characters.	My retelling names the characters correctly and describes the characters so my listeners know about the characters.
Setting	My retelling does not include when and where the story takes place.	My retelling provides some information about when and where the story takes place.	My retelling gives all of the information about when and where the story takes place.
Problem	My retelling does not tell the listeners about the problem.	My retelling states the problem but does not talk about how or why the problem happened.	My retelling states the problem and talks about how and why the problem occurred.
Solution	My retelling does not talk about how the characters in the story solved the problem.	My retelling talks about some of the important events that helped characters solve the problem.	My retelling talks about all of the important events that helped the characters solve the problem.

Source for Table 12.1 and 12.2: From Checking for Understanding: Formative Assessment Techniques for Your Classroom (Figure 2.5, p. 29 and Figure 2.6, p. 31) by Douglas Fisher & Nancy Frey, Alexandria, VA: ASCD. Adapted by permission. Learn more about ASCD at www.ascd.org

The four components of narrative—character, setting, problem, and solution—are identified in the left-hand column and are highlighted. The criteria for performance at each level—needs improvement, meets the standard, exceeds the standard—for each component are described in the next three columns and assigned a number of 0, 1, or 2. We have found that even lower-level proficiency learners are easily able to differentiate among the three different levels of performance on the rubric.

Retelling can also be used with types of informational texts. The rubric for informational texts would include different components, such as main ideas, details, sequence of information, and conclusion (see Table 12.3).

Rubrics can be used in a variety of ways. The rubrics above are meant to be used by individual learners to assess their own retelling; however, they can be easily modified for peer (i.e., simply change *my* to *your*) or teacher use. In addition, retelling can be used as a springboard for assessing writing. Instead of using the formula and rubrics to promote oral language, students can use them as springboards for organizing their writing. With the structure provided by the formula and the rubrics, students transform the ideas they have talked about into written prose. For beginning learners who are not yet able to speak or write sufficiently to retell as described above, graphic organizers can be used for assessment of learner understanding of a reading or oral narrative.

Table 12.3 Rubric for Retelling with Informational Text

Components of Informational Text	Needs improvement (0)	Meets standard (1)	Exceeds standard (2)
Main Ideas	My retelling does not identify the main ideas from the text.	My retelling identifies some of the main ideas from the text.	My retelling identifies all of the main ideas from the text.
Details	My retelling does not identify the important details.	My retelling identifies some of the important details.	My retelling identifies all of the important details.
Linking Information	My retelling does not link the details to the main ideas.	My retelling links some of the details to the main ideas.	My retelling links all of the details to the main ideas.
Conclusion	My retelling does not include a conclusion that summarizes the text.	My retelling includes a conclusion.	My retelling includes a conclusion that summarizes the text.

QUESTIONING STRATEGIES

The use of effective questioning strategies is essential if teachers are to escape the initiate–respond–evaluate cycle identified by Cazden (1988) and Sinclair and Coulthard (1975) and illustrated in the vignette at the beginning of this chapter. One of the models for effective questioning that we have found most useful in working with teachers is known as QUILT (questioning understanding to improve learning and thinking). It is the work of Walsh and Sattes (2005) and includes five distinct steps in the questioning process (see Table 12.4).

Rather than the two-step process of question and answer, QUILT proposes five distinct steps that assist teachers in creating questions to determine what students know and do not know. Teachers who think about questioning in advance of instruction and who follow specific steps in questioning can avoid many of the pitfalls that trap teachers into the initiate-respond-evaluate cycle. For example, in the first step of QUILT, teachers are asked to think about the purpose of their questions. At this stage, teachers must think about the nature of the question being asked. Is the question factual in nature? Is it being asked to get students to recognize or recall information? Perhaps the question is asking students to apply the information they have learned.

Cognitive demand is tied closely to determining the purpose of the question. In fact, when teachers determine the purpose of a question, such as to find out whether students can find or recall a fact about the text, they also determine the cognitive demand the question requires of the learner. Factual questions, such as *Who is . . . Where is . . . How many were . . .* place the least demand on cognition because they simply ask students to recall information from a text or to find information in a text. Evaluative questions, such as *Do you think this story could have happened today? Who was your least favorite character? Why?* place the highest demand on cognition because they require learners to analyze a text and make a judgment.

Table 12.4 QUILT Framework for Questioning

QUILT Framework

Stage 1: Prepare the question
Identify instructional purpose.
Determine content focus.
Select cognitive level.
Consider wording and syntax.

Stage 2: Present the question
Indicate response format.
Ask the question.
Select the respondent.

Stage 3: Prompt student responses
Pause after asking question.
Assist nonrespondent.
Pause following student response.

Stage 4: Process student responses
Provide appropriate feedback.
Expand and use correct responses.
Elicit student reactions and questions.

Stage 5: Reflect on questioning practice
Analyze questions.
Map respondent selection.
Evaluate student response patterns.
Examine teacher and student reactions.

Based on *Quality questioning: Research-based practice to engage every learner* by J. A. Walsh and B. D. Sattes (2005). Thousand Oaks, CA: Corwin Press

In order to interpret demands on cognition, we use the six levels in Bloom's Taxonomy (see also Chapter 10, this volume, for a complete discussion of Bloom's Taxonomy)—knowledge, comprehension, application, analysis, synthesis, and evaluation (Bloom, 1956)—and think of questions in terms of the demand on cognition associated with each level (see Table 12.5).

Simple recall of information (i.e., knowledge) is at the lowest level and determining the value of something (i.e., evaluation) is at the highest level.

All stages of QUILT are important in developing effective questioning strategies for second language learners; however, experience in observing hundreds of practising teachers in the past decade has heightened our awareness concerning how teachers respond to students (Stage 3 & 4 in QUILT). We frame our observations in the form of guidelines for practising teachers below:

1. Provide wait time for students. Wait time is extremely important for all learners, but critical for learners who are at risk[3] (Rowe, 1986). Wait time can be structured in several different ways. Of course, you can simply ask the question and then provide at least a 10-second wait before calling on anyone to answer the question. You can also create the wait time in advance of the question. You might say something like, "My next question is a difficult one, so I'm going to ask everyone to think about it for a few moments before responding."

Table 12.5 Questioning and Demands on Cognition

Level in Bloom's Taxonomy	Description of the level	Sample question
Knowledge	The ability to recall data or information.	Wh- questions Where is . . .? How many . . .? Who was . . .?
Comprehension	The ability to show that one understands the meaning of something by such activities as rewriting, interpreting, predicting, translating, giving examples, or explaining in one's own words.	Can you tell me in your own words? Can you give me two examples of . . .? Describe what happened.
Application	The ability to use a concept in a new situation.	If you were the character in that story, what would you have done? How would you solve the problem?
Analysis	The ability to separate concepts into their component parts or the ability to identify the organizational structure of something.	What part of the story did you find the scariest? What kind of a person do you think . . . is? What things are similar and different about the two experiments?
Synthesis	The ability to bring together parts or ideas to form a new structure or a new way of thinking.	Create a new ending for the story. What would have happened in the experiment if we had added more water? Why do you think this happened? What would you change to make the experiment work?
Evaluation	The ability to determine the value of something based on a set of criteria.	Do you think this story could have really happened? Why or why not? Which character in the story was the bravest? Why didn't this experiment work?

2. Avoid answering your own questions. Adjusting to the response patterns of different groups of second language learners can sometimes be difficult for teachers. The wait time is often longer and students develop strategies for not responding, such as avoiding eye contact or looking like they are searching for an answer in the text or in their notes. These response patterns may seem foreign at first, and silence in the classroom can be an unnerving event. Attempting to answer one's own questions is often a natural response to silence and reluctance on the part of the learners. Unless you are aware of these probable patterns, you may fall into answering your own questions in an attempt to make adjustments to the altered pace of your instructional delivery. However, it is important to remember that with language learners, silence is not necessarily negative (e.g., students need more thinking and processing

time in a second language) and focusing on strategies for eliciting responses takes time and practice.

3. Develop strategies for responding to incorrect answers. Students will answer incorrectly; that is a given. The job of a teacher is to develop strategies for responding effectively to incorrect answers. For example, you might give students cues to help them (e.g., "Look at the chart on page 181. What does it say in the top line in the left column?"). You might also rephrase questions and give students time to talk over their answers with a partner. Another way to respond to incorrect answers is to tell students you want them to think about it or confer with a partner. Then, tell them that you will come back to them later.

4. Develop a system for calling on students. Teachers have typical patterns for calling on students. These patterns include calling on students who sit closest to the front and center of the classroom, who frequently raise their hands, and who have the correct answers most of the time. Teachers avoid engaging students who do not make eye contact, who sit at the back of the room and on the far sides of the classroom, and who seldom have the correct answers. In order to avoid falling into patterns of interaction with students that exclude some students, it is helpful to develop a system for calling on students beforehand. For example, one teacher we observed used a set of small cards with student names on the cards. She rotated through the cards. Another teacher targeted different parts of the room with each question, "I'd like an answer to this question from the back of the room." Yet another teacher gave out colored cards to students when they answered a question. At various points in the lesson she would make requests of students, "Let me see who has cards?" or "Who doesn't have a card yet?"

5. Use response practices that promote student involvement. Practices that involve many students in giving a response are extremely valuable in checking for student understanding. We have seen teachers use small white boards with students. After the teacher asks a question, students respond on the white board and then hold up their boards. Another teacher used colored cards when asking true/false questions. She said, "Hold up green if the statement is true and red if the statement is false." Another version of this same technique is to hold up one finger if the statement is true and two if it is false. Some teachers ask students to close their eyes with this last technique. With these practices teachers can check answers quickly, and, in addition, more than one student is involved and responding to the questions.

Task: Explore

In addition to the strategies given above for effective questioning, add two more strategies to your list by thinking about your own experiences and talking to other teachers. Share your completed list with at least two other teachers or peers.

Alternative Assessment

Alternative assessments can either be formative or summative. In this section, we discuss alternative assessment in terms of summative assessment. We call it alternative assessment because it is an alternative to the traditional forms of assessment, such as true/false or multiple choice. In traditional forms of assessment the required answers are generally predetermined (e.g., the answer to Number 1 is [a]), but in alternative assessment, students have latitude in crafting their responses; there is not just one predetermined answer possible.

Alternative assessments can differ from traditional summative assessments in other ways as well. First, alternative assessments can give language learners an opportunity to demonstrate what they know about language and content based on criteria that have been set up in advance of the assessment. Second, learners can get involved in the evaluation of their own work, thereby increasing motivation. Third, learners can show, demonstrate, or display what they have learned to their teachers, peers, or family members and can explain why they were evaluated in the way they were. Finally, alternative assessment is by definition criterion-referenced since it is based on activities that represent instructional activities or activities from real-life settings.

Alternative assessment has become a critical issue with English language learners (ELLs) in public schools in English-dominant countries around the world. Both accurate and effective assessment of ELLs is essential to ensure that ELLs gain access to instructional programs that meet their needs. The assessment of ELLs in public school settings is far more complex (Short & Fitzsimmons, 2007) and challenging than with native speakers of English. Because the most common summative assessments have not proven to be effective with ELLs (Cummins, 1984; Cummins, 2001; Short & Fitzsimmons, 2007), second language educators have begun to experiment with alternative assessments (O'Malley & Valdez-Pierce, 1996).

Types of Alternative Assessments

We have worked with eight different types of alternative assessments. Although there is an almost endless list of possible assessment types, we focus on the eight outlined below since they are the ones with which we are most familiar.

Constructed Responses

Students respond orally or in writing to open-ended questions, such as, *Two examples of conductivity from real life are . . ., In today's story, Bill tried to . . ., The story "The Pearl" took place in . . ., The part of this story that I liked best was when . . .* Prompts are usually based on a text or perhaps an in-class experience. Students respond to the prompts with their own ideas, and there is generally more than one appropriate answer possible.

Experiments/Demonstrations

Students complete experiments or demonstrate the use of materials, such as showing the class how to play the guitar or conducting an experiment to show solubility as a property of matter.

Observations

Teachers and students observe students' attention, responses to instructional materials and tasks, or student/teacher and student/student interactions. The observations are recorded on an observational rubric which delineates the specific behaviors one wants to observe.

Oral Interviews

Teachers ask students questions about personal background, readings, and interests. Oral interviews are often given to language learners to determine their level of proficiency with oral language development. The questions that teachers use can vary within a general framework for questioning, but teachers use specific criteria for evaluating students in areas such as grammar, pronunciation, use of vocabulary, etc. These criteria are shared with students in advance of and after the interviews so that students know precisely on what they should focus in order to make progress.

Portfolios

A portfolio is a focused collection of student work. A portfolio can show progress over time, it can show only one's best work, or all work related to a specific short-term project, depending on the goals of the teacher and student in using a portfolio. A portfolio needs to be systematic, not just a random collection of student work. Pierce and O'Malley (1992) list the following criteria as essential for the development of portfolios. Portfolio assessment:

- is the use of records of a student's work over time and in a variety of modes to show the depth, breadth, and development of the student's abilities
- is the purposeful and systematic collection of student work that reflects accomplishment relative to specific instructional goals or objectives
- can be used as an approach for combining the information from both alternative and standardized assessments
- has as key elements student reflection, assessment, and self-monitoring.

Projects

Students complete a project in a content area, working individually, in pairs, or small groups. Projects usually contain a specific list of requirements with an accompanying rubric so that students know what to include in their project and how their project will be evaluated.

Retelling

Students retell main ideas or select details of the text through listening or reading. Retelling is a good example of a strategy that can be used as both a formative and a summative assessment, depending on when the retelling occurs—during or at the end of a learning episode. A detailed description of this strategy has been dealt with previously in this chapter.

Writing Samples

Students generate a narrative, expository, persuasive, or reference paper in response to a specific prompt. Peers and instructors use rubrics to respond to and evaluate the paper. The rubric is given to students in advance of the assignment and is used as a guide for the writing.

Task: Explore

Which of the alternative assessments above have you tried in your own classroom? What were the results? What challenges did you face? Which of these alternative assessments do you think you might try? In what class and with what type of student?

Conclusion

In this chapter we have dealt with issues related to both formative and summative assessment and have outlined the ways in which they are different from each other. In addition, we have provided you with two specific strategies for formative assessment—retelling and questioning—and provided a list of eight alternative assessments for you to work with in your classroom. Assessment is not so much about cataloging students' mistakes as it is about helping students grow and learn (Tomlinson, 1999). We hope that we have been able to communicate clearly this point of view about assessment with you.

Task: Expand

If this chapter has piqued your interest in assessment, you may want to explore the following books in order to deepen your understanding.

Bachman, L., & Palmer, A. (1996). *Language testing in practice.* London: Oxford University Press.

Language Testing in Practice presents an in-depth discussion of the six qualities of useful language tests—reliability, construct validity, impact, interactiveness, practicality, and authenticity—and three principles for considering the qualities of usefulness in test construction and selection. In addition, the book provides sections on designing useful scoring for language tests.

Fisher, D., & Frey, N. (2007). *Checking for understanding. Formative assessment techniques for your classroom.* Alexandria, VA: ASCD.

In this book the authors show how to increase students' understanding with the help of creative formative assessments. They explore a variety of engaging activities that can build understanding, including: interactive writing, portfolios, and multimedia presentations. In addition, *Checking for Understanding* further explores how teachers can effectively use traditional tests and collaborative assessments to improve instruction and increase student comprehension.

O'Malley, M., & Valdez-Pierce, L. (1996). *Authentic assessment for English language learners*. New York: Addison Wesley Publishers/Longman Publishing Group.

Authentic Assessment for English Language Learners is a practical guide for teachers, teacher trainers, administrators, and assessment specialists who work with ESL/bilingual students at all grade levels. The book offers a comprehensive selection of practical strategies for assessing oral language, reading, writing, and the content areas. In addition, it provides a research-based framework for linking assessment to instruction. There are reproducible checklists, rating scales, and rubrics that can be adapted for local assessment needs.

Coombe, C. A., & Hubley, N. J. (Eds.). (2003). *Assessment practices*. Alexandria, VA: TESOL, Inc.

This volume showcases assessment in its myriad forms—classroom, formal, program evaluation, curriculum, self-assessments of teaching and learning. The studies in this volume are internationally situated.

Questions for Discussion

1. What are the ways in which formative and summative assessments differ?
2. How does a test differ from other types of assessments? Give an example.
3. Describe two strategies for formative assessment.
4. What is QUILT? How can it help teachers assess students more accurately and fairly?
5. What is an alternative assessment? Give an example.

Notes

1. Students were asked to identify all false statements, change all false statements to true statements, and explain their reasoning. There were at least two changes that could be made for each false statement to make it true. It was up to the students to decide.
2. The genre of retelling an event that one experienced is called recount in systemic functional linguistics and the Australian school of genre. Recount is different from narrative in its generic structure.
3. "At-risk" is a term used in Inner Circle countries. Learners are referred to as at-risk when certain societal factors are present, such as low socioeconomic status, language and cultural differences, dysfunctional family situations, or residence in a disadvantaged community.

References

Bachman, L., & Palmer, A. (1996). Language testing in practice. London: Oxford University Press.
Bloom, B. S. (1956). *Taxonomy of educational objectives: The classification of educational goals: Handbook I, Cognitive domain*. New York: Longman.
Cazden, C. B. (1988). *Classroom discourse: The language of teaching and learning*. Portsmouth, NH: Heinemann.
Coombe, C. A., & Hubley, N. J. (eds.). (2003). *Assessment practices*. Alexandria, VA: TESOL, Inc.

Cotton, K. (1989). *Expectations and student outcomes*. Portland, OR: Northwest Regional Educational Laboratory. www.nwrel.org/scpd/sirs/4/cu7.html.

Cummins, J. (2001). *Negotiating identities: Education for empowerment in a diverse society*. (2nd ed.). Ontario, CA: California Association of Bilingual Education.

Cummins, J. (1984). *Bilingualism and special education: Issues in assessment and pedagogy*. San Diego, CA: College-Hill Press.

Durkin, D. (1978). What classroom observation reveals about reading comprehension instruction. *Reading Research Quarterly, 14*(4), 481–533.

Fisher, D., & Frey, N. (2007). *Checking for understanding*. Alexandria, VA: ASCD

Lingard, B., Hayes, D., & Mills, M. (2003). Teachers and productive pedagogies: Contextualizing, conceptualizing, utilizing. *Pedagogy, Culture and Society, 11*, 399–424.

O'Malley, M., & Valdez-Pierce, L. (1996). *Authentic assessment for English language learners*. New York: Addison Wesley Publishers/Longman Publishing Group.

Pierce, L. V., & O'Malley, J. M. (1992). *Performance and portfolio assessment for language minority students*. NCBE 9. Washington, D.C.: NCBE.

Rothenberg, C., & Fisher, D. (2007). *Teaching English language learners: A differentiated approach*. Upper Saddle River, NJ: Pearson/Merrill/Prentice Hall.

Rowe, M. B. (1986). Wait time: Slowing down may be a way of speeding up. *Journal of Teacher Education, 37*, 43–50.

Short, D., & Echevarria, J. (2004/2005, December/January). Teacher skills to support English language learners. *Educational Leadership, 62*(4), 8–13.

Short, D., & Fitzsimmons, S. (2007). Double the work: challenges and solutions to acquiring language and academic literacy for adolescent English language learners. A report to the Carnegie Corporation of New York. Washington, D.C.: Alliance for Excellent Education.

Sinclair, J. M., & Coulthard, M. R. (1975). *Towards an analysis of discourse: The English used by teachers and pupils*. London: Oxford University Press.

Stipek, D. (2004). Teaching practices in kindergarten and first grade: Different strokes for different folks. *Early Childhood Research Quarterly, 19*, 548–568.

Tomlinson, C. A. (1999). *The differentiated classroom: Responding to the needs of all learners*. Alexandria, VA: ASCD.

Walsh, J. A., & Sattes, B. D. (2005). *Quality questioning: Research-based practice to engage every learner*. Thousand Oaks, CA: Corwin Press.

Chapter 13

Large-Scale Assessment

VIGNETTE

Delia teaches in an intensive English program that prepares international students to enter English-speaking universities. The program includes courses that teach academic skills, that teach specific skills for various fields (ESP), and that prepare students to take the test. She is an expert in the large-scale assessment instrument used for entrance, having been an examiner for many years. Faculty in departments that have a number of international students consider that the international students who pass the test in their own country are not fully prepared either in English or in university study skills. Students in their departments have been failing courses at a much higher rate than local students. The University President and the Office of International Students are alarmed at this failure rate and have told the faculty such a high failure rate is unacceptable. They are worried that word will get out that international students can't succeed at their university and this important revenue stream will dry up. But, they feel they need to respond to faculty concerns. They have therefore proposed raising the admissions score for university entrance. Delia has been asked to give advice on what the admissions score should be. Their university has the same admissions score as most other regional universities that compete with them for international students. [Murray, research notes]

Task: Reflect

1. If the university raises the admissions score, what might international students do?
2. Why do you think students who pass the test in their own country have more difficulty than those who take intensive English courses at the university or pass the test after taking a preparation course at the university?
3. To what extent do you think these students' difficulties are a result of their English proficiency? To what extent might they be the result of a lack of familiarity with the culture of a university in an English-speaking country?

4. What alternatives might Delia be able to offer instead of raising the admissions score?

Introduction

In the previous chapter, we discussed formative and alternative assessments, with a primary focus on how teachers might develop and use such assessments. However, there are a range of assessments used in English language education that are not focused on the teacher and the classroom, namely large-scale assessment, which serves different needs than those assessments of teachers in classrooms. Hamp-Lyons (2003) elaborates those differences:

> The large scale needs to discriminate, to separate, to categorize and label. It seeks the general, the common, the group identifier, the scaleable, the replicable, the predictable, the consistent, the characteristic. The teacher, the classroom, seeks the special, the individual, the changing, the changeable, the surprising, the subtle, the textured, the unique. Neither is better but they *are* different. (p. 26)

In this chapter, we focus on one particular type of large-scale assessment, namely large-scale tests. Tests are but one type of assessment, but are the type used in large-scale assessment. Large-scale tests are **proficiency** tests, that is, they measure the level of learners' language competence, regardless of how they learned the language. Most teachers do not help develop or assess large-scale test items; however, they and their students are consumers of such tests. However, teachers and other educators often do contribute to test development and pilot testing of test items. These tests are also **high-stake** because they determine major life events for students, such as whether they are accepted into a university, whether they can graduate, or whether their school is considered effective. We consider it vital for teachers to understand how these tests are developed, what they do and do not measure, and how their results are interpreted. We believe it is important because teachers are the best judge of their learners' language use and they need to be able to advocate for their learners when test results do not seem to be an adequate measure of their learners' proficiency. They are often asked to recommend tests or test cut scores by administrators and they are often instructors of classes designed to help learners pass such a test.

We will begin with what these tests are designed to measure and how they are determined to be accurate measures. As part of this discussion, we will confront the issue of the abuse of large-scale tests. Then we will discuss some of the major large-scale tests.

Measuring Language Proficiency

In order to discuss how to measure language proficiency, we first need to discuss the concept of language proficiency itself. Then we will present the types of measures used and how to evaluate the efficacy of the tests.

What is Language Proficiency?

Although most people have a folk idea of what proficiency means, they would not be able to identify its components. For example, people often make comments about NNSs of English, saying things like, "She's not very fluent." Or "He's got a really thick accent." Or "They need to employ people who are more competent in English." But, what do people mean by "fluent," "thick accent" or "competent?" Language proficiency is clearly a scale along different dimensions of the four skills of listening, speaking, reading, and writing. Consequently, the field of ELT talks about **proficiency levels**. Different scales have been developed to define such levels. For example, the European Common Framework of Reference for Language has six levels that can be used to set targets for instruction and also **benchmark** language proficiency. The framework begins with three broad levels—basic, independent user, and proficient user, with two levels in each. The three broad levels "are an interpretation of the classic division into basic, intermediate and advanced" (Council of Europe, n.d.). They include the major categories of language use in each of the six levels. For example, the European Common Framework of Reference for Language has six levels (See Table 13.1).

The Interagency Language Roundtable (IRL) in the U.S. uses a six-point scale, originally developed by the United States Foreign Service Institute (FSI): no proficiency, elementary proficiency, limited working proficiency, professional working proficiency, full professional proficiency, and native or bilingual proficiency (Interagency Language Roundtable, 2009). There are descriptors for the scales for each language skill—listening, speaking, reading, and writing. The American Council on the Teaching of Foreign Languages (ACTFL) based their proficiency levels on those of IRL, but, because ACTFL scales were designed for use in schools and universities, they conflated the top IRL levels and expanded the lower levels. There are five levels—novice, intermediate, advanced, superior, and distinguished—for listening and reading, but only four for speaking and writing. They recognized that most learners would not achieve the well-educated native speaker level at the top of the IRL scale in speaking and writing (American Council for the Teaching of Foreign Languages, 1999).

These different scales demonstrate the nature of the psychological construct called "English language proficiency." This wide range of different descriptors demonstrates just how difficult it is to describe language and language proficiency even though we all seem to know it when we see it! How then can this construct be measured since the scales only provide criteria for each level? Large-scale assessments use two types of measures—indirect and direct.

Indirect Measures

The primary indirect measure is **multiple choice**, although true/false and matching have also been used. Multiple choice refers to a test item where there is only one best answer and the test taker has to choose among several answers, usually four. The other possible answers are called **distractors**. Distractors have to be carefully designed and tested because they should not provide nonlinguistic hints to the test taker and nor should they be impossible linguistically. So, for example, the distracters should be around the same length as the best answer and should be in

Table 13.1 Common European Framework of Reference for Language: Level Descriptors

Proficient user	C2	Can understand with ease virtually everything heard or read. Can summarise information from different spoken and written sources, reconstructing arguments and accounts in a coherent presentation. Can express him/herself spontaneously, very fluently and precisely, differentiating finer shades of meaning even in more complex situations.
	C1	Can understand a wide range of demanding, longer texts, and recognise implicit meaning. Can express him/herself fluently and spontaneously without much obvious searching for expressions. Can use language flexibly and effectively for social, academic and professional purposes. Can produce clear, well-structured, detailed text on complex subjects, showing controlled use of organisational patterns, connectors and cohesive devices.
Independent user	B2	Can understand the main ideas of complex text on both concrete and abstract topics, including technical discussions in his/her field of specialisation. Can interact with a degree of fluency and spontaneity that makes regular interaction with native speakers quite possible without strain for either party. Can produce clear, detailed text on a wide range of subjects and explain a viewpoint on a topical issue giving the advantages and disadvantages of various options.
	B1	Can understand the main points of clear standard input on familiar matters regularly encountered in work, school, leisure, etc. Can deal with most situations likely to arise whilst travelling in an area where the language is spoken. Can produce simple connected text on topics which are familiar or of personal interest. Can describe experiences and events, dreams, hopes and ambitions and briefly give reasons and explanations for opinions and plans.
Basic user	A2	Can understand sentences and frequently used expressions related to areas of most immediate relevance (e.g., very basic personal and family information, shopping, local geography, employment). Can communicate in simple and routine tasks requiring a simple and direct exchange of information on familiar and routine matters. Can describe in simple terms aspects of his/her background, immediate environment and matters in areas of immediate need.
	A1	Can understand and use familiar everyday expressions and very basic phrases aimed at the satisfaction of needs of a concrete type. Can introduce him/herself and others and can ask and answer questions about personal details such as where he/she lives, people he/she knows and things he/she has. Can interact in a simple way provided the other person talks slowly and clearly and is prepared to help.

Available at: http://www.coe.int/T/DG4/Portfolio/?L=E&M=/main_pages/levels.html

the same linguistic form. Nor should there be a pattern of the placement of the best answer over the test, such as always appearing last. However, they must also appeal to learners who are not at the level of language being tested. The best answer needs to be exactly that so that there should not be two possible answers, depending on context. In listening tests, it is important to ensure that the item can only be answered if the test taker has understood what they have listened to. Often listening test items can be answered without any reference to the listening passage. This may be because the item really tests grammar. Similarly, many reading test items can be answered without reference to the reading passage. Or, they can be answered merely by pattern matching, as in the following example.

Reading passage (section)

Tourists visit Africa to see wild animals. They take a safari tour. They stay in huts and are driven to national parks. On safari, they see many animals, such as elephants, tigers, and lions. They also see deserts and mountains.

Sample questions

1. Tourists visit Africa to:

     a. go on safari
     b. stay in huts
     c. see wild animals
     d. kill elephants.

2. Where do tourists stay?

     a. In national parks
     b. In huts
     c. In a safari
     d. In deserts

The first question can be answered by someone who doesn't know English at all. The second may appear a little more difficult, but also only requires pattern matching. To illustrate this point, in teacher education classes on assessment, we usually give students a passage in a language none of them speaks, with a couple of multiple-choice comprehension questions such as those above, and have students take the test. They can all achieve 100%. Although it may seem an easy task to write multiple-choice questions, they are notoriously difficult to write well and item analysis is a highly technical field for testing the efficacy of such items.

Task: Explore

Compare the following two, sample multiple-choice items. How do they differ? How do you think learners might respond to each? Why? Discuss with a colleague.

1. There was _____ snow that the roads were closed.

     a. so much
     b. a lot of
     c. many
     d. hardly

2. We should put meat in the refrigerator _____ bacteria from developing.

---

a. to retard
b. so that it won't happen that
c. to prevent
d. and

Along with the difficulty of designing each item is the difficulty of developing a range of items that discriminate between test-takers. So, item analysis is also concerned with how test-takers perform on each item. For example, if several items rank all test-takers exactly the same, then most are redundant. On the other hand, if one item is failed by test-takers who score well on all other items, and is passed by those who score poorly on all other items, the item is measuring something different. We have only briefly touched on the issues in designing multiple-choice test items so that teachers will understand the difficulty of constructing their own multiple-choice items and also ensure that any large-scale test used in their institutions have been carefully analyzed and found to be reliable and valid (we discuss reliability and validity below).

Direct Measures

For teachers, **direct** measures (also called **performance assessment**) often appear to be more authentic measures of learner proficiency. However, they bring their own particular problems. Direct measures are used for both writing and speaking.

Writing

Direct measures of writing provide learners with a **prompt** to which they should respond. They are usually given instructions concerning the response—such as the time they have or the number of words or pages required. The responses then need to be assessed. The prompt needs to be carefully chosen so that test-takers can display their ability. In one large-scale assessment, test-takers were asked to write a for/against essay on a particular topic and were given the written instruction *provide concrete examples*. One test-taker wrote an essay on the pros and cons of concrete (the material). While it is easy to dismiss this learner as not being very proficient, he did write a reasonable essay on the topic he thought was being asked, although he still would have scored quite low. He certainly displayed that his reading skills were not highly developed, but the test was a test of writing, not reading. A further aspect of the prompt is the genre it requires that test-takers use in their response. As we discussed in Volume I, Chapter 9, learners may have mastered one genre, but not another (recall the young child who mixed report and recount). Therefore, the genre needs to be carefully chosen for the particular purposes of the test. So, for example, it would seem inappropriate to choose a prompt leading to a narrative for university entrance since narrative is not commonly used at university. However, if the previous schooling (e.g., secondary schooling) only taught narrative, we have a disjunct between what test-takers can be reasonably expected to know and what is being required of them. In order to appear more authentic, one large-scale test used for university entrance has required a letter stating a position for/against a particular proposition. However, while students at university usually have to use a for/against/take a position genre in their university studies, they are not in letter form.

The responses are then scored by trained examiners. The most common assessment is through the use of a **scoring rubric** that has several different levels, usually six. An even number is usually chosen to prevent scorers from choosing the middle score when in doubt. Scoring guidelines are usually detailed and parallel at each level, but scorers are required to provide a **holistic** score, not an **analytical** one. While they apply the guidelines, they do it quickly and from a position of expertise. Analytical scoring, on the other hand, scores on each of the different criteria such as grammar, organization, spelling, fluency, vocabulary, or supporting details. The following scoring guidelines were used at one of our universities for a large-scale graduation writing test.

Use the following guidelines for assigning your scores. Some aspects of the topic may be dealt with by implication. Reward students for what they do well.

6 A 6 essay demonstrates **high competence** in writing on both rhetorical and syntactic levels.
A 6 essay:

- is well organized and well developed
- effectively addresses the topic
- uses appropriate details to support a thesis or illustrate ideas
- shows unity, consistent facility in use of language
- demonstrates syntactic variety and appropriate word choice
- is nearly free of error.

5 A 5 essay demonstrates **clear competence** in writing.
A 5 essay:

- is generally well organized and well developed though it may offer fewer details than a 6 paper
- may address some parts of the topic better than others
- shows unity, coherence and progression
- demonstrates syntactic variety and range of vocabulary
- displays facility in language.

4 A 4 essay demonstrates **competence** in writing on both the rhetorical and syntactic levels.
A 4 essay:

- is adequately organized
- addresses the topic adequately, though perhaps not completely
- uses some details to support a thesis or illustrate ideas
- demonstrates adequate but not distinguished facility with language and syntax
- may contain some errors of the sort that are easily remedied.

3 A 3 essay, while it may demonstrate some **developing competence** in writing, remains flawed on either the rhetorical or syntactic level or both.

A 3 essay may reveal one or more of the following weaknesses:

- inadequate development or organization
- failure to support or illustrate generalizations with appropriate or sufficient detail
- multiple errors in sentence structure and/or usage
- inappropriate choice of words or word forms.

2   A 2 essay suggests **limited competence** in writing.

A 2 essay may be seriously flawed by one or more of the following weaknesses:

- failure to organize or develop
- little detail or irrelevant specifics
- serious and frequent errors in usage or sentence structure
- problems with fluency or focus.

1   A 1 essay demonstrates **incompetence** in writing. An essay to which this score may be given may reveal the writer's inability to comprehend the question, may be incoherent or impressively illogical. An essay that is severely underdeveloped or exhibits no response also falls into this category.

In direct writing tests, **moderation** is used to ensure reliable scoring. Scorers are given a set of sample papers at each level in order. These **range finders** demonstrate how test-takers responded to the particular prompt. They are then given other samples, but not in order, and are asked to score them. These are then discussed and scorers try to align their scoring. This calibration is essential for ensuring that all scorers are using the criteria in the scoring rubric. During the scoring sessions, samples are taken from scorers and checked by master scorers. In most large-scale assessments, two readers score each paper and their scores are compared. If they differ by more than one (on a 6-point scale), the paper is read by a third reader. At the end of the session, statistical analyses are conducted to ensure **inter-rater reliability**, that is, that the raters are essentially scoring the same way.

As well as appearing to be authentic assessments (i.e., the types of writing tasks in the world outside the classroom), in many ways, direct writing samples are authentic for particular purposes. It depends on the decisions that will be made based on the scores. For example, if a direct writing sample is used for entrance to a program and the program requires that students already have acquired a certain level of English and know how to write a particular genre, then if the prompt requires that genre and the scoring aligns with the program practices, it is an authentic measure. However, as we mentioned above, often the genre elicited by the prompt has no relation to what test-takers already know or will be required to do in the future.

Speaking

Speaking can also be tested directly, either through an interview or through a prompt eliciting a speech. These speaking tests raise more issues of authenticity than do written tests. This is because speaking is a largely interactive medium (writing is, too, in one sense). Conversations, the most common form of spoken language, are co-constructed. How then can the examiner engage in a conversation without co-constructing the language with and for the test-taker? This has led to the interview and a speech being the preferred genres for testing speaking. In an interview, turns are more prescribed than in conversation. There is none of the overlapping prevalent in casual conversations. Rather, the interviewer asks a question, the interviewee responds, and the interviewer asks another question, without responding to the text in the interviewee's turn. However, while everyone undergoes an interview at some stage in their lives, interview is a very specific genre and does not substitute for conversation. Similarly a monologic speech is not the same as interactive genres. Therefore, while direct measures may appear more authentic than indirect measures, they too are only partial measures of test-takers' proficiency.

Such speaking tests can be rated by the interviewer or by a separate person. In the former case, the interviewer has two conflicting roles—one as maintainer of the interview and the other as evaluator. This requires extensive training. In the latter case, the interview or speech is audiotaped. In both cases the scorer rates on the base of criteria. The principles for developing the criteria are the same as for writing. However, while having a second person rate the interview removes the conflict, it also makes such testing expensive and the rater is rating without all the visual cues that accompany speech and help in naturally occurring interactions.

Measuring Test Ability

We have already mentioned how test items need to be carefully designed and studied to ensure they are performing how the test users want them to perform. A number of issues revolve around this issue of measuring a test's ability to perform as required. We shall briefly discuss some of these below, namely norming of tests, validity, reliability, and practicality.

Norm-Referenced or Criterion-Referenced Tests

Norm-referenced tests compare one test-taker's score with scores of a sample of people who have already taken the test. This sample should come from the target population, that is, the group with which the test will be used. Tests are **normed** so that the scores usually fall on a normal distribution curve (also called a bell curve), which has standard statistical properties. Norm-referenced tests are mostly multiple choice with perhaps some one-word short answer items.

However, a number of issues arise, especially regarding the population on which the test is normed. Often tests that are normed on an English native speaker population are used for ESL/EFL speakers. Or the best answer is only correct for a standard variety of English. (Note: In Volume I, Chapter 2, we discussed in detail the varieties of English.) If the standard is the norm, then speakers of other varieties will be disadvantaged in taking the test. It is vital therefore for teachers to ensure that any large-scale, high-stakes tests that their learners are required to take have been normed on a population that is similar to that of the learners. Many high-stakes tests in the U.S., for example, have, in fact, been normed on white, middle-class learners (The National Center for Fair and Open Testing, 2007).

Criterion-referenced tests, on the other hand, are not normed against a sample population, but against criteria. In such tests, there is no expectation that scores will fall on a normal distribution curve. In fact, most test-takers could pass if the test were measuring achievement and the test-takers had all acquired the level of proficiency for passing. The direct writing and speaking tests we described above are examples of criterion-referenced tests.

Validity

Whether norm-referenced or criterion-referenced, large-scale tests need to be measured for validity. In general terms, **validity** refers to "the degree to which a test measures what it claims, or purports, to be measuring" (Brown, 1996, p. 231). There are a number of types of validity. The most important is **construct validity**, which refers to how we use and interpret the results of a test. So, the score needs to reflect the ability (in ELT case some aspect of language) the test maker is trying to measure. The ability we are trying to measure is called a construct. One of the problems many teachers have with large-scale tests is that they are often indirect measures of language use. **Predictive validity** means the test can accurately predict what it should theoretically be able to predict. So, a test used for entrance to a university would have predictive validity if it correctly predicted who succeeds (and fails) in their university studies. **Concurrent validity**, on the other hand, is when the test discriminates accurately between groups. Often a new test is compared with an established, reliable, and valid test with similar objectives and specifications. If both tests differentiate similarly between different test-takers, it is an example of **criterion-related validity**.

Reliability

As well as being valid, whether norm-referenced or criterion-referenced, tests need to be reliable. **Reliability** refers to the consistency of measurement, that is, how consistent is the test result from occasion to occasion and in different settings. The same test-taker should achieve the same score on different occasions and in different settings, as long as the conditions do not change (for example, additional instruction or different time limits in one setting). Additionally, the ranking of the same test takers should be the same on the different occasions and settings. A change in the setting might include a different room with perhaps outside noise, or a different form of the test, where both forms have been considered to measure the same proficiency.

The scoring of the test needs to be reliable. Therefore, in indirect tests, analyses are performed to ensure that two different raters produce the same result (**inter-rater reliability**), as we discussed above under direct writing tests.

Practicality

In addition to being reliable and valid, tests also need to be practical. It is because of this that so many large-scale assessments use standardized, indirect measures. While the development stage of such tests is lengthy and needs to be quite exhaustive, administration and scoring are relatively straightforward. This is not the case for direct measure such as a writing sample or interactive spoken assessment. As well as the development effort needed to ensure valid and reliable prompts and scoring guidelines, raters need to be trained and constantly calibrated. Furthermore, for international tests, trained examiners are needed in all the countries where the test is administered. Additionally they take more time for students to complete. Overall they are more costly for students. Test developers therefore have to balance content and face validity against practical concerns of affordability, security, and reliability of scoring across test centers.

Cut Scores

Above, we have alluded to "passing" a test, but determining the pass score is not only a statistical act, it is also a political one, whether the test is norm-referenced or criterion-referenced. While each test taker receives a score, the raw score is not in itself useful. If the test is norm-referenced, the score may be reported in terms of percentile. So, for example, a particular test taker who is found to be in the 95th percentile has scored higher than 95% of the other test takers. While this information may be useful, often the purpose of a test is to decide whether a student will enter a university, receive a high school diploma, graduate from college, or get a job where English is required. Therefore institutions that use the test have to determine the **cut score** which will differentiate between test takers who were successful and those who were not.

Usually, the testing company can provide guidance about what the test scores mean. Even so, individual institutions may want to develop their own cut scores, as in the case in the vignette at the beginning of the chapter. To determine the cut score, experts read (and sometimes take) the test items to decide which ones they consider essential. This results in a raw number that could be the cut score. However, there is usually a second stage. The test is piloted with a sample of the target population and the cut score applied. The institution then knows how many students would be successful. In some cases, they might judge that the number who would be unsuccessful is not appropriate—too many students would fail to graduate or to enter university. For example, in the case of the vignette, once the administrators found out how many students would not be admitted, they might decide to keep the current cut score, but institute other ways of ensuring students are prepared for their university studies (for example, additional English classes before entry, adjunct English classes while taking discipline classes).

Consequences of Tests

We have already referred to a number of possible consequences of tests. Here we want to introduce the concept of **washback**, the technical term for the consequences of tests. We have mostly above referred to negative washback or the potential for such negative washback. However, sometimes tests have positive washback. One large university in the U.S. decided to use portfolios of student work to make decisions about admitting students (see Chapter 12, this volume), rather than the standardized, norm-referenced national tests they had been using previously. This resulted in the local school districts implementing an extensive system of performance-based assessments, resulting in portfolios of student work. When the university received these extensive portfolios, they realized that they did not have the personnel to read everything. So, they chose to read the initial entry in which the student selected their best piece of work, explained why it was their best piece and described what they had learned in the subject. After extensive research over a number of years, the university decided this was sufficient and the admissions decisions they were making were superior to those based on norm-referenced tests. Furthermore, they found over time that local students were better and better prepared for their university work. Their decision to use portfolios had the washback effect of encouraging the local schools to use performance-based assessment and "teach to the test." In this case, because the test was performance-based and required skills the university was looking for, such as critical thinking, analysis, and evaluation, students were better prepared.

Major Large-Scale Tests

A range of large-scale tests that measure language ability are used around the world, some are country-specific, while others are designed for and used by many countries. We will only discuss those tests that are the most commonly used worldwide, namely TOEFL, TOEIC, and IELTS, and make some reference to some local tests. We will discuss the purposes and features of these international tests so that teachers will have a better understanding of what these tests do and don't measure. We are not advocating use of any of these tests, nor is our discussion extensive. Rather, we are trying to make them less mysterious and less threatening.

TOEFL

The Test of English as a Foreign Language (TOEFL) is developed by the Educational Testing Service (ETS), a nonprofit organization that develops, administers, and scores a wide range of educational assessments. "The TOEFL test measures the ability of nonnative speakers of English to communicate in English in the college or university classroom" (ETS, 2009). TOEFL provides the test in both Internet and paper-based versions,[1] but Internet-based is not available in all testing centers. The test is an indirect measure of how well test takers read, listen, and write in English. Writing is further tested using the direct assessment, the Test of Written English (TWE), while speaking is tested using the Test of Spoken English (TSE). The TWE is an automatic part of the paper-based test, but the TSE is a separate test and not all universities require a score on the TSE for admission. TOEFL consists of three sections, in addition to the TWE: a 30–40-minute listening comprehension with 50 multiple-choice questions, a 25-minute structure and written expression section with 40 multiple-choice questions, and a 55-minute reading section with 50 multiple-choice questions. The TWE is a timed, 30-minute writing test on one topic. The listening portion uses North American English as the variety, while the entire test uses the standard, rather than regional, varieties. The listening section has three parts—one with short conversations, one with longer conversations, and one with short talks. The comprehension questions all have four possible answers—the best answer and three distractors. The structure and written expression section includes sentences where the test-taker has to fill in the gap from four choices, and ones where four words are underlined and the test-taker has to choose which word needs to be changed to make the sentence correct. The reading section consists of a series of passages chosen because they are similar to those students find in universities. The comprehension and inferencing questions have four choices—the best answer and three distractors.

Task: Explore

The ETS website (http://www.ets.org) has sample questions, with answers, for each section of the TOEFL test. Go to the website and try the items. Do you think TOEFL has face and content validity? Why? Share your ideas with a colleague.

The direct writing test, TWE, has a prompt for students to respond to in 30 minutes. The topic requires test takers to respond using the genres of "take a position for/against" or "compare and contrast." The papers are scored as described above. Sample prompts are provided in the following task.

Task: Reflect

Read the two sample prompts. How do they differ? What different language do they require of test-takers? To what extent do you think these are useful prompts to decide who is ready for university?

Nowadays, food has become easier to prepare. Has this change improved the way people live? Use specific reasons and examples to support your answer.

It has been said, "Not everything that is learned is contained in books." Compare and contrast knowledge gained from experience with knowledge gained from books. In your opinion, which source is more important? Why?

TOEIC

The Test of English for International Communication is also an ETS product. "The TOEIC tests directly measure the ability of nonnative speakers of English to listen, read, speak and write in English in the global workplace" (ETS, 2009). TOEIC includes a listening and reading test, a writing test, and a speaking test.

The listening and reading test is a timed, multiple-choice, pen-and-paper test, with two sections, each of which contains 100 test items. In the listening portion are a number of questions and extended texts, to which test-takers respond. Four types of items are used: statements about photos, question with three possible answers (the answers are not on the text booklet; they are spoken with their corresponding letter), conversations with three questions (question and possible answers are printed), and short talks (questions and possible answers are printed). In the reading section are three types of reading materials: incomplete sentences, error recognition or text completion, and reading comprehension. This test differs from TOEFL in its semantic field. Test item situations and vocabulary are from the business world, rather than from the general fields studied at university. It also differs in the types of test items.

The writing test is Internet-based and includes the following test items:

- writing a sentence based on a picture
- responding to a written request in email
- writing an opinion essay.

The speaking test is Internet-based and includes the following test items:

- reading a text aloud
- describing a picture
- responding to questions
- responding to questions and using the information
- proposing a solution
- expressing an opinion.

IELTS

The International English Language Testing System (IELTS) is administered by the University of Cambridge ESOL Examinations.[2] IELTS has two test types: Academic and General Training. The Academic is used by English-medium universities for admissions, while the General Training is used by countries for immigration decisions and by companies for hiring. Both have four sections: listening, reading, writing, and speaking. The listening and speaking test is common to both. The listening, reading, and writing tests are taken the same day. The listening section has 40 test items to be completed in 40 minutes; the reading section has 40 test items to be completed in one hour; and the writing section has two different tasks, one of 150 words, the other of 250 words, to be completed in 60 minutes. The speaking test is often administered over more than one day because of the number of examiners needed. The listening and reading portions use multiple-choice test items, while the writing and speaking tests are direct measures. While IELTS strives to include a range of native-speaker accents, standard English is still the variety being measured. Although listening and reading tests produce actual scores, all IELTS test scores are reported on a 9-point scale, as shown in Table 13.2.

The listening test includes conversations and a monologue; the reading test uses passages with comprehension questions. Academic reading passages cover a wider range of genres and include analytical, whereas the General Training passages are narrative, factual, and descriptive. Like TOEFL, the IELTS speaking test uses the interview genre for its prompt. It asks general questions about the candidate, asks them to talk about a topic they are given on a card, and then the examiner asks them

Table 13.2 IELTS Band Scale

The IELTS 9-band scale
Each band corresponds to a level of English competence. All parts of the test and the overall band score can be reported in whole and half bands, e.g., 6.5, 7.0, 7.5, 8.0.

Band 9: Expert user: has fully operational command of the language: appropriate, accurate and fluent with complete understanding.

Band 8: Very good user: has fully operational command of the language with only occasional unsystematic inaccuracies and inappropriacies. Misunderstandings may occur in unfamiliar situations. Handles complex detailed argumentation well.

Band 7: Good user: has operational command of the language, though with occasional inaccuracies, inappropriacies, and misunderstandings in some situations. Generally handles complex language well and understands detailed reasoning.

Band 6: Competent user: has generally effective command of the language despite some inaccuracies, inappropriacies, and misunderstandings. Can use and understand fairly complex language, particularly in familiar situations.

Band 5: Modest user: has partial command of the language, coping with overall meaning in most situations, though is likely to make many mistakes. Should be able to handle basic communication in own field.

Band 4: Limited user: basic competence is limited to familiar situations. Has frequent problems in understanding and expression. Is not able to use complex language.

Band 3: Extremely limited user: conveys and understands only general meaning in very familiar situations. Frequent breakdowns in communication occur.

Band 2: Intermittent user: no real communication is possible except for the most basic information using isolated words or short formulae in familiar situations and to meet immediate needs. Has great difficulty understanding spoken and written English.

Band 1: Nonuser: essentially has no ability to use the language beyond possibly a few isolated words.

Band 0: Did not attempt the test: no assessable information provided.

Available from: http://www.ielts.org/institutions/test_format_and_results.aspx

questions about that topic. The Academic writing prompts include a graphic such as a diagram, and test-takers are asked to summarize, describe, or explain. The second task prompt is an argument or problem to which the test-takers respond. The General Training prompt presents a situation and test-takers write a letter. The second prompt is similar to that used in the Academic format, but the response can be more personal.

As with TOEFL, examiners for the writing and speaking sections are trained and moderated and score according to criteria. The Academic format has tasks, topics, and vocabulary that are likely to be found at university, while the General format focuses on basic skills for people intending to live in an English-speaking country. However, it is also used by companies in some countries to make decisions about hiring into a firm that has international clients. While institutions can determine their own cut score, IELTS makes recommendations based on how linguistically demanding particular courses are. So, for example, they recommend a score of 7.5 (and possibly 7) for fields such as medicine, law, and linguistics, but 5.5 for training courses in catering (International English Language Testing System, 2009).

Other Large-Scale Tests

Many countries have developed their own large-scale English language assessments, either to measure student performance at various levels or to make decisions about university entrance. Most of these are standardized, indirect tests, such as in Korea or Japan.

While the Hong Kong Examinations and Assessment Authority examines most senior secondary subjects using standardized, indirect tests that act as gatekeepers to decide whether the student continues in high school, aiming for university, or leaves school. Recently, however, they have required school-based assessments, performed by teachers. For English, the aim is to use authentic, reading-based, interactive assessments to measure students' oral proficiency (Hamp-Lyons, 2009).

Conclusion

In this chapter we have introduced some of the major issues in large-scale assessment, from their development to scoring, to their use and consequences. We have provided some details of three of the most widely used large-scale assessments, but acknowledge that many countries have developed their own English tests, especially for university admissions. We would recommend that teachers get to know the testing instruments used in their own contexts and examine them in the light of the issues we have raised in this chapter.

Task: Expand

http://www.ets.org

The ETS website provides a range of resources for language teachers, including TOEFL and TOEIC test preparation tools, online tutorials, and publications. Some of these resources are free on the websites; others are in books for sale.

http://www.fairtest.org

This is the website for The National Center for Fair and Open Testing. While its focus is on the U.S., it draws information from other countries. In addition, it provides excellent analyses of different issues around tests and their use.

http://www.ielts.org

The IELTS website explains the test for both test takers and teachers, and also has a downloadable guide. Most other resources are available for purchase.

Gottlieb, M. (2009). *Assessing English language learners: Bridges from language proficiency to academic achievement*. Thousand Oaks, CA: Corwin.

This book focuses on K–12 in the U.S. and includes extensive information on both language proficiency and content-area assessment. It provides an important critique of large-scale standardized testing of English language learners in North America.

Questions for Discussion

1. Discuss the advantages and disadvantages of using norm-referenced indirect standardized tests to assess English language proficiency.
2. Do you think that indirect tests are appropriate for communicative curricula? Why?
3. Why is language proficiency such a difficult construct to measure?
4. How can test developers ensure positive washback from their tests?

Notes

1. We will only discuss the paper-based version in this chapter. If you want to learn about the Internet-based version, please refer to the official website (http://www.ets.org).
2. UCLES administers other ESOL tests and information about them is available at: http://www.cambridgeesol.org/

References

American Council for the Teaching of Foreign Languages. (1999). *ACTFL proficiency guidelines: Speaking*. Retrieved from http://www.actfl.org/files/public/Guidelinesspeak.pdf

Brown, J. D. (1996). *Testing in language programs*. Upper Saddle River, NJ: Prentice Hall Regents.

Council of Europe. (n.d.). *European language portfolio: Levels*. Retrieved from http://www.coe.int/T/DG4/Portfolio/?L=E&M=/main_pages/levels.html

ETS. (2009). Tests Directory. Retrieved from http://www.ets.org/portal/site/ets/menuitem.36b6150d13d7bab7b1935b10c3921509/?vgnextoid=e63ce3b5f64f4010VgnVCM10000022f95190RCRD

Gottlieb, M. (2009). *Assessing English language learners: Bridges from language proficiency to academic achievement*. Thousand Oaks, CA: Corwin.

Hamp-Lyons, L. (2003). The impact of testing practices on teaching: Ideologies and alternatives. In G. Poedjosoedarmo (Ed.), *Teaching and assessing language proficiency* (pp. 26–37). Singapore: SEAMEO Regional Language Centre.

Hamp-Lyons, L. (2009). Principles for large-scale classroom-based teacher assessment of English learners' language: An initial framework from school-based assessment in Hong Kong. *TESOL Quarterly, 43*(3), 524–530.

Interagency Language Roundtable. (2009). *Introduction to ILR*. Retrieved from http://www.govtilr.org/Skills/ILRscale1.htm

International English Language Testing System. (2009). *IELTS Guide*. Retrieved from http://www.ielts.org/PDF/IELTS%20Guide%20for%20Stakeholders%20March%202009.pdf

The National Center for Fair and Open Testing. (2007). *Norm-referenced achievement tests*. Retrieved from http://www.fairtest.org/norm-referenced-achievement-tests

Chapter 14

Program Evaluation

VIGNETTE

I have been hired by a large English language teaching center in Brazil to conduct an evaluation of their program and provide a report to the Board of Directors. I have five days to collect the quantitative and qualitative data and two additional days to analyze the results and write a written report before I present to the Board of Directors. I am working alone, so I know that I have a huge task ahead of me. Three months ago, at the request of the Director, I submitted a proposal to the Board that included an outline of the scope of the work, including a budget. I have since worked with the center's administrators to prepare a statement that outlines the scope of the work that I will do for them. The administrators have answered all of my preliminary questions, and in the last two months, we agreed on the evaluation questions and scheduled the classroom observations, interviews, and meetings for the next five days. Prior to my arrival here, I also received a document that outlined the goals and objectives for the center and a letter from the Director outlining what they expected and wanted from the evaluation. In addition, I have reviewed all of the teaching materials and tests that had been created for the different levels. I have done as much work as I could have done in advance, but I am worried that I will not be able to compile all of the information and analyze the data in the time I have and in a way that will be useful to the Center. For the next five days, it seems that I have every minute scheduled from 8:00 a.m. until 7:00 p.m. in the evening. I will observe 18 classes and meet with every senior teacher and level supervisor. I also have three scheduled meetings with the center directors, short meetings with all support staff, and three focus groups with students in the different programs. In addition to all of the qualitative data, I have three different questionnaires that must be collected from the stakeholders and analyzed and test scores from all six levels. [Christison personal notes, 2000]

Task: Reflect

Work with a partner or a small group of three to five to answer the following questions.

1. Have you ever participated in a program evaluation? If so, what was it like for you? In what sort of activities did you participate? How was it different from the evaluation in the vignette above?
2. The author of the vignette suggests that the process of evaluation began before her actual arrival on site. What sort of activities did she do before she arrived on site? What sort of activities will she do on site?
3. Can you see some of the activities associated with program evaluation in this context appropriate for other contexts? Which ones are appropriate and which ones are not?
4. Do you think it is unusual that she is working alone in the evaluation process? What are the advantages and disadvantages (for the evaluator(s) and for the program) of having one evaluator as opposed to a group of evaluator(s) participate in the program evaluation?

Introduction

There are a number of key components that must be addressed in program evaluation no matter what the context may be. These components include texts and materials, financial resources, support staff, physical facilities, and quality of instruction. In this short chapter, it is hard to do justice to the complex nature of program evaluation in all of these areas; therefore, we have had to make some decisions about how to focus this chapter. We divide the chapter into two parts. In the first half we focus on the general components of program evaluation and in the latter half on teacher evaluation. We first discuss English language program evaluation in Inner, Outer, and Expanding Circle countries (Kachru, 1986) in both private and public school contexts by looking at the characteristics of programs in different contexts and the challenges that such diversity in programs creates for program evaluation. In order to address this diversity, we focus on key elements of program evaluation that are common to all contexts, such as determining the purpose of the evaluation, the models that govern the design of the evaluation, the types of evaluation available, and the specific processes associated with each type. We then turn our attention to teacher evaluation within the context of program evaluation and review the purposes of teacher evaluation and present a structural framework for teacher evaluation.

Contexts and Program Characteristics

English language teaching programs exist in many different social contexts (see Chapters 5–9 in this volume) throughout the world in Inner, Outer, and Expanding Circle countries (Kachru, 1986). They can be both public and private entities and serve a broad range of learners who are at different ages and levels of proficiency and who have very different reasons for studying English. These programs also have different missions, goals, and models for the delivery of instruction and this diversity presents a challenge for program evaluation. Among both public and private entities English language teaching is a competitive, multibillion dollar business. Top-quality programs in any context get the competitive edge in attracting language learners; consequently, many private and public programs seek external program evaluation for the purposes of maintaining their competitive edge in marketing their programs, as well as for improving and maintaining the quality of English language instruction. In some settings regular program evaluation is mandated by accrediting agencies.

In the section that follows, we will briefly review the different types of English language teaching programs that seek evaluation in Inner, Outer, and Expanding Circle countries. Program evaluation in English language teaching is not a one-size-fits-all model but is varied in terms of program structure, the design of instruction, and the course offerings.

K–12 Programs

Within K–12 programs there are a number of different types of instructional models that make program evaluation in this particular context a challenge. The principal K–12 models for Inner Circle countries were reviewed in Volume I, Chapter 3. Table 14.1 presents a summary of the different types of programs in K–12 schools that may need to be evaluated.

TESOL's ESL Pre-K–12 Standards (1997) have motivated many schools to analyze their current ESL programs from a data-driven and standards-based perspective (National Study of School Evaluation, 2002). The Standards encourage schools to reflect on the degree to which they are meeting the content and academic language learning needs of their students who are learning English.

Table 14.1 Types of English Language Programs in K–12 Schools

Program	Description
Pull-out	Students are pulled out of their regular content classes to receive instruction from an ESL specialist.
Push-in	ESL specialists work in content classrooms with content-area teachers and all grade level students.
Sheltered Immersion	"Sheltered" content classes are taught by ESL specialists or content-area teachers with ESL endorsements. ELLs do not compete academically with native English speakers.
Structured Immersion	ELLs are taught by content-area teachers who have developed specific skills for working with English language learners.
Newcomer Programs	Programs and schools are made up of only ELL students, who are given intensive ESL instruction that focuses on the integration of language and content.
Bilingual Education	Content information (i.e., science, math, social studies, and language arts) is presented to the students in two (or more) languages. The two main types of bilingual programs are transitional (one-way), with its purpose to transition minority language speakers to the majority language as quickly as possible, and dual (two-way), with its purpose to produce bilingual and biliterate individuals who can use both the minority and majority languages in social and academic environments.
EFL Classes	English is a foreign language and offered for a limited number of hours per week with a non-English curriculum.

Adult ESL Programs for Immigrants and Refugees

In Chapter 7 in this volume, we discussed English programs for adult immigrants and refugees in different contexts. Adult ESL programs vary greatly using different approaches to literacy and different orientations towards instruction. Consequently, the evaluation of adult education programs will also vary to a large extent. Most adult programs receive funding from the country in which the immigrants or refugees reside. In order to receive the funding, the program must meet certain criteria; however, few, if any, of the criteria are directed towards meeting standards for effective instruction. For example, the U.S. Department of Education completed a national evaluation of federally supported adult education programs in 1994 (Murray, 2005) that focused on who was being served by adult education programs, the size of the classes, the retention of learners, employment profiles, and data relative to independent study and/or computer-assisted instruction. TESOL's Standards for Adult Program Delivery (TESOL, 2002) become important in the evaluation of adult ESL programs that are inherently so diverse in terms of the number of hours of instruction, the curriculum, access to materials, and methods of instruction both within the same country and across BANA countries because they contain standards for key elements of instruction (see Chapter 7 for more information on standards for instruction in TESOL's adult program delivery).

Intensive English Programs

Intensive English programs (IEPs) typically offer between 18 and 24 hours of instruction per week at different levels and in a course of study designed to assist students in achieving a particular set of goals, such as completing a program of study in a U.S. institution of higher education. The phenomenon of university-related IEPs began in the U.S. at the University of Michigan in 1948, but they now exist in other Inner Circle countries as well as in Outer and Expanding Circle countries in institutions of higher education with English curricula. IEPs may be university or college administered or independent English language institutions operating under contract with the college or university to offer courses to its students. An IEP may also be an English language institution that exists independently of any institution of higher education, and its students may or may not be university of college bound. The curricula offered by IEPs vary from ESP and EAP courses (see Chapters 8 and 9, this volume) to integrated language and content courses (see Chapter 10, this volume). The focus of IEP curricula is to prepare adult learners for academic study in English.

Binational Centers and Private Language Schools

Although binational centers and private language schools can serve the same learners as K–12 public schools, they are not part of a K–12 school system. Binational centers (BNCs) are private, autonomous, nonprofit institutions, created to increase mutual understanding between the peoples of the host country and an English-speaking country (Morghen, 2010). The United States and Australia are two countries that have both participated in establishing and, to varying degrees, maintaining binational centers. These language centers are binational in that they promote the values of the two cultures. The difference between private language schools and binational centers is that private language schools do not promote allegiances to a specific culture or type of English, but provide students with exposure to many different forms of English from many different cultures. Most binational centers and private English language schools offer a general English curriculum at different proficiency levels for pre-K–12 learners and adults. In addition to the general English curriculum, they sometimes offer ESP courses (e.g., English for business). Some programs have also been experimenting with integrated content and language curricula for young adults with academic content. Binational centers and private language schools can also provide services for adult learners; however, the typical student studies between 2 and 10 hours per week, so they are not IEPs, and the adult curriculum is not specifically academically oriented.

Nonintensive Academic English Programs

Most colleges and universities in English-speaking countries have nonnative English speaking (NNES) learners seeking both undergraduate and graduate degrees. Many of these universities have IEPs (see discussion above) associated with them; however, some universities do not or they have nonintensive academic English programs in addition to the intensive English programs. These programs are intended to provide academic English language support to NNES learners who may already be admitted to the university on the basis of a standardized test score such as IELTS or TOEFL (see Chapter 13, this volume). Even though NNES learners may have satisfied a minimal requirement for English proficiency on a standardized exam, they may still struggle with academic English and require additional support. Nonintensive academic English programs also support NNES learners who have been provisionally or conditionally admitted (with provisions and conditions established by individual universities and often related to English proficiency). Nonintensive programs offer between 3 and 15 hours of instruction in academic content specific to reading and writing across disciplines (EAP) or integrated language and content-specific courses, for example in business, engineering, or science (EST or ESP), which may be offered as adjunct to content-specific courses.

Workplace Literacy Programs

In Chapter 9, we described the diversity in workplace literacy programs for adults. Because the workplace determines the content and adults are seeking employment in so many different workplace environments around the world, differences in learner profiles, design of instruction, length and intensity of instruction are to be expected (Snow & Kamhi-Stein, 2006).

Program Evaluation

Determining Purpose

Program evaluations are designed to meet the needs of the program or institution requesting the evaluation. As is evident from the descriptions of programs that reside in the different contexts above, it is no small task to conduct a program evaluation that achieves this goal. We suggest beginning with design features that focus on the general purpose of the evaluation.

There are generally four types of evaluations—**progress-oriented, decision-oriented, research-oriented**, and **standards-oriented**. The purpose of a progress-oriented program evaluation is to determine the progress the program has made towards achieving certain goals. These goals are set by the individual programs, their funders, or accrediting agencies and could be related to almost any facet of the program—teacher retention, budget goals, student learning, etc. Because programs vary so much, there is great variation in the goals set by individual programs. Decision-oriented evaluations are carried out in order to help the program make decisions about future developments and change. For example, a program director may request an evaluation because she may be trying to decide whether to keep a 4-hours-a-week conversation program for Levels 5 and 6 for the coming year. She knows how much the program costs, and she wants to know if the program is worth the extra money so that she can make a decision about its future. The job of a program evaluator would be to determine what information could be used in order to make this decision, and then collect and analyze the data for decision-making purposes. In the example given above, analyzing student ratings for fluency on the program's oral interview exam both before and after the conversation program began might be useful in the decision-making process. Students' self-assessments of the value of the conversation program might also help in making this decision, as would attendance records. In research-oriented evaluation the purpose of the evaluation is to explain effects and identify the causes of effects in order to make decisions about the program's effectiveness. For example, a program evaluator or team of evaluators might look at the exit scores of the students who received jobs or published their research or analyze exit scores before and after a curriculum change in order to determine program effectiveness. The purpose of a standards-oriented evaluation is for the program to demonstrate that it has met a set of standards, usually for the purposes of accreditation; however, there is nothing to preclude a program from conducting a standards-based evaluation without the possibility of accreditation since accreditation is only possible when there is a licensed accrediting body (e.g., see the discussion of CEA and intensive English programs below).

Program Evaluation Models

Once the purpose of the program evaluation has been identified, program administrators must decide on a model for the evaluation. There are three different models for program evaluation. These models are based on the type of data collected and desired outcomes. **Quantitative evaluation models** are used to measure program effects. For example, scores on an oral interview might be compared with established norms. The emphasis with this type of model is on measuring, summarizing, and comparing measurements. Quantitative evaluation models can help us answer questions such as the following:

- Does it work?
- Does it work better than . . .?
- What variables affect performance (e.g., class size, teacher education, available texts)?

Qualitative evaluation models approach evaluation from a holistic perspective and can help us gather information to do the following:

- provide analyses of major program processes
- describe different types of participants
- describe different types of participation
- describe how programs affect participants
- analyze the strengths and weaknesses as reported by the participants.

Data are collected through classroom observations, interviews with stakeholders, case studies, analysis of teaching materials and assessments, and sometimes surveys and questionnaires, depending on how they are structured. A qualitative approach to program evaluation uses the data to make sense of the existing situation without imposing pre-existing expectations on the program. The third type of program evaluation model is a **mixed–methods evaluation model**. Qualitative data can be presented in combination with quantitative data, particularly if the mixed method approach is the best way of getting the information necessary to answer the questions the program has generated. The author of the vignette above was using a mixed methods model by collecting data from observations, interviews, and scores on exams.

Types of Program Evaluations

For the purposes of discussion in this chapter, we will consider two different types of evaluations for programs. We will refer to the first type as **program-motivated evaluations**. Most evaluations will fit into this type of evaluation. In this type of evaluation the program itself determines the focus of the evaluation and its purpose. The second type of program evaluation is called **program evaluation for accreditation**. In this type of program evaluation the accrediting body determines the focus of the evaluation, and its purpose is to demonstrate that the program meets a set of standards.

Program-Motivated Evaluation

Although program evaluation differs depending on the individuals involved and the context in which the evaluation is being done, there are some general guidelines that can be applied broadly regardless of the context. What we share here is a process based on our experiences with program evaluation when the goals are set by the individual entity and not by an external entity, as in the case of accreditation (see "Program evaluation for accreditation" below).

PREPARING A SCOPE OF WORK STATEMENT

A scope of work statement is an important first step in clarifying the parameters of the upcoming evaluation for both the program personnel and the evaluator(s). In order to determine whether an evaluation should be carried out, the following pieces of information must be assembled:

- the stated goals and objectives of the program including the board of trustees, funders, or employers
- a description of the most important characteristics of the program—activities and services
- a description of staff—instructional, support, and administrative
- a description of the questions that the evaluation should answer
- a plan for data collection, including the sources to be used, the instruments, and methods of collecting data
- a time frame for the process
- a list of tasks and responsibilities that staff and others will undertake in support of the evaluation
- a tentative agenda for on-site activities
- a budget estimating anticipated costs.

A scope of work statement includes the questions that are normally part of conducting a needs analysis (e.g., What are the goals and objectives of the program? What are the main characteristics of the program?), but it also moves beyond the needs analysis to clarify the desired outcomes, as well as the roles and responsibilities of staff and the evaluator. A scope of work statement gives the evaluator(s) and the program the tools they both need to conduct an effective evaluation that will be useful for all stakeholders[1] involved.

DATA COLLECTION

The data collection phase of program evaluation can consist of a number of different activities designed to collect the information needed to make decisions. Data collection is determined by the model chosen for evaluation and the type of questions being asked. A site visit from the program evaluator(s) is generally part of this stage. The activities associated with this stage include activities such as direct observations, interviews, written documents, review of teaching materials, analyses of surveys and questionnaires, scores on level tests, oral interviews, and other quantitative data collected by the program. When standards are available, for example TESOL's ESL Pre-K–12 Standards and Adult Program Delivery Standards, a program may want to be evaluated relative to a specific set of standards.

DATA ANALYSIS

Depending on the model of evaluation selected, evaluators may be working with quantitative, qualitative, and/or mixed types of data. The emphasis in the data analysis phase is on being able to use the data collected to create a detailed description about the quality of the program's activities and its outcomes. If working with both types of data, the analyses for quantitative and qualitative data should be presented separately. The presentation of the data analysis should be directed to the stakeholders involved. Care should be taken to explain carefully the statistical analyses used, including the reasons for their use. In the case of qualitative data analysis, care should also be taken to explain how the data were analyzed and what types of tools were used for the analysis.

FINAL REPORT

The final report should provide a summary of each of the steps in the process of the evaluation. In preparing the final report, the evaluator(s) should focus on presenting the data in a way that makes sense to all of the stakeholders involved. The quantitative and qualitative data should be presented separately. Program evaluations may or may not include a request for interpretation of the data and recommendations. Many programs conduct external evaluations for the purpose of collecting data and prefer to have an internal group work with interpretations and recommendations. Other groups prefer that the interpretations and recommendations come from the external evaluator(s). Still other programs adopt a model wherein recommendations are made from both internal and external groups who make their recommendations separately.

Program Evaluation for Accreditation

English language teaching programs seek program evaluation for accreditation for many of the same reasons they seek program-motivated evaluation: they want to determine that the educational offerings and administrative practices in the program are consistent with best practices in the field. In addition, they want to have the professional and public recognition that accreditation brings. For the public and the students, accreditation means that the quality of instruction and the services rendered by the program will be of the highest quality. In some countries, programs cannot be offered without accreditation.

An example of one such accrediting agency is The Commission on English Language Program Accreditation (CEA).[2] We will use CEA as an example of how program evaluation for accreditation works. CEA was founded in 1999 by English language professionals as a specialized accrediting agency. CEA's purpose is to improve the quality of English language teaching and administration through accepted standards. As such, CEA conducts accreditation reviews in the U.S. and internationally.[3]

CEA's primary focus[4] is the accreditation of U.S.-based intensive English language programs (IEPs). CEA's mission is to promote excellence in the field of English language teaching and administration, and it achieves its mission by using widely held standards to foster continuous program development. The *CEA Standards for English Language Programs and Institutions* are available to download on www.cea-accredit.org/standards.php#length. CEA standards cover 10 specific areas with a varying number of standards in each area for a total of 52. The 10 areas of focus for the CEA Standards are:

- mission
- curriculum
- faculty
- facilities, equipment, and supplies
- administrative and fiscal capacity
- student services
- recruiting
- length and structure of program of study

- student achievement
- student complaints.

In order for the standards to reflect current practice in the profession, the Commission's Standards Review Committee has an ongoing standards review project.

Programs wishing to receive accreditation go through a process that is in many ways similar to the one described above for program-motivated evaluation as well as in the vignette. The commonalities include the overlap in the preliminary steps that must be taken and the site visitation; nevertheless, there are also important differences. Accrediting bodies evaluate only those programs that meet specific criteria; consequently, the first step for any program is to meet basic eligibility requirements and submit an application form to the accrediting body. Generally, programs must agree to host a preliminary visit, receive training on how to conduct a self-study, and submit a plan for how it will conduct its self-study and get it approved. All of these steps must be taken and completed before the accrediting body agrees to become involved in accrediting the program. Once an agreement has been reached, the program must then complete the self-study, addressing how the program meets the standards and, in addition, host a site visit by a team of peer reviewers who verify the contents of the self-study. Finally, a body of appointed commissioners who make the final decision on accreditation evaluate the self-study and site review documents.

Teacher Evaluation

Purposes of Teacher Evaluation

Teacher evaluation is an essential component of program evaluation. The process of evaluating teachers can be part of program evaluation or it can be dealt with separately. For the purposes of this chapter, we focus on teacher evaluation separately because we believe that the evaluation of teaching should be constant and ongoing and not reserved only for occasions when the entire program is evaluated. This view does not preclude a teacher evaluation component included in a program evaluation; however, in this section, we consider components of teacher evaluation that may go beyond the scope of program evaluation so that if they were all included in a general program evaluation, they might create an imbalance in the focus of the evaluation and leave other features of program evaluation (e.g., physical facilities, access to materials, staff support, student outcomes, and budget and finance) somewhat shortchanged.

Almost every teaching program includes a procedure (either formal or informal) for the evaluation of teachers. Traditionally, this procedure often consisted of one or two observations of teaching by a supervisor who completed an evaluation that was placed in a teacher's personnel file. Sometimes, the evaluation was not even shared with the teacher. This type of approach to teacher evaluation, which is summative (see Chapter 12, this volume) and focused solely on making decisions (mostly about retention and promotion), is no longer adequate (Danielson & McGreal, 2000), especially in an educational climate that is focused on student learning and on standards for student learning. We also believe that formative assessments that focus on helping teachers develop their professional skills and, thereby, encourage students to meet higher standards are important. The above statements are not meant to place formative and summative assessments of teacher performance in a dichotomous position. We believe that teacher evaluation is important for both quality assurance in the decision-making process and also for the professional development of teachers (see Volume I, Chapter 14).

Haefele (1993) outlined seven specific purposes of teacher evaluation that include both those reasons associated with professional teacher development. Teacher evaluation should:

- screen out unqualified or ineffective teachers from employment
- identify teachers who need more intensive professional development (as a requirement for continued employment)
- provide constructive feedback to individual teachers for the purposes of improving the quality of instruction
- recognize outstanding and exemplary teaching
- provide a focus for in-service professional development
- terminate incompetent and ineffective teachers
- unify teachers and administrators in their efforts to provide quality instruction for learners.

Different stakeholders will view the purposes of teacher evaluation in different ways, with some groups, such as policymakers in the case of public education, placing a higher value on summative measures, and teachers and program super-visors placing a higher value on formative measures of teacher evaluation.

For the past 50 years, evidence has been amassed to support various instructional methodologies relative to both teaching and language teaching, for example research on teacher effectiveness, learning styles, cooperative learning, brain research, critical thinking, multiple intelligences, cognitive learning theory, and learner engagement. Regardless of the growing body of research that connects certain teacher behaviors to positive outcomes for learners (Marzano, Pickering, & Pollock, 2004; Marzano, Marzano, & Pickering, 2003), and therefore to effective teaching, teachers are often reluctant to make changes in their teaching. The reasons for this reluctance are often embedded in the teacher evaluation program. Programs may lack the resources and the time to promote teacher professional development; therefore, teachers feel discouraged about investing time and energy in teaching effectiveness that is not supported by their program. Second, program evaluators may lack the background in teaching and sometimes in English, making it difficult for experienced and educated teachers to respect a process that has little to do with professional growth and effective teaching. Third, despite the evidence emerging from research on effective teaching as it relates to positive outcomes for learners, some teachers and administrators find it easier to pretend they do not know about the research so that they do not have to go through the painful process of making changes in their teaching.

A Structural Framework

We believe that an effective system for evaluating teaching for the purposes of improved professional development can address the problems with teacher evaluation outlined above. An effective framework for teacher evaluation comprises three essential characteristics (Danielson & McGreal, 2000). The first component consists of "what" is being evaluated and requires a complete and coherent description of exemplary instruction. Standards for professional practice (e.g., TESOL's Pre-K–12 ESL Standards), observation protocols based on research on L2 teaching (e.g., SIOP), and internally created protocols based on research on L2 acquisition and research on teaching are all appropriate ways of addressing the "what" in a teacher evaluation program. In order to ensure the quality of teaching, programs must have specific evaluative criteria and communicate the criteria to teachers and other stakeholders.

Effective teacher evaluation programs must also make certain that all teachers can demonstrate "how" they will show they have met the expectations for exemplary instruction. The "how" of teacher evaluation is rather complex, requiring that programs think about procedures that allow teachers multiple avenues to demonstrate exemplary instruction (i.e., not just one classroom observation), differentiate between novice and experienced teachers, make resources and observation protocols available in advance (e.g., the observation instrument), create a manageable time line, and provide equitable support for all teachers.

The final feature of an effective teacher evaluation program is trained evaluators. Individuals making evaluative judgments on teaching must be adequately educated with formal backgrounds and experience in teaching and trained with the forms and instruments so their judgments are accurate, consistent, and based on evidence (Danielson & McGreal, 2000). Evaluators must not only be familiar with the evaluative criteria, but they must also be able to recognize these criteria in action. In addition, they must be able to interpret the actions against the criteria. A skilled evaluator also recognizes that there may be more than one interpretation of an event possible and recognizes that it is sometimes necessary to gather additional information (e.g., additional observations, discussion, and interviews of teachers and learners) to determine how to evaluate the action. Finally, evaluators must be able to provide feedback to teachers in such a way that the evaluation promotes the professional development of teaching.

Teaching is a complex mental activity that involves not only specific teaching behaviors but also includes such factors as how we process contextual information, make use of our background knowledge, and respond to learners. Although in reality teaching is not reducible to a simple set of teaching behaviors; nevertheless, teaching evaluation based on specific teaching behaviors associated with research and positive outcomes for learners is a place to begin in efforts to improve teacher effectiveness.

Programs may elect to use standards as the basis for teacher evaluation (e.g., TESOL's Pre-K–12 ESL Standards that focus on learner behaviors as indicators of effective instruction). There are also commercially available observation protocols, such as SIOP (Echevarria, Vogt, & Short, 2008), which have been used by programs to focus on effective instruction. In SIOP there are 30 teacher indicators associated with positive L2 learner outcomes, divided into eight areas of instruction. In addition to standards and commercially available protocols, a number of programs create their own observation protocols based on research on teaching and other agreed upon measures of effective instruction (see Volume I, Chapter 13, for an example observational protocol). These protocols are used by evaluators, supervisors, and peers, and, with few modifications, as instruments for self-observation.

Task: Explore

Work with a partner or a small group. Discuss the structural framework for program evaluation as it relates to either a program in which you work or a program in which you plan to work in the future. How might this structural framework address some of the problems that you have experienced or anticipate experiencing in the future?

Conclusion

In this chapter we have discussed the contexts and the characteristics of different English language teaching programs from the perspective of program evaluation; namely, that the wide array of differences in programs creates challenges for program evaluation. We then turned our attention to program evaluation by discussing the different purposes of program evaluation and how to determine the purposes. We then introduced three program evaluation models based on the types of data collected and discussed the process of evaluation with two different types of program evaluation. In the final section of the chapter, we turned our attention to teacher evaluation by discussing how the research on teaching can be used in conducting teacher evaluation for professional growth and providing a structural framework for this type of evaluation.

Task: Expand

Visit at least one of the following websites for accreditation. Find out what the requirements are for accreditation and be prepared to share the information with your classmates.

Commission on English Language Program Accreditation (CEA)

http://www.cea-accredit.org/international.php

If you visit the CEA website, find out how the international accreditation process with CEA differs from the IEP U.S.-based accreditation process.

In Australia, English language programs, both IEPs and adult programs for immigrants/refugees, have to be accredited by The National ELT Accreditation Scheme (NEAS). Details on their program evaluation standards are available at their website:

http://www.neas.org.au/home/

In the U.K., Accreditation U.K., which is run by the British Council, is responsible for quality assurance in the ELT sector. Information on the scheme can be found at their website:

http://www.britishcouncil.org/accreditation.htm

In Canada, Languages Canada is responsible for quality assurance. Their standards are available at:

http://www.languagescanada.ca/en/accreditation-quality-assurance

In New Zealand, the authorized accrediting agency is New Zealand Qualifications Authority (NZQA):

http://www.nzqa.govt.nz/

Questions for Discussion

1. Imagine you are a program administrator for an English language teaching program in one of the contexts described in this chapter. Describe the context for the program evaluation and outline the steps that you would follow in carrying out the evaluation. Be certain to include the purpose of the evaluation and the model being used. Try to discuss your plan with a partner who has selected a different context.
2. Discuss the structural framework offered for teacher evaluation in this chapter. How might this framework alleviate some of the common fears that teachers have about being evaluated?
3. What observation protocols have you used in your teaching? How did you use them? Did you find the experience useful? Why? Why not?

Notes

1. Stakeholders include learners, parents, investors, boards of trustees, potential employers, employees, etc.
2. Accrediting agencies also exist for other types of programs, for example AdvancED is creating a global K–12 accreditation system. Currently it is focused on the United States, the Navajo Nation, Department of Defense Schools, and 65 countries around the world. Other accrediting bodies include North Central Association Commission on Accreditation and School Improvement (NCA CASI) and Southern Association of Colleges and Schools Council on Accreditation and School Improvement (SACS CASI). These groups accredit K–12 schools and districts and use standards created by other groups and professional associations (e.g., TESOL).
3. CEA is recognized by the U.S. Secretary of Education, and this recognition allows English language institutions in the U.S. to use CEA accreditation for the purposes of certification to admit international students and issue Form I-20.
4. In 2007 CEA expanded its accreditation to international programs that meet the specific guidelines.

References

Commission on English Language Program Accreditation (CEA). Retrieved from http://www.cea-accredit.org.

Danielson, C., & McGreal, T. L. (2000). *Teacher evaluation to enhance professional practice*. Alexandria, VA: Association of Supervision and Curriculum Development.

Echevarria, J., Vogt, M. E., & Short, D. (2008). *Making content comprehensible for English language learners: The SIOP Model* (3rd ed.). New York: Pearson Education.

Haefele, D. L. (1993). Evaluating teachers: A call for change. *Journal of Personnel Evaluation, 7*, 21–31. Boston, MA: Kluwer Academic Publishers.

Kachru, B. B. (1986). *The alchemy of English: The spread, functions and models of non-native Englishes*. Oxford: Pergamon Press.

Marzano, R. J., Marzano, J. S., & Pickering, D. J. (2003). *Classroom management that works: Research-based strategies for every teacher.* Alexandria, VA: Association for Supervision and Curriculum Development.

Marzano, R. J., Pickering, D. J., & Pollack, J. (2004). *Classroom instruction that works: Research-based strategies for increasing student achievement.* Alexandria, VA: Association for Supervision and Curriculum Development.

Morghen, V. (2010). Binational centers. In M. A. Christison, & F. L. Stoller (Eds.), *A handbook for language program administrators.* Provo, UT: Alta Book Center Publishers.

Murray, D. E. (2005). ESL in adult education. In E. Hinkel (Ed.), *Handbook of research in second language teaching and learning* (pp. 65–84). Mahwah, NJ: Lawrence Erlbaum Associates.

National Study of School Evaluation (2002). *Program evaluation: English as a second language: A comprehensive guide for standards-based program evaluation for schools committed to continuous improvement.* Tempe, AZ: NSSE.

Snow, M. A., & Kamhi-Stein, L. (Eds.). (2006). *Developing a new course.* Alexandria, VA: Teachers of English to Speakers of Other Languages, Inc.

TESOL Pre-K–12 ESL Standards (1997). Alexandria, VA: Teachers of English to Speakers of Other Languages, Inc.

TESOL Standards for Adult Program Delivery (2002). Alexandria, VA: Teachers of English to Speakers of Other Language, Inc.

Index